SHARPENING THE FOCUS OF THE CHURCH

SHARPENING THE FOCUS OF THE CHURCH

GENE A. GETZ

Extensively Revised

VICTOR BOOKS®

A DIVISION OF SCRIPTURE PRESS PUBLICATIONS INC.
USA CANADA ENGLAND

6 7 8 9 10 Printing/Year 94 93 92 91 90

Recommended Dewey Decimal Classification: 262.7
Suggested Subject Heading: NATURE OF THE CHURCH

Library of Congress Catalog Card Number: 84-50150
ISBN: 0-89639-393-8

ABOUT THE AUTHOR

Gene Getz serves in two primary positions. He is senior pastor at Fellowship Bible Church North, a rapidly growing church located in Plano, Texas. Fellowship Bible Church North is one of many "Fellowship" churches that Dr. Getz and his associates helped start in the Dallas metroplex.

He also serves as director of the Center for Church Renewal, an organization founded to serve the church at large in the area of both church planting and renewal. Consequently, Dr. Getz and his CCR staff minister to pastors, missionaries, and other Christian leaders literally in all parts of the world. Many of Dr. Getz's books on biblical renewal have been translated into numerous languages.

Asked about the relationship between the church and the center, Dr. Getz stated: "When God began to open doors to minister to other Christian leaders, I felt it was important to continue to serve the body of Christ at the grass-roots level. This is what gives our Center for Church Renewal staff credibility. We too are constantly involved in facing the same challenges as spiritual leaders everywhere—and trying to meet those challenges in a biblical way."

Dr. Getz wrote *Sharpening the Focus of the Church* in the early '70s. This thorough revision includes what he has learned in the last number of years in church planting and renewal.

5

Commenting on his experience, he says: "Generally, I still believe firmly in everything I wrote in the early '70s. However, I now have a lot more experience in applying these principles. The last twelve years have helped me greatly in 'sharpening my own focus' on what I originally researched and wrote."

Dr. Getz still serves as an adjunct professor at Dallas Theological Seminary, teaching in the area of church renewal. He has authored numerous books in the area of biblical renewal, including *Building Up One Another, Loving One Another, Encouraging One Another, Praying for One Another*, and *Serving One Another* —all published by Victor Books. He has also authored *The Measure of a Man, The Measure of a Woman, The Measure of a Marriage, The Measure of a Family,* and *The Measure of a Church,* as well as a number of Old Testament studies.

CONTENTS

8

FOREWORD

There is no end to the making of books. But there are few books with distinct, relevant, and directive messages. Such books are hard to produce. They demand an imaginative and creative mind. Such books do not die by criticism and crucifixion. They blaze new trails for the daring pioneer and explorer in the kingdom of God. Such a book, I believe, is *Sharpening the Focus of the Church* by Dr. Gene A. Getz.

According to the New Testament, the church of Jesus Christ is a glorious church. Christ loved the church and gave Himself for it. He builds it. He walks in the midst of the golden lampstands. It is His church and He will present it unto Himself without spot or wrinkle.

However, the glory of the church has not always and fully been reflected by the local churches in history. This tragic fact we must humbly admit. Because of this many churches are bitterly criticized, cruelly attacked, sadly neglected, and by many coldly rejected as irrelevant, antiquated, and meaningless. In some places church buildings are not much more than historic monuments or even museums.

No doubt the judgment of the world is harsh and at times unfair. But is it altogether without reason? Have the churches been true to their divine calling? Have they faithfully served the total purpose God chartered for them? Must we not say even to the churches: You did run well: who did hinder you . . . ? This then is our present situation.

But our Lord is not through with His church. He is walking in the midst of the lampstands right here and now. He is graciously leading some of His servants to apply their skills and knowledge to diagnose the ills of the churches and assist them in finding paths of renewal and reconstruction. I believe that Gene Getz has been led of the Lord in his diagnoses and in pointing a way out of a dilemma.

The threefold lens of Scripture, history, and culture is effectively and consistently applied and is most searching and helpful. Such an approach points up the fact that the churches are not to live *in* the Bible but *by* the Bible and *in* history and *in* cultural milieu. And while the former—the Bible—remains constant and is our absolute norm for church life, the latter—history and culture—constantly change and demand form and structural changes in order to remain related to the world in which they are to serve. The process of institutionalization can "freeze" churches into patterns that invite stagnation and death. The way out is the continuous metamorphosis of the churches without changing the changeless message and yielding the standards, ideals, and purpose as stated in the Scriptures.

Dr. Getz's scriptural presentation of the New Testament churches is practical ecclesiology made alive and is well documented from the Bible. It puts local churches in the center of the Christian and evangelical movements—where the New Testament places them. It clearly defines their purpose, describes the function and functionaries in the churches and delineates between essential and incidental, the functional and the structural, the content and the form, the pneumena and the phenomena, the biblical dynamic organism and the culturally related organization.

There are details in word distinctions and definitions of preaching, teaching, evangelizing, and witnessing, and the description of offices and officers. The author divides between ministries to and in the local churches and the church universal where differences of opinion and interpretation are permissible without becoming disagreeable.

The book has a message for the churches today and we will do well to ponder it.

GEORGE W. PETERS
Professor Emeritus of World Missions
Dallas Theological Seminary

INTRODUCTION

From Theory to Practice

I am deeply indebted to a number of Christian men and women who have helped to make this volume a reality. Special appreciation is due my students and brothers in Christ at Dallas Theological Seminary who initially and over a period of several years continued to prod my thinking regarding the needs and problems of the twentieth-century church. Their forthright questions, their comments, and particularly their positive responses to the concepts in this volume were a perpetual source of stimulation and encouragement.

Two students particularly—both missionaries now in Europe—dared to challenge me to become involved in church planting. "This sounds like great theory," they often implied in our discussions after class, "but when are you going to demonstrate that it can work in a real-life setting?"

Initially, my response was that it was their task to apply these principles in various cultural situations. It was mine to research, teach, and prepare others—like them—to both plant and renew churches.

But their words lingered in my mind. Little did I realize I would leave the academic halls of sacred learning after twenty years as a full-time professor to become a full-time pastor. Though I still teach part time at Dallas Seminary, I've spent most of my time since 1973 at the "grass-roots" level planting and pastoring churches.

What a great learning experience! What I discovered several years ago about the principles of New Testament church life—the main subject of this book—I still believe with all my heart. However, I now know a lot more about how to apply these principles. And, I'm still learning! And what I'm learning I'm trying to share with others. This rather extensive revision of *Sharpening the Focus of the Church* is a reflection of that effort.

PART ONE
THE LENS
OF SCRIPTURE

Part One is designed to help you view the church today through the lens of Scripture. It is the largest section because it is foundational. It's a biblical study, and these chapters have been written to raise and answer some bedrock questions regarding the church in the New Testament and, in turn, to look for principles which will serve as guidelines for the twentieth-century church.

What were its functions and what were the results? What were its directives and objectives? How did the church relate to the first-century culture and community? What were the significant experiences of New Testament believers as they gathered for edification? Who were their leaders? How were they chosen, and what were their qualifications? How did members of the New Testament church communicate with one another and with the world? What were their structures and forms?

This study, of course, is not exhaustive, for who alone can plumb the depths of the eternal Word of God? But it is hoped that it is comprehensive enough to confront you in a new and vital way with the dynamic group of people who changed the course of history—the first-century church.

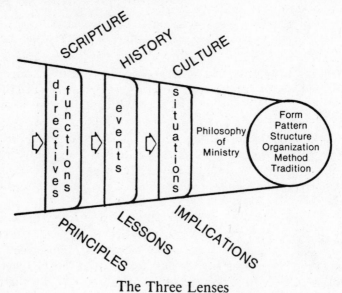

The Three Lenses

14

ONE

CHURCH RENEWAL IN PERSPECTIVE

What has transpired in evangelical churches over the last two decades is not unrelated to what has happened in our culture at large. It never is. "Cultural spillover" is inevitable.

During the late '60s and early '70s, America began to experience an anti-institutional mood that actually threatened the very foundations of our society. It was during these years that university students particularly were rebelling.

These cultural upheavals and crises indeed "spilled over" into our evangelical subcultures. Most of us who were teaching on Christian campuses during those days vividly remember the threatening questions and verbal attacks on the various institutions we were teaching in as well as negative student attitudes toward the institutional church (see figure 2).

A number of educators, theologians, and churchmen began to sincerely face these questions and to attempt to unravel the problem and sort out what was indeed valid in these reactions and what was simply unhappiness, frustration, and disillusionment caused by a society in crisis.

What was transpiring then in culture generally and in the evangelical subculture particularly also had significant historical roots. No crisis is ever precipitated in a vacuum. In the secular world the "sacred cow" of science and its promised results were not working. There were no signs of the "great society." Furthermore,

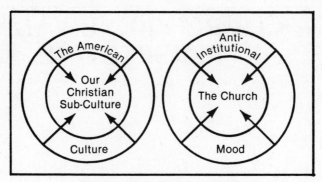

Figure 2. Cultural Spillover

the adult world was in the process of changing its moral value system, particularly causing disillusionment among our youth. Also, more and more young people were becoming very dissatisfied with what they felt was a depersonalized society that was swallowing them up, squelching their individuality, and destroying their creative urges. They felt lost in a huge cultural machine that was running out of control. They felt let down. Their main recourse was to vent their anger on the institutions of America. And the crisis in Vietnam only added fuel to the fire.

Intricately interwoven with these institutions in America stood the churches and the Christian schools. The negative "spillover" was immediate. But there were some valid reasons. Christian institutions along with secular institutions appeared to many to be void of meaning and reality. Christianity seemed merely academic and cognitive, many times legalistic and often superficial and unreal. In its present form it seemed to lack acceptable solutions to the big issues of the day. The facts are that in many instances we were not even talking about these issues.

THE CHURCH RENEWAL MOVEMENT
It was in those days that church renewal writers began to speak to these issues. The book titles themselves form a unique profile regarding the primary concerns occupying the thinking of many Christian leaders.

The Company of the Committed. In the early '60s Elton True-blood published *The Company of the Committed.* Quoting Karl Heim in his book, *Christian Faith and Natural Science,* he saw the church as:

> A ship on whose deck the festivities are still kept up and glorious music is heard, while deep below the waterline a leak has been sprung and masses of water are pouring in, so that the vessel is settling hourly lower though the pumps are manned day and night.[1]

A Quest for Vitality in Religion. Findley Edge picked up the same theme as Trueblood a couple of years later. Experiencing disillusionment himself, particularly over the continual growth in his own denomination and yet what he felt was a lack of Christian reality, he wrote *A Quest for Vitality in Religion.* He stated:

> At the present time churches are experiencing a period of almost unparalleled popularity and prosperity. Such a situation normally would be the base for unrestrained optimism and rejoicing. Strangely, such is not the case. Many thoughtful religious leaders and mature Christian laymen evidence a growing ferment of uneasiness and concern. In spite of plush church buildings, growing membership, and many vigorous activities that are carried on within the churches, something is seriously wrong with modern Christianity. Something is wrong at its center. It is in danger of losing its life and dynamic.[2]

A New Face for the Church. A few years later the spectrum of concern broadened when a group of Christian educators representing various Christian schools met at Wheaton College's Honey Rock Camp during successive summers in 1967 and 1968. The result was Larry Richards' *A New Face for the Church,* representing the thinking of the Honey Rock group generally, and his own thinking particularly.

To most, the book was radical and idealistic. It called for a complete evaluation and overhaul of our present church forms and structures and, if necessary, beginning anew. However, it was a stimulating book. It motivated many of us to go back to the New Testament to take a fresh look at what God has said about the church.[3]

The Church at the End of the Twentieth Century. The second book that appeared in the early '70s was *The Church at the End of the Twentieth Century*, authored by Dr. Francis Schaeffer. Writing out of a very comprehensive understanding of history and culture, he spoke directly to the problem of differentiating absolutes from nonabsolutes in Scripture. "In a rapidly changing age like ours," he wrote, "an age of total upheaval like ours, to make nonabsolutes absolutes guarantees both isolation and the death of the institutional, organized church."[4] This was an especially perceptive church renewal book.

The Problem of Wineskins. Also beginning in the early '70s we began to hear another voice. Howard A. Snyder, a missionary stationed in Sao Paulo, Brazil, began to submit articles to various American magazines. The titles themselves focused his concerns: "The Fellowship of the Holy Spirit,"[5] "Church Renewal through Small Groups,"[6] "Does the Church Suffer an Edifice Complex?"[7] " 'The People of God'—Implications for Church Structure,"[8] and "Should the Protestant Pastor be a Superstar?"[9] After returning to the States he used these articles as a base for publishing a book entitled *The Problem of Wineskins.* "Leaving the North American scene and becoming involved in the work of the church in another culture," he wrote, "prompted me to a fundamental rethinking of the mission and structure of the church in today's world."[10]

Both Snyder's and Schaeffer's insights were directly related to their experiences with the church after leaving the American culture and becoming involved in ministry in another part of the world. This is a significant observation because many times our own cultural experiences blur our vision regarding the supracultural nature of Scripture. As people who live in the United States particularly, we often times "Americanize" the Bible and inadvertently superimpose upon the Word of God cultural forms and structures that are not there. Both Schaeffer and Snyder helped cut through some of these misperceptions.

Full Circle. Here and there Christian leaders experimented with new forms and structures. David Mains, especially impressed with the writings of Elton Trueblood, launched a bold experiment in downtown Chicago. We were all impressed and excited about Circle Church, made popular by Mains' own story in his book

Full Circle.[11] Those of us who followed Mains' efforts admired his willingness to confront the inner city and the problems of integration and class distinction that plagued not only our American society but the evangelical subculture.

Yet the experiment did not measure up to Mains' expectations and hopes. One reason he gives is that he did not heed the principle being propounded by church growth specialists regarding the need to consider structuring to reach the "homogeneous unit." He later stated that he would have been wise to have heeded Wagner. Mains wrote,

> He warned me not to try to reach too many different people in one church. Sure enough, the congregation eventually split in our attempt to extend our imperfect love too far, too fast. We were young and obsessed with solving in a few years problems that had been centuries in the making."[12]

The House Church. Some (including myself) tried the house-church concept in the early '70s and were often disappointed because we ignored twentieth-century problems. Lifestyle demands placed on American families soon made it a burden to continually have a home available for a church meeting, especially involving all ages. Furthermore, in these experiments we did not calculate the tremendous impact of the "church building" mentality that has evolved in our present culture, which is undeniably related to our sense of security and the need for permanence.

This experience taught me how important it is to not only look through the "lens of Scripture" but also through the "lens of culture" when we attempt to develop contemporary forms and structures for the church today.

Some Christian leaders attempted to do away with the traditional educational ministries to children and youth to focus more on the total family unit. Though it was a noble objective, these people again ignored culture. Many were soon to learn that this approach worked only for singles and young couples without children. As soon as children came along, educational programs were added, or people graciously excused themselves and began attending more traditional churches with nursery facilities and educational programs for their children. Though they often missed the dynamics generated by a simple church structure, the needs of their children outweighed their own in the eventual choice of a place to worship.

With this constant exodus and/or the inability to attract families, these new churches were often made up of singles or young couples. This posed another problem. These churches lacked mature leaders, older men and women who had well-ordered households. Furthermore, these churches lacked a dynamic that a total family brings to a body of believers.

Dr. George Peters, a missionary statesman in his own right and who has influenced my own thinking as much as any other evangelical leader, believes that in order to be healthy, "churches should be built of family units rather than individual believers."[13]

Brethren Hang Loose. Some church renewal enthusiasts overreacted to structure per se and attempted to design "structureless" and "leaderless" churches, which can best be illustrated in Bob Girard's book *Brethren Hang Loose.*[14] Though Girard did not actually think it was possible to function without form or to have groups without leaders, he seemed to convey an uneasiness when the church began to become organized. On the other hand, his concern for "body function" under the leadership of the Holy Spirit is certainly noble and is, in my opinion, a biblical emphasis. But, it represented at that time an overreaction and swing of the pendulum away from the institutional syndrome. He seemed to want "organism" without "organization"—a functional impossibility.

Body Life. During this time some traditional churches began to make significant changes. Peninsula Bible Church in Palo Alto, California is a prime example. Under the leadership of Ray Stedman, this church popularized the "body-life" service. Stedman's book *Body Life* spread the concept and encouraged numerous traditional churches to incorporate more body function into their structures.[15]

I was much inspired by Stedman's ministry. In fact, I spent time at the church observing the phenomenon and videotaping Peninsula Bible Church's body-life services and sharing them with my students at Dallas Theological Seminary.

But it soon became obvious that much of the dynamic at Peninsula Bible Church was directly related to the West Coast culture and the Jesus movement that was rapidly gaining momentum at that time. Nevertheless, Ray Stedman's ministry inspired many Christian leaders.[16]

REVIVED TRADITIONALISM

Ironically, another strong movement began basically at the same time with the quest for church renewal we've just described. While many were questioning the traditional approach to church structure, both educationally and for the total congregation, some began to promote the traditional Sunday School. When Richards and many others were questioning the validity of traditional educational agencies and their contribution to church nurture, Elmer Towns, for example, published a book titled *The Bright Future of the Sunday School*.[17] The same year he published *The Ten Largest Sunday Schools and What Makes Them Grow*.[18]

This emphasis was destined to be more than a Sunday School influence. It involved pastors, since one of Town's findings was that "great pastors" create "great Sunday Schools" and "great Sunday Schools" build "great churches."

Towns was able to capture the imagination of numerous church leaders, primarily because he had at that time a channel and public expression for his research statistics and conclusions in *Christian Life* magazine. Corresponding with his own publications, he began to promote large Sunday Schools, their statistical growth, and how they ranked in both size and growth rate. And perhaps, most significantly, he identified each pastor.

This was an ingenious idea, building on an inherent motivational technique. Unfortunately, the primary emphasis was on numerical growth. It fostered unhealthy competition and in some instances generated unethical reporting of statistics. It did, however, generate a great deal of activity in reaching new people with the Gospel.

One of the most important things that has resulted from this emphasis is that pastors of some of these large churches have conducted seminars that are designed to motivate and convince young pastors that they also can be just as successful in growing a large Sunday School and church if they follow certain *techniques* and *methods*. Unfortunately, these leaders have ignored the cultural milieu that contributed significantly to their own growth phenomenon. Furthermore, they have ignored the strengths and uniqueness of their own personalities in causing these churches to grow.

William J. Petersen, editor of *Eternity* magazine, has pointed out that these "smaller churches which followed the example of superaggressive evangelism and spent money for buses, television, church campuses, and larger facilities (even salaries of church evangelists) often did not fare so well."[19] The facts are that some of these churches went bankrupt.

THE CHURCH GROWTH MOVEMENT

In the early '70s another simultaneous movement began with the church renewal movement and the revived emphasis on Sunday School growth. It is what I identify as the "official" church growth movement, involving such notables as Donald A. McGavren, Winfield Arn, and Peter Wagner. Writing such books as *How to Grow a Church*,[20] *Your Church Can Grow*,[21] and *Ten Steps for Church Growth*,[22] these men took a more sophisticated approach to this process. Applying good techniques of research, they surfaced numerous principles and guidelines which cause church growth.

Though these writers emphasize a need for evangelism and nurture and a commitment to the authority of Scripture, the practical outworking of this emphasis is still focused on quantitative growth. Though they attempt to integrate biblical principles with scientific guidelines, emphasizing the need for qualitative Christian experience, the pragmatic and scientific often seem to overshadow the scriptural. It appears they purposely focus on *general* ecclesiological principles so as to be able to relate to a wide variety of churches and denominations on the religious continuum.

My main concern personally is that most church-growth writers do not start with biblical study and exposition to support their positions. Rather they start with "what works" and then attempt to integrate scriptural support into their pragmatic system. This often results in a nebulous perspective on what the Bible actually teaches about the church. However, these men and many inspired by them are having a significant and continual influence on churches and Christian leaders. What they are saying cannot and should not be ignored. Keen insights from culture and sophisticated research methodology make this movement commendable, particularly in terms of helping reach more people for Christ.

A TURNING POINT

In the latter part of the decade of the '70s new dynamics entered the culture at large, affecting the mainline church renewal movement. As just outlined, there was initially a flurry of activity, articles, books, and experiments. But almost simultaneously the church renewal movement was overshadowed by the church growth movement. At the same time the radical anti-institutional movements in the culture at large began to subside, which even made some radical evangelicals more content with the institutional church. Further impetus was added by the Jesus movement, in a sense a quasi-return by the youth culture to institutional structures for security and hope. The charismatic renewal movement also added greatly to this impetus, particularly in some mainline denominations that were characteristically void of both good Bible teaching and relational Christianity. In fact, this movement is impacting missions and the church substantially in the decade of the '80s. It has focused the attention of the official growth specialists.[23]

It became clear to everyone that evangelicals were becoming a force in society to be reckoned with. In 1978 George Gallup, Jr., "predicted a continued upsurge of evangelical strength."[24] Richard Quebedeaux added to this analysis when he wrote:

> The evangelicals are a talking point everywhere. Their growing churches, highly visible campus ministries, phenomenally successful publishing and other media efforts, and unlikely "twice born" national celebrities . . . have caught the eye of Protestant liberals, Roman Catholics, and secular journalists.[25]

To most Christians this was no time to splinter and divide but to forget our differences and unite for the glory of God. Many writers who had been critical of the church now began to see in the rebirth of evangelicalism potential answers to their concerns.

But where is all of this heading? Predictably, the church-growth writers are excited. They see in this flurry of activity the movement of God's Spirit. And who can deny that God is at work in this world? Furthermore, it is certainly ego satisfying to be a part of a movement that has often been ignored.

Frankly, however, I'm concerned. I'm excited about church growth. I've experienced it first hand, helping start a number of churches in the past several years. And as I write this chapter, I'm pastoring a rapidly growing church in the Dallas metroplex.

However, as I travel around the country sharing with pastors, as I read what is being written relative to the church, as I observe what is happening in evangelical Christianity generally, and as I draw upon my own experience as a pastor, I am convinced that both the average church as well as the average parachurch organization definitely lacks a clear grasp on what the Bible teaches about the church. We still confuse function and form, principles and patterns, absolutes and nonabsolutes and that which should be supracultural and that which is strictly cultural. Many Christian leaders have no clear-cut philosophy of ministry based on an adequate ecclesiology that emerges from a careful study of Scripture. Without this foundation, many Christian leaders evaluate success based on personal and corporate experience rather than on biblical theology. Furthermore, quantitative response still seems to be the "bottom line."[26]

The need for church renewal is just as great today, if not greater, as it was in the late '60s and early '70s. Evangelical popularity, as exciting as it has been, has only sidetracked us from the basics and contributed to the process of growing institutionalization. The influence of humanism abounds in many Bible-believing churches, both in function and form. The concerns stated in the early '70s can still be stated today. In some respects we've come full circle. What is needed, however, is not theory, overreactions, and superficial experiments that characterized the initial efforts in church renewal. We need a comprehensive biblical perspective that will guide pastors, missionaries, and all church leaders through a maze of viewpoints that are often confusing.

BIBLICAL RENEWAL

What is a biblical perspective on renewal? Paul was the only New Testament writer to use various forms of the word, but the concept behind the words permeate the New Testament literature. Renewal is at the heart of Christianity. It is an active word and describes the conversion experience as well as the process of growing in Christ.

Renewal and Salvation. Writing to Titus, Paul described "renewal" in terms of the work of the Holy Spirit in regenerating an unsaved heart. God "saved us," he wrote, "not on the basis of deeds which we have done in righteousness, but according to His mercy, by the washing of regeneration and *renewing by the Holy Spirit*" (Titus 3:5).

"Biblical renewal" then involves the very experience of salvation itself. It is a work accomplished by God's Spirit. In this sense, it happens at the moment we put our faith in Jesus Christ. It involves a moment in our personal history when we pass from darkness to light and become a member of God's eternal family.

Renewal and Spiritual Growth. Paul also used the word "renewal" to describe the process of becoming conformed to the image of Christ once we have been initially renewed by the Holy Spirit. *Initial renewal* takes place instantaneously the moment we trust Christ for salvation. *Ongoing renewal* that conforms us to the image of Christ is ongoing and progressive.

The most graphic and comprehensive use of the word "renewal" by Paul in this sense is found in his letter to the Romans. After laying down a broad theological foundation in the first eleven chapters of this letter, and which he summarized in Romans 12:1 as "God's mercies," Paul urged these Christians to present their bodies to God as a living and holy sacrifice. "Do not be conformed to this world," he wrote, "but be transformed by the *renewing of your mind*." This process, said Paul, is the means whereby the Christian is able to determine the will of God (Rom. 12:1-2).

Paul referred to the same process in his letters to the Ephesians and Colossians. "Lay aside the old self," he wrote to the Ephesians, and *"be renewed in the spirit of your mind*, and put on the new self, which in the likeness of God has been created in righteousness and holiness of the truth" (Eph. 4:22-24; see also Col. 3:9-11).

Renewal—Both Personal and Corporate. The initial renewal experience is definitely personal. It involves a one-to-one relationship with Jesus Christ. Conversion is a transaction between each individual and God. However, progressive renewal for the Christian is both personal *and* corporate. To present my body to Christ is certainly a personal experience. To conform my life to Christ by the renewing of my mind is also a personal experience. But, contextually Paul made it clear that renewal is also corporate. Not only should individuals develop the mind of Christ, but a church should develop the mind of Christ. This is why Paul spoke to the *entire body* of believers at Ephesus exhorting them to be renewed in the spirit of their mind. This is also why the Scriptures speak of Christians being *one* in heart and mind (Acts 4:32).

Personal renewal will not happen as God intended it unless it happens in the context of *corporate renewal.* On the other hand, *corporate renewal* will not happen as God intended it unless it involves *personal renewal.* Both are necessary. This is why we see the concept of renewal in Scripture used at times in a corporate sense and at times in a personal sense.

A biblical perspective on renewal can be illustrated with the following circles:

Biblical Renewal

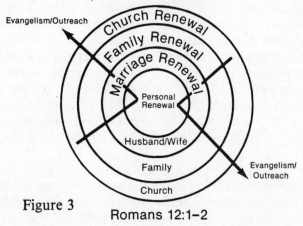

Figure 3

Romans 12:1–2

Church Renewal. The total circle represents "church renewal." This is the most comprehensive concept in the New Testament and extends right on into the center of the circle. In most instances scriptural injunctions are directed at local bodies of believers— not at individual Christians.

It is important to note, however, that even though God intended every body of local believers to be His most basic and dynamic unit of people in society, the body also consists of smaller, self-contained, but interrelated social units—marriage and the family.

Family Renewal. The family (the next inner circle) in Scripture emerges as the "church in miniature." By its very nature, every local church is made up of a number of family units. Thus, the Christian family is an intricate part of the local church. What God says to the church, He also says to the family, although He at times said some special things to members of each family unit. (See Ephesians 5:22—6:4; Colossians 3:18-21; 1 Peter 3:1-7.)

Marriage Renewal. The family, in turn, is made up of an even smaller unit—husband and wife. In fact, the husband/wife relationship is to be a constant reminder of the relationship that should exist between Christ and the church. It is to be the most intimate of all human relationships.

Personal Renewal. The inner circle represents personal renewal which is inseparably linked to all of the other basic units. For example, *marriage* is made up of *two separate individuals* who become one. Furthermore, the *family* is made up of parents and children who are, as a family unit, also to reflect the mind of Christ. And the church is not only made up of individuals but of couples and families.

Biblically speaking, it is impossible to renew the *church* without renewing families, husbands/wives, and individual Christians. On the other hand, it is not possible to renew *individual Christians* without renewing husbands/wives, families, and the church.

THE PROCESS OF RENEWAL

It is possible to begin biblical renewal within any separate social unit included in figure 3. But wherever you begin—with the church, with families, with husbands/wives, or with individuals—you immediately touch all of the other social units in God's scheme of things. Furthermore, unless we understand the functions and principles that God has outlined for each unit, we will not be as successful in bringing about positive Christlike change as God intended. In fact, we can make serious errors in judgment and in some instances "box people in" to what we *think* God is saying to a particular social unit or individual, when in reality we have tunnel vision. On the other hand, we may unwittingly go *beyond* the principles of Scripture and give too much freedom, not realizing we are being affected by our humanistic culture.

Therefore, biblical principles of renewal must include what God says, *first* to the church, and *then* to parents and children, next to husbands and wives, and finally to individual Christians. This is important, because it is difficult to understand and to discern the *special* things God says to families, couples, and individual Christians without understanding what He has said to the church. As stated earlier, what is said to the church makes up most of what God says in the New Testament letters. Without this total perspective, we develop blind spots in our philosophy of ministry.

Let me illustrate how a restricted approach can lead to an inappropriate interpretation of Scripture. I was talking one day with two people who are deeply involved in the process of marriage renewal. Through a study of Scripture, they have concluded that "headship" is not a scriptural concept. They believe that Paul emphasized this responsibility because of the cultural context in the New Testament. They insisted that Jesus never intended it to be that way on a continual basis. In other words, to them "headship" in marriage is not an absolute but a cultural adaptation.

At that point I asked them about authority in the local church. "What about elders?" I asked. "What about *their* authority?" Their response to my question was enlightening. They had no problem with the fact that elders were to be the leaders of the church with God-given authority; however, they believed that God's plan for marriage was different.

At this juncture it became clear—in my own thinking at least— that their biblical interpretation was influenced by the fact that they had not developed a proper ecclesiology; that is, what the New Testament teaches about the church. They did not seem to perceive the consistency that is present in the New Testament. We see this consistency in that *elders* are to lead the church, *fathers* are to lead their families, and *husbands* are to be the head of their wives as Christ is the head of the church. In fact, it is impossible to separate *family function* and *marriage function* from *local church function*. All of these social units are interrelated. It is not logical that God would have one set of supracultural principles for the church, another for the family, and another for husband-wife relationships.

This helps focus a problem faced by founders and leaders of many parachurch organizations that come into being because of specialized needs in the body of Christ at large. There are many examples. One organization may come into existence because of a burden for *personal evangelism*. Without a proper ecclesiology, leaders often neglect what the Bible says about *corporate evangelism*. Another organization may come into existence with a burden for *personal discipleship*. Without an adequate ecclesiology, leaders will neglect the importance of *body function* in bringing people to maturity in Christ.

The problem is complicated when some organizations begin with a ministry to smaller social units and then attempt to expand their ministry to include the larger context treated in the Scriptures. For example, I can think of one organization that began by helping young people relate to their parents. A set of principles was developed out of context of what the Bible says to the local church. The next step was to become involved in the area of husband-wife relationships. Again, a set of principles was developed outside of the context of what the Bible says about the local church. Eventually, however—out of necessity—the principles were expanded to include the local church. The problem is that when we move from the inside of the circle to the outside of the circle, we can develop "blind spots" in our biblical interpretation. This is why it is so vital to develop all principles to guide the family, marriage, and individuals in view of the overarching principles that God has established for the church. After all, this is the essence of the New Testament. The bulk of the New Testament is written to the corporate body, not to individual Christians, or even to family units.

BIBLICAL RENEWAL—AND EVANGELISM

We must remember that biblical renewal is not an end in itself. The body of Christ is to build itself up in love so that the unity produced will serve as a bridge to reach a lost world for Jesus Christ—as individuals, as married couples, as a family, and as a total church. This was the essence of Christ's prayer for believers: "May they be brought to complete unity *to let the world know that You sent Me and have loved them even as You have loved Me*" (John 17:23, NIV).

SUMMARY

Biblical renewal is a comprehensive process. It is the essence of Christianity, the ultimate purpose of the church, and the primary message of the Bible. It excludes no segment of the Christian community. The task before us then is to first discover those principles that God has established for the church. From that point, we can focus biblical principles of renewal for the family, for husband-wife relationships, and for personal growth in Christ. There is a means for accomplshing these goals—the subject of our next chapter.

Footnotes

[1]Elton Trueblood, *The Company of the Committed*, Harper Brothers, p. 5. (Quoted from Karl Heim, *Christian Faith and Natural Science*, (Harper Brothers. p. 24.)

[2]Findley B. Edge, *A Quest for Vitality in Religion*, Broadman Press, p. 9.

[3]Larry Richards, *A New Face for the Church*, Zondervan Publishing House, p. 9. [Larry Richards has continued to write in the field of church renewal. Though I consider Larry a good friend and colleague and admire his disciplined pen, I personally believe he has more and more moved down the road of idealism. His views on leadership particularly and how the church body functions are not based on realistic experience. If taken seriously, his leadership theory is unworkable, particularly in a growing church. In fact, under certain circumstances, it can ultimately lead to chaos and church divisions. See "A Biblical Style of Leadership?" an article where I debate Larry Richards on the subject of leadership, in *Leadership* (Vol. 2, Number 2, Spring 1981), pp. 68-78. See also Richards' books *A Theology of Church Leadership*, Zondervan Publishing House, and *A Theology of Personal Ministry*, Zondervan Publishing House.]

[4]Francis Schaeffer, *The Church at the End of the Twentieth Century*, InterVarsity Press, p. 67.

[5]Howard Snyder, "The Fellowship of the Holy Spirit," *Christianity Today*, pp. 4—7.

[6]_____, "Church Renewal through Small Groups," *United Evangelical Action,* Summer 1971, pp. 29-31.

[7]_____, "Does the Church Suffer an Edifice Complex?" *World Vision,* September 1971, pp. 4-5.

[8]_____, " 'The People of God'—Implications for Church Structure," *Christianity Today,* October 27, 1972, pp. 6-11.

[9]_____, "Should the Protestant Pastor Be a Superstar?" *The Other Side* March-April 1973, pp. 8-11.

[10]_____, *The Problem of Wineskins,* InterVarsity Press, p. 11.

[11]David Mains, *Full Circle,* World Book Publishers, p. 22.

[12]_____, "A Balanced Stride," *Christianity Today,* August 18, 1971, p. 22.

[13]George W. Peters, *Saturation Evangelism,* Zondervan Publishing House, p. 153.

[14]Robert Girard, *Brethren Hang Loose,* Zondervan Publishing House.

[15]Ray Stedman, *Body Life,* Regal Books.

[16]Following are some books written during this period of time that tell the story of various churches that were making significant changes in their structures:

Dan Baumann, *All Originality Makes a Dull Church,* Vision House Publisher.

Bernard Palmer, *Pattern for a Total Church,* Victor Books.

Larry Richards, *Three Churches in Renewal,* Zondervan Publishing House.

Mike Tucker, *The Church That Dared to Change,* Tyndale House.

Frank Tillapaugh, *The Church Unleashed,* Regal Books.

[17]Elmer Towns, *The Bright Future of the Sunday School,* F.C. Publications.

[18]_____, *The Ten Largest Sunday Schools and What Makes Them Grow,* Baker Book House.

[19]William J. Petersen, "Thinking Big," *Eternity,* February 1978, p. 21.

[20]Donald A. McGavren, *How to Grow a Church,* Regal Books,.

[21]C. Peter Wagner, *Your Church Can Grow,* Regal Books.

[22]Donald A. McGavern and Winfield Arn, *Ten Steps for Church Growth,* Harper and Row Publishers.

[23]See *Christian Life* magazine, October 1982, an issue devoted to the charismatic movement and church growth.

[24]Albert J. Menendez, "Who Are the Evangelicals?" *Christianity Today,* January 27, 1978, p. 42.

[25]Richard Quebedeaux, *The Worldly Evangelicals,* Harper and Row Publishers, p. 3.

[26]For an excellent study that speaks to these concerns, see George W. Peters, *A Theology of Church Growth,* Zondervan Publishing House.

TWO

A LOOK THROUGH THREE LENSES

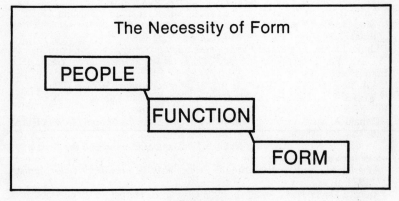

Figure 4.

Wherever you have people, you have function. And wherever you have function, you have form. In other words, "form" and "structure" are inevitable. Put another way, you cannot have "organism" without "organization." Wherever you attempt to achieve a goal or apply a principle, you must develop a procedure or pattern for doing it. You cannot communicate a "message" without a "method." You cannot teach "truth" without developing some kind of "tradition." And to quote Dr. George Peters, "Wherever you have 'pneumena,' you have 'phenomena.' "

The local church is no exception. Wherever you have people

actively functioning in various roles, you have form and structure. You cannot have one without the other.

Note! It is possible *to describe function without describing form.* The authors of Scripture did it all the time. But in the outworking of the New Testament functions, you can be sure there was always some kind of cultural form.

All of us can identify with this reality. We live within the circle of form and structure (see figure 5). It is what gives us a sense of security. But the important question facing every church leader is, What kind of form and structure should we have in *our* church?

AN ADEQUATE PHILOSOPHY OF MINISTRY

We cannot answer this question for ourselves or for anyone else unless we have an adequate philosophy of the ministry, which raises one basic question—the question "why?" *Why* do we do what we do? Even as individuals we all have a philosophy that determines the way we function in life. We may not have spelled it out or articulated it to ourselves or others. But it is there, nevertheless, determining our actions and the way we function.

So it is in the church. All church leaders have a philosophy of ministry. Though it may not be obvious to the leaders themselves or the congregations they serve, it is there, nevertheless, determining *how* each church functions (see figure 6).

My concern in writing this book is to help Christians develop

Figure 5. Circle of Form

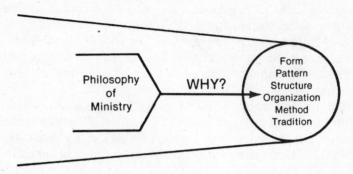

Figure 6. Philosophy of Ministry

a *biblical* philosophy of ministry. It is only then that we can structure and organize our churches properly. It is only then that we can choose methods and patterns that will help the church become what God intended it to become in this world.

Interestingly, the "church growth" writers emphasize how important it is for church leaders to focus their philosophy of ministry in order to experience numerical growth. However, they seldom specify, at least in detail, what that philosophy should be. In fact, they often recognize various philosophies of ministry as being valid and acceptable.[1]

Is it possible to develop *a* philosophy of ministry that is truly biblical—one that is recognized as what the Scriptures illustrate and teach? I believe it is—if we use an adequate research methodology that helps us arrive at a clear focus regarding what God is saying. Though we may have differences of opinion on minor matters, I believe it is possible to understand God's specific plan for local churches just as surely as it is possible to discover the truth regarding Christ's deity, the Trinity, salvation—and other important biblical doctrines.

To develop an adequate philosophy of ministry—one that God espouses—we must look through at least three lenses (see figure 7). The first is basic and foundational—the lens of Scripture. The lenses of history and culture are not unrelated in content to the lens of Scripture, but they also reveal extra biblical insights and are very important in avoiding "tunnel vision" and ecclesiastical

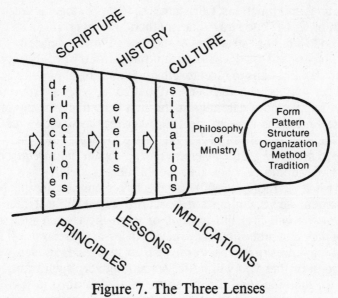

Figure 7. The Three Lenses

myopia as we develop a personal philosophy of ministry. Stating it positively and following through on our analogy, the three lenses can assist us in developing 20-20 vision regarding God's plan for the church.

How can we use the three lenses? This is the purpose of this book. What follows this chapter are the *results* of this process. What follows immediately in this chapter, however, is an explanation with illustrations of *how to use* this process. In that sense, the three-lens approach comprises a method for biblical, historical, and cultural research.

The Lens of Scripture. This is the place to begin in formulating a *biblical* philosophy of ministry. Let me illustrate. Consider the following exhortations in the letter to the Hebrews:

> Let us not give up *meeting together*, as some are in the habit of doing, but let us *encourage one another*—and all the more as you see the day approaching (Heb. 10:25, NIV).

This Scripture passage delineates clearly two New Testament

directives and functions. Christians are to "meet together regularly" in order to "encourage one another;" however, it is also clear that no "form" or "structure" is mentioned in this verse for these two functions. This does not mean that the author of this epistle expected Christians to meet together without form. Neither could they "encourage one another" without some type of structure.

Let's look more carefully at the first directive (see figure 8). These Christians were to meet together regularly. However, the passage does not specify *when* they were to meet, *how often* they were to meet, *where* they were to meet, or what the *specific order of service* should be when they would meet together.

If we look more carefully at the larger context in the New Testament—a very important aspect in accurate biblical interpretation—we will find illustrations of *when* the church met, *how often* they met and *where* they met. To a lesser degree we will find a few references *to how they ordered their services.* However, when you look further you will notice something very significant.

First, functions and directives are often described in the New Testament without a description of forms, just as they are in the passage in Hebrews. For example, Luke recorded in the Book of Acts that the apostles "never stopped *teaching* and *proclaiming*

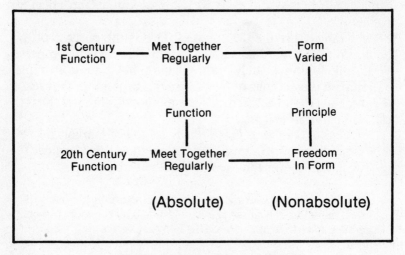

Figure 8. Function and Form

the Good News that Jesus is Christ" (Acts 5:42c, NIV). "Teaching" and "proclaiming" are functions. Though Luke made references to these functions, he did not describe the apostles' teaching and preaching methodology (form); however, we know that it is impossible to "teach" and "preach" without some kind of form and methodology.

Second, when form *is* described it is always *partial* or *incomplete.* It is never possible to duplicate biblical form and structure exactly because certain details and elements are always missing in the biblical text. For example, Luke recorded in the same passage that the apostles "kept right on teaching and preaching" as they went "from house to house" (5:42b). Going from "house to house" is definitely form and structure. However, the process is not delineated in detail. Did they stop at every house? Or did they go only to the homes of those who had already believed in Christ? Did people invite their neighbors to come and hear the apostles? Did the apostles go "inside the house" or "stand outside" or "go to the rooftop"—as they would be able to do in this culture? We do not know the answers to these questions because the form described (going "from house to house") is incomplete and partial.

Third, form and structure that is partially described varies from one New Testament setting to another. In fact, we see variations within the text we're looking at. Not only did the apostles teach and preach from house to house, but they also went to the "temple courts" (5:42a, NIV).

This poses a problem immediately. We may not have too much trouble in some cultures going "from house to house" teaching the Gospel of Christ. However, we would have to select our methodology carefully, for if we used the apostles' approach described in the Book of Acts, we would probably be in violation of most city ordinances and find ourselves in trouble with local authorities.[2]

The problem of cultural restrictions on Christianity impacted me forcefully several years ago when I was sharing principles of New Testament church life with pastors behind the Iron Curtain. In this particular country, it was illegal for groups of people to meet in private homes. Even relatives could not get together in large numbers. It was not just a regulation directed toward Christians. This government policy was established to avoid any possibility of a conspiracy against state authority. Naturally it restricted Christians greatly in being able to use their homes for any kind of religious service involving more than their immediate families.

Our biggest challenge, however, in any culture today would be to teach the Gospel in "the temple courts." This was a cultural phenomenon related to the early days of Christianity, which was exclusively Jewish. However, it wasn't long until even the "temple courts" were off limits to Jewish Christians.

Let me summarize.
• The Bible often teaches function without describing form.
• Where it does describe form it is partial and incomplete.
• What form is described varies from situation to situation.

This leads to a very important conclusion. In church-renewal conferences, I'm often asked how it is possible to distinguish absolutes from nonabsolutes in Scripture. The answer is found in these three observations regarding form in the New Testament. It is not possible to absolutize something that is *not described;* that is always *incomplete;* and that is *always changing* from one setting to another. This is why form and structures are not absolutes in the Bible. I have not found any that do not fit this threefold criteria. In fact, there is only one structure in the entire Bible that is described in detail—the tabernacle in the Old Testament. But even then, it is not possible to reconstruct this Old Testament place of worship without adding some details of our own.

On the other hand, functions and principles *are* absolute—*if* they appear consistently throughout New Testament history and are not self-delimiting.[3] Our challenge is to "look through the lens of Scripture" and isolate those functions and directives that are absolute and supracultural.

The Lens of History. Note, first of all, that we can superimpose the lens of Scripture over the lens of history. Scripture *is* history—that is, divine history, inspired history, or "God-breathed" history. It is here that we find absolute directives and functions that enable us to lay the foundations for a biblical philosophy of ministry.

Furthermore, we can learn valuable lessons from our forefathers. Paul illustrated this point in his letter to the Corinthians when he wrote: "Now these things happened to them [the Children of Israel] as an example, and they were written [the Old Testament] for *our instruction,* upon whom the ends of the ages have come" (1 Cor. 10:11). Today Christians have not only Old Testament history but New Testament History—God's divinely inspired history of the church. It too has been recorded for "our instruction" to teach us how to order His church.

However, there is history that extends beyond the sacred pages of Scripture. *Church history* is filled with lessons for twentieth-century Christians. It is this lens that enables us to turn the spotlight on the church the latter part of the first century and throughout the centuries that followed. It is this process that gives us insights that will enable us to accentuate what Christians have done right, hopefully eliminate what we've done wrong, and correct what we have done poorly. This process, like the study of the church in Scripture, is open-ended.

There is, however, a special kind of history that can also be studied that offers unusual insights for Christians. Let me illustrate. Not surprisingly, social historians have discovered that wherever you have people, you have function, and wherever you have function, you have form. But they have discovered something else that is extremely relevant to our overall concern in this book.

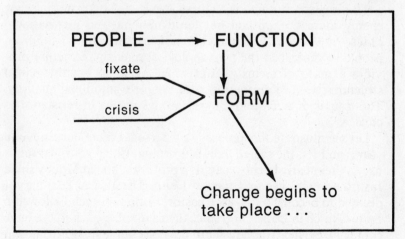

Figure 9. Fixation, Crisis and Change

Resistance to change. Social historians have made two important observations (see figure 9). First, in studying people and their societal structures, they have discovered that over a period of time people tend to fixate—particularly on forms. People do not want to change. Studies show there is one constant in history. That constant is fixity.

However, social studies also point out that people *do* change their forms and structures in society, basically under one condition—some kind of *crisis.* Then, and then only, people are open to change. Usually this crisis comes because forms and structures are no longer relevant. They are no longer serving as an effective means to meet the needs of people in that particular society.

Recently this has been illustrated in an unusual way in our own society and others. For years we have built our national economy on such important energy sources as oil, gas and coal. Understandably, these resources will someday be depleted.

What has happened? This energy crisis has precipitated extensive research projects to overcome this problem. If the Lord tarries, we'll no doubt develop *new* energy sources, perhaps to eventually replace the old ones entirely. Already we've learned how to use solar energy in new and different ways and we'll refine this process in the years to come.

The important point is that we would not be exploring new energy sources if we had not faced national and international crises. And so it is with the church. Christians differ little from people in general in their psychological makeup. Structure provides a sense of security. And when we tamper with societal structures, we are tampering with people's emotional stability. This causes anxiety, and anxiety always results in resistance to change.

Let me illustrate this point with a personal experience. Several years ago I left the sacred halls of learning—the theological seminary. After nearly twenty years as a professor, first at Moody Bible Institute in Chicago and then at Dallas Theological Seminary, I decided to become a full-time pastor. I helped launch Fellowship Bible Church in Dallas, and since then a number of churches have come into existence as a result of the first church in 1972. Though in these early days I was enjoying this experience greatly, for a number of months I also experienced unusual anxiety. I couldn't understand why.

Then one day I got the answer to that question. It suddenly dawned on me that after twenty years in one kind of structure—a structure that I knew very well—I had made a dramatic change. In fact, I was pastoring a renewal church, one that started with functions first, allowing forms to develop naturally in our own cultural setting. I knew the forms forward and backward in a traditional church. I had been down that road before. But here I was, exchanging academic forms for local church forms that were new and innovative. I had not been down that path before. Had I stopped to think before I made the change, I could have predicted the anxiety that followed. It was natural. Once I understood the source of my anxiety, I was able to cope with it and eventually develop security in the new forms I was helping create.

I have often seen this psychological phenomenon in people who visit our services for the first time, particularly if they are unusually entrenched in traditional church structures. At first they feel uncomfortable. It is an understandable emotional reaction.

Lack of understanding. We must therefore understand why people resist change. But we must also understand that Christians sometimes have "double-trouble." Because we believe there are things that should *never* change, we often confuse nonabsolutes (those things that *should* change) with absolutes (things that should *not* change). Often this resistance is rooted in insecurity and fear and leads to rationalization. After all, what better way to rationalize than to *think* we are standing for the truth of Scripture?

However, many Christians resist change because they are honestly confused. They don't understand the differences between absolutes and nonabsolutes. They put "beginning the service with the doxology" in the same category as the "virgin birth." Or, they think that "meeting at 11 o'clock on Sunday morning" is just as significant as what the Bible teaches about the "second coming of Christ." Though I'm speaking hyperbolically, these illustrations point to our problem.

It is important to help Christians understand the difference between absolutes and nonabsolutes (see figure 10), between functions and forms, between principles and patterns, between truth

ABSOLUTES	NONABSOLUTES
Function	Form
Principle	Pattern
Organism	Organization
Truth	Tradition
Message	Method
SUPRACULTURAL	CULTURAL

Figure 10. Absolutes vs. Nonabsolutes

and tradition, between organism and organization, between message and method, between that which is supracultural and that which is purely cultural. This is why it is important to look carefully at the New Testament churches through the lens of Scripture. And, as illustrated, the lens of history will help us discover our successes and failures in making these differentiations in the past.

Furthermore, as Christian leaders, we have a God-given means to bring about crisis in the lives of Christians that can bring significant change. I'm speaking of the Word of God. Wherever and whenever God's truth is taught, it should create a Spirit-directed crisis in the life of every believer who is out of harmony with that truth. If we are to be in the will of God, we must change our attitudes and behavior and conform our lives to God's Word.

This is why it is important to use the lens of Scripture to help Christians understand God's plan for the church. As believers begin to comprehend what is absolute and what is not absolute; what is supracultural and what is cultural; and as they understand that the Bible teaches "freedom in form" in order to effectively carry out the Great Commission of our Lord Jesus Christ in every place in the world and at any moment in history, most will be open to change in areas where they should change. At the same time, they'll be secure in the fact that they are not changing those things God intended to remain the same. When this happens, they'll understand what Paul really meant when he wrote: "And to the Jews I became as a Jew, that I might win Jews . . . to those without law, as without law . . . . I have become all things to all men that I may by all means save some" (1 Cor. 9:20-22).

The Lens of Culture. Once again, this lens is clearly related to both the lens of Scripture and of history. You can't study the Bible without seeing the influence of culture. And you cannot study history—particularly social history—without encountering culture.

Jesus carried on His ministry within several cultures, and He understood those cultures very well. This was dramatically illustrated when He encountered the Samaritan woman at Jacob's well. Her culture was different. Her viewpoint on religion and life in general was very different from the individual who had a typical Jewish background. Jesus used His cultural insight to communicate effectively with this woman. It had a decided effect on His methodology in approaching her and teaching her divine truth. It also had a decided effect on her response.

Paul, more than any other apostle, illustrated how important it is to understand culture. We would expect this since his ministry was primarily to the Gentiles. As we'll see in our chapter on New Testament leadership functions and principles, Paul's insights into the Greek and Roman cultures, for example, affected his use of language.

Thus, we can build a strong case from the lens of Scripture itself showing the importance of understanding culture and how it affects the way people think and feel about life. But, as with history, we need to look beyond Scripture to gain insight and implications from culture.

Secular analyst Alvin Toffler has helped all of us understand the influence on culture much better. His book *Future Shock* was a stimulating study relative to where history is headed. However, his book *Third Wave* was particularly helpful to me personally, especially in contributing to my understanding of how culture affects form and structure. Interestingly, I first read much of this book on my way to Quito, Ecuador to speak to missionaries on the subject of New Testament church principles. I found Toffler's insights helpful as I entered this setting to minister to Christian leaders who were ministering in several different cultures vastly different from my own.[4]

Toffler has pointed out that for years much of civilization existed in an agrarian culture. Society's forms and structures were relatively small because form "conforms" to the number of people involved in any given situation. Generally speaking, this describes the biblical culture, though certainly there are exceptions, particularly in the Roman Empire that boasted some very large cities. Even then, most structures were relatively small, with the exception of the amphitheaters and some religious temples.

Toffler further states that all of this was destined to change several hundred years ago. We moved from the "agricultural wave" to the "industrial wave" which gave birth to centralization of population, which in turn gave birth to large societal structures—such as towns, cities, and suburbs. These population centers also gave birth to factories, universities, hospitals, and also churches. Large forms and structures came into existence to accommodate functions that involved thousands of people living in a particular geographical area.

This is a significant cultural insight. For a time in my own church planting experience in the Dallas metroplex, I determined to keep church structures small to encourage body function. To achieve this goal, we've made multiple use of buildings and started a number of branch churches. However, the more churches we started, the more growth we experienced, primarily because we were in a growing population area. The churches we started in other areas of the city did not resolve the growth problem in our home-base church.

A couple of things happened that were directly related to culture. First, we soon used up the culturally acceptable times for worship and teaching periods. Second, in about four years we had exhausted geographical areas that were potential areas to start new churches, particularly in relationship to our home-base congregation. Third, we soon reached the maximum number of people we could accommodate in our own building. Fourth, this began to lead to an "ingrown mentality"—a desire to stop reaching new people. Also, we began turning people away, causing negative feelings on the part of newcomers as well as those who were regulars.

It was then I saw that we were beginning to violate the very principles that we believed in—one being that form follows function. To solve the problem we had to change form—in short, we had to build a larger building. This, in turn, would affect the service form. And here the "church-growth" people have also made a very significant cultural observation. As the church grew in size, it was necessary to move to "celebration" when the church met corporately. The challenge we faced was to encourage and develop forms that would continue to accommodate body function. To do this, we developed home cells—which we call Fellowship Families and mini-churches.

In essence, I'm saying you cannot force church structures to remain small if you are located in a cultural situation that is permeated with people and large structures. That is, you cannot remain small if you're about our Father's business of reaching people for Christ. And if you are reaching these people, you must then design structures to accommodate these people in their own cultural environment without violating New Testament principles of church life.

SUMMARY

This is a book designed to help the church develop forms and structures that are effective in carrying out the Great Commission in any given cultural setting. It is not a book *about* form and structures. Rather, it is a book that focuses first and foremost on New Testament directives and functions, which, in turn, can be translated into absolute principles that are applicable in every culture of the world since the first century. In that sense, if they are focused correctly, they become supracultural guidelines that are normative for all time.

The lens of Scripture is basic in formulating these principles. The lens of history and the lens of culture add additional insights, particularly in helping us discern and apply these biblical principles. Together, all three lenses help any seeking person to formulate an adequate philosophy of ministry. It is this kind of philosophy that will enable every church leader to develop forms and structures and use methods and techniques that are contemporary and relevant but yet in harmony with biblical absolutes. It is this combination that creates dynamic churches that reflect God's purposes and plans in any culture of the world and at any moment in history.

Footnotes

[1]See C. Peter Wagner, *Leading Your Church to Growth*, Regal Books, pp. 175-181, 214-216.

[2]The apostles definitely got in trouble for preaching the Gospel. In fact, some ended up in prison. However, they were incarcerated for challenging their fellow Jewish and religious leaders theologically. Twentieth-century city codes in most instances are designed to guarantee the right of privacy to local citizens. In this sense, we would be in violation of Paul's admonition to obey local magistrates and authorities (Rom. 13:1-7).

[3]A "self-delimiting" function or directive is incapable of being repeated. For example, Paul asked Timothy to bring his cloak and parchments (2 Tim. 4:13).

[4]Alvin Toffler, *Third Wave*, William Morrow and Company, Inc.

THREE

WHY THE CHURCH EXISTS

Anyone who attempts to formulate a biblical philosophy of the ministry and develop a contemporary strategy and methodology that stands foursquare on scriptural foundations *must* ask and answer some very fundamental questions. Why does the church exist? What is its ultimate purpose? Why has God left it in the world in the first place?

Jesus Christ, before ascending to the Father, spoke directly to these questions. One day on a mountain in Galilee He spoke in clear and simple language: "Go therefore and make disciples of all the nations, baptizing them in the name of the Father and the Son and the Holy Spirit, teaching them to observe all that I commanded you; and lo, I am with you always, even to the end of the age" (Matt. 28:19-20).

Earlier, He had said in the presence of the disciples, and more specifically to Peter, "I will build My church; and the gates of Hades [the power of death] shall not overpower it" (16:18).

Now prior to leaving them to carry on His work and to fulfill His prophetic words, He told them what they must do: "MAKE DISCIPLES OF ALL THE NATIONS!" The command is clear, concise, comprehensive! First, they must wait in Jerusalem for the Holy Spirit (Acts 1:4-5). Then they would "receive power" and become His witnesses, "both in Jerusalem and in all Judea and Samaria and even to the remotest part of the earth" (1:8).

47

The disciples began to understand. The Book of Acts demonstrates this beyond doubt. Luke's document is a precise record of the disciples' activities and accomplishments as they seriously and systematically carried out Jesus Christ's marching orders.

A CLOSER LOOK

Look more carefully at the content of this enormous command. They were to *make disciples*—an imperative. In verse 19 the word "go" in the original text is a participle, along with two additional participles in verse 20, "baptizing" and "teaching." But all of these verb forms imply *action* and spell out in greater detail what Christ wanted them to do. In essence, Jesus was saying, "As you *go, make disciples; baptize* these disciples, and *teach* them to do what I have taught you." Stating it still more simply, the disciples of Christ heard Jesus say that day, "Go everywhere and win men to Christ [that is, make Christians], and then baptize them and teach these Christians the truth that I have taught you."

People who became followers of Christ were immediately identified as "disciples." They were not called Christians until the church was founded in Antioch (Acts 11:26). A clear illustration of the fulfillment of Jesus' instructions to *make disciples* as well as *to teach* them is seen in Acts 14:21-22a: "And after they had preached the Gospel to that city [Derbe] and had *made many disciples*, they returned to Lystra and to Iconium and to Antioch, *strengthening the souls of the disciples*, encouraging them to continue in the faith."[1]

In other words, on Paul's first missionary journey, he and Barnabas preached the Gospel and won many to Christ (made many disciples). Later, on the same journey, they returned to Lystra, to Iconium, and to Antioch, and strengthened the new Christians (the disciples)—a direct fulfillment of Christ's commission in Matthew 28:19-20.

The church therefore exists to carry out two foundational functions—*evangelism* (to make disciples) and *edification* (to teach them). These two functions in turn answer two questions: First, why does the church exist in the world? and second, why does the church exist as a gathered community?

When you ask, "Why does the church exist in the world?" you

are asking what God expects to do through His people as they come in contact with the unbelieving world! When you ask, "Why does the church exist as a gathered community?" you are asking what God intends to happen to believers as they meet together as members of the body of Christ.[2]

AN OVERVIEW

Evangelism and edification are separate but interrelated functions in the New Testament. Both types of activity are very clear and observable, but not always mutually exclusive. The church as a "gathered community" is shown as having distinctive activities and objectives. The church as it ministers to the world likewise has distinctive activities and objectives.

This can best be illustrated with the table that follows entitled "Why Does the Church Exist?" Though space prohibits an exhaustive presentation of all of the New Testament content which illustrates how the early church carried out the Great Commission of our Lord, most of the basic Scripture references and passages are categorized so you can make your own study.

The two tasks of *evangelism* and *edification* are classified into two columns. Scripture texts are included which illustrate both the *functions* and *directives* (that is, *how* these tasks are carried out), as well as the *results* and *objectives* which were achieved. In some instances *evangelistic* and *edification* functions are so interrelated in Luke's records they are indistinguishable. In these cases the Scripture texts appear in the middle of the table.

As you read through the New Testament with these two basic questions in mind (that is, "why does the church exist in the world?" and "why does the church exist as a gathered community?"), you will discover that the correspondence which makes up a large segment of the New Testament was written for the primary purpose of edification. These letters were to be read and studied by the churches for the purpose of spiritual growth and development. Therefore, all of this biblical content could be included in column two in the table. Consequently, each Epistle is identified (in name only) somewhere in the table.

However, many of the Epistles include biographical material and other information and instructions which are particularly illustrative of and pertinent to both *evangelism* and *edification*. Therefore, in addition to including the name of each letter per se in the *edification* column, selected references from the Epistles are also included in *both* columns.[3]

SUMMARY

This is where we must begin a study of the New Testament church. Christ's commission states in general terms *why* He left the church on earth. The Book of Acts and the Epistles demonstrate, first, that His disciples took Christ's instructions seriously, and, second, the *way* in which they carried out His command. Matthew 28:19-20 outlines the basic tasks and the rest of the New Testament fills in that outline with dynamic examples and additional instructions, which help us understand in a more comprehensive way what Christ had in mind for His church on earth.

Chapters 4 to 8 of this book present a detailed report and interpretation of the Scriptures which are outlined in the following table. However, before proceeding to read *my* interpretations, make your own inductive study. The research model illustrated in figure 11 will help you understand how to work through this exciting process. To assist you with your own inductive study, Appendix A includes a *written* compilation of the Scriptures outlined in the chart which follows. Specific instructions are also given regarding *how* to do this study.

Footnotes

[1]Note that the words "make disciples" in Matthew 28:19 and "made . . . disciples" in Acts 14:21 represent the same verb form in the Greek New Testament.
[2]It will be shown later that the "church gathered" exists to carry on *more* than a teaching function. Teaching, however, is the first step in developing a body of mature believers. This is demonstrated clearly in the Book of Acts.
[3]An unusual example of this is found in 1 Thessalonians, particularly in chapters 1 and 2 where Paul reflects upon his ministry in Thessalonica where the church was first founded. (See Acts 17.) Paul states ideas and concepts in 1 Thessalonians that are very illustrative of both his evangelistic work among them (1 Thes. 1), as well as his ministry among the new converts in carrying out the process of edification (1 Thes. 2).

WHY DOES THE CHURCH EXIST?

	EVANGELISM — Going—Make Disciples / Why the Church Exists in the World		EDIFICATION — Baptizing—Teaching Them / Why the Church Exists as a Gathered Community		
	Functions and Directives	Results and Objectives	Functions and Directives	Results and Objectives	ACTS / EPISTLES
ACTS	Declaring Speaking Proclaiming Preaching Testifying Etc.	Many believed The Word of God kept spreading Some were persuaded Etc.	Baptizing Teaching Encouraging Strengthening Reporting Etc.	Were of one mind Were of one heart and soul Were being built up Etc.	
EPISTLES	Love your neighbor as yourself Keep your behavior excellent among the Gentiles	So that . . . they may glorify God in the day of visitation	Encourage one another Build up one another We admonish and teach every man	That we may present every man complete in Christ	

Figure 11. A Research Model

WHY DOES THE CHURCH EXIST?

Why Does the Church Exist in the World?		Why Does the Church Exist as a "Gathered Community"?	
GOING—MAKE DISCIPLES		BAPTIZING—TEACHING THEM	
EVANGELISM		EDIFICATION	
Function and Directives	Results and Objectives	Functions and Directives	Results and Objectives
Acts 1:8		Acts 2:41-42	

Acts 2:46-47

Acts 4:1-2, 4
Acts 4:31
Acts 5:12-14   Acts 4:32
Acts 5:19-21a
Acts 5:25

Why the Church Exists

Acts 5:27-28	
Acts 5:42	
Acts 6:4, 7	
Acts 8:1b-4	
Acts 8:5	Acts 8:12
Acts 8:25	
Acts 8:35	Acts 8:36, 38
Acts 9:20	
Acts 9:31	
Acts 10:42-43	
Acts 11:19-21	Acts 11:22-26
Acts 12:24	
Acts 13:5a	
Acts 13:13-16, 42-44	
Acts 13:45-49	

THE EPISTLE OF JAMES
James 3:1-2

Acts 14:1	
Acts 14:5-7	
Acts 14:19-21a	Acts 14:21b-23
Acts 14:25	Acts 14:26-28
	Acts 15:2-4
Acts 16:31-32	Acts 16:33-34, 40
Acts 17:2-4	

THE THESSALONIAN LETTERS
(written from Corinth)

1 Thessalonians 1:5-10	1 Thessalonians 2:7-12
	1 Thessalonians 3:1-5
	1 Thessalonians 3:10-13
	1 Thessalonians 5:11
	1 Thessalonians 5:14-15
2 Thessalonians 3:1	
Acts 17:10-12	
Acts 17:16-17	
Acts 17:22, 34	
Acts 18:4-5	
Acts 18:8-11	

THE CORINTHIAN LETTERS
(written from Ephesus and
Macedonia)

1 Corinthians 1:17	1 Corinthians 1:10
1 Corinthians 1:21-24	1 Corinthians 4:17
1 Corinthians 2:1-5	
1 Corinthians 5:9-10	
1 Corinthians 9:16	
1 Corinthians 11:26	
1 Corinthians 14:23-25	

1 Corinthians 15:58

2 Corinthians 1:9	
2 Corinthians 4:5	
2 Corinthians 5:18-20	
Acts 18:19-21	Acts 18:22-23
	Acts 18:24-28
	Acts 19:1-7
	Acts 19:9
Acts 19:8	Acts 19:23; 20:1-2

Acts 19:10, 20

	THE ROMAN LETTER
Romans 1:8	Romans 1:9-13

Romans 1:14-16

Romans 13:8-10

Romans 16:25-27

	Acts 20:6-7
	Acts 20:17-21
Acts 20:22-24	Acts 20:25-35
Acts 22—26 (Paul's	
testimony in Jerusalem,	
before Felix,	
Festus, and Agrippa)	
Acts 28:23-24	
Acts 28:30-31	
	THE PRISON EPISTLES
	Philemon
Ephesians 3:8-9	Ephesians 1:15-19a;
	3:14-19
	Ephesians 2:19-22
	Ephesians 4:11-16
	Ephesians 6:1-4
Colossians 1:25-28a	Colossians 1:9-12
Colossians 4:5-6	Colossians 1:28b-29
	Colossians 2:2-5
	Colossians 3:16

	Colossians 3:18-23
Philippians 1:12-14	
Philippians 1:27-28	
	Philippians 2:1-4
	Philippians 2:19-24
	Philippians 4:9
	THE PASTORAL EPISTLES
1 Timothy 2:1-7	1 Timothy 1:3-7
	1 Timothy 4:11-16
	1 Timothy 5:17
1 Timothy 6:1	1 Timothy 6:2
	2 Timothy 1:6-11
	2 Timothy 2:2
	2 Timothy 3:14-17
	2 Timothy 4:1-2
2 Timothy 4:4-5	
	Titus 1:5
	Titus 2:1-15
ADDITIONAL CORRESPONDENCE	
	Hebrews 3:12-14
	Hebrews 5:12-14
	Hebrews 6:1
	Hebrews 10:24-25
1 Peter 2:12	1 Peter 2:1-5
1 Peter 2:18	1 Peter 4:10-11
1 Peter 3:1-2	1 Peter 5:1-3
1 Peter 3:15	
	2 Peter
1 John 1:1-2	1 John 1:2-4
	2 John
	3 John
	Jude 3
	Jude 20-21
	Jude 24
	Revelation 1-3

The list of the Epistles in the "edification" column is not meant to be completely chronological and sequential. In some instances they are; in other instances, they are included so as to be in close proximity to the record of the founding of that particular church in the Book of Acts. The general chronologies, however, are based upon Merrill C. Tenney's *New Testament Survey*, rev. ed., Eerdmans.

FOUR

MAKING DISCIPLES

Before you read this chapter, complete the inductive study in Appendix A, then study Appendix B. These will provide you with a biblical foundation for the following material.

A PANORAMIC VIEW

Jesus Christ spent three and a half years ministering on this earth. He went everywhere preaching the kingdom of God to the *multitudes*, teaching people who He was and demonstrating His deity by working miracles (John 20:30-31).

But He also spent much of His time with *twelve men* He had carefully selected and then trained, not in a formal educational setting, but in a "field-type," real-life learning situation. They associated with Him in His ministry, and they saw Him demonstrate with His own life how to do God's work. He eventually sent them out on their own and then carefully helped them learn from their successes and failures.[1]

At the end of these three and a half years, Jesus had basically accomplished two major goals in terms of strategy: He had *saturated the minds of the multitudes* with His teachings, and *prepared a small group of men* in depth to enter into His labors and bring in the harvest (4:35-38). After His death and resurrection (His primary purpose in coming into this world), He gave His followers a great evangelistic commission—"Make disciples!"

They did! They built immediately upon the foundations which Jesus had laid. They began in Jerusalem where He had taught, died, and rose again. They went everywhere—in the temple, from house to house, before the Jewish council, in the synagogues, and on the streets.[2]

Hearts were prepared. The Holy Spirit worked in power! The harvest was great!—*so great* the Jewish leaders were threatened and responded with hatred and counteraction.

But this response only served to fulfill the ultimate plan of God, for believers were scattered everywhere throughout Judea and Samaria and to the uttermost parts of the then known world. Everywhere they carried the message of Christ's death and resurrection and that He truly *was the promised Messiah*—not only for the Jews but also the One spoken of to Abraham so many years before—the One in whom "all the families of the earth" would "be blessed" (Gen. 12:3). "And I have other sheep," Jesus said, "which are not of this fold; I must bring them also, and they shall hear My voice; and they shall become one flock with one Shepherd" (John 10:16). Both Jews and Gentiles entered the family of God after the church expanded its outreach and its impact upon the world.

As a result a new phenomenon came into being—something which had not existed while Christ was on earth. It began in Jerusalem after Christ's ascension and then spread throughout the New Testament world. Wherever believers *made disciples*, local churches came into being. People who lived in various communities and cultures were brought together to form new relationships. They became brothers and sisters in Christ—members of the family of God. A new force was established, not to form as a "traveling group" but as a people "settled in a community," where they lived, worked and carried on the other routine responsibilities in life. And as they were taught and edified, they soon discovered that they had two basic responsibilities—one "to the world" and the other "to each other."

The Power of Love. Interestingly, the Epistles contain few instructions regarding direct evangelism as it was practiced by those who "traveled" in the Book of Acts. Great emphasis was placed on "corporate" responsibility. Emphasis on "verbal presentation" of the Gospel was subordinated to "maintaining a dynamic relationship within the church" and "maintaining a loving, exemplary relationship" with those in the world.

Opportunities to present the Gospel of Christ verbally were to grow naturally out of the saturation that took place in the community, saturation that reflected "love and concern for all men." Lifestyles were to be so different and dramatically changed by Christ that unbelievers could not help but notice and inquire what made the difference.

Above all, the love that existed among the local group of believers was to be so forceful that unbelievers would notice that they were *disciples of Jesus Christ*. Further, they would become convinced that Jesus truly *was* who He said He *was*.

As Christ was approaching the time of His crucifixion, He remarked to His disciples one day, "A new commandment I give to you, that you love one another, even as I have loved you, that you also love one another." Notice the objective which follows this directive from the Lord Jesus: "By this all men will know that you are My disciples, if you have love for one another" (13:34-35).

Community evangelism was to be preceded by a corporate example of "love" among believers. It would be "proof positive" that the disciples of Christ reside there. For no other sect, religion, or group was ever capable of rising to the level of love that was potentially possible in the true family of God. And without its existence, evangelistic efforts would be thwarted.

The Power of Unity. But there is another factor here that is basic to community evangelism. It is actually a reflection of "love." Francis Schaeffer has called it "the final apologetic."[3] Jesus spoke of it in John 17:21, 23 while praying for His disciples. He asked the Father "that they may all be *one*, even as Thou, Father, art in Me, and I in Thee, that they also may be in Us; that the world may believe that Thou didst send Me. . . . I in them, and Thou in Me, that they may be perfected in *unity*, that the world may know that Thou didst send Me, and didst love them, even as Thou didst love Me."

Here Christ speaks of the results of love—that is, unity and oneness. By seeing love, non-Christians would come to *know* and *understand* that people are Christians, followers of Jesus Christ.

But by observing *unity* and *oneness* they would become *convinced* of who Christ really was—that He came from God—that He was truly the Son of God, the Saviour of the world.

In the Book of Acts this phenomenon was demonstrated forcefully. It was the love and unity among Christians in Jerusalem that provided the base for effective witness. And this idea, as demonstrated earlier, is reinforced again and again throughout the Epistles. But it will be demonstrated even more as we look later at the edification process as it is illustrated in the churches in the New Testament.

A CLOSER LOOK

Evangelistic Communication in the Book of Acts. Though a number of words are used to recount the evangelistic activities and functions of first-century believers, Luke used several basic words to describe the process of communication with non-Christians. Those which follow appear most frequently, and although similar in meaning, each, as used in context, contributes to our understanding of *how* the unsaved world was reached with the Gospel of Christ in the first century.

They spoke. One of the most common words is the one translated "speaking" or "spoke." The word *laleo* simply means "to talk" or "to tell." We read that Peter and John were in the temple "*speaking* to the people" (Acts 4:1). Later as the congregation of the disciples was filled with the Holy Spirit, they all "began to *speak* the Word of God with boldness" (4:31).[4]

Though this word (*laleo*) is the most common one used in describing the way the message of Christianity was presented, we can learn several lessons about the process from the context in which the word was used. Frequently, we are told they "spoke the word" (their message); they spoke "in the name of Jesus" (their authority); and they spoke with "boldness" (their manner). They were to speak "the whole message of this Life"; and they spoke "in such a manner that a great multitude believed."

They evangelized. This word is frequently translated that the followers of Christ "preached the Gospel" or "told the Good News." Unlike the word "to speak," this word (*euangelidzo*) is a "content" word in itself. It refers to the *message* that was being spoken as well as the *process* of communication. In Acts 5:42, Luke recorded that "every day, in the temple and from house to house, they kept right on . . . *preaching Jesus as the Christ*"; that is, "they kept right on . . . *telling the Good News:* Jesus is the Promised Saviour" (BECK).[5]

This process was carried on by both groups and individuals. It was carried out by *all* believers; it took place in the temple, from house to house, from village to village, from city to city, on a desert road, and its outreach was constantly expanded to regions beyond. They went everywhere telling the Good News.

They taught. Though *didasko* (meaning to teach) is one of the most common words in the New Testament used to describe edification, it is also used to describe evangelism. In this latter sense, the word appears most frequently in the opening chapters of the Book of Acts and on several occasions was used in a context of displeasure and unhappiness on the part of the Jews. They were "greatly disturbed because they [Peter and John] were *teaching* the people" (4:2).[6]

Following the apostles' secret release from jail, they all entered the "temple about daybreak, and began to *teach*" (5:21). Surprised by their appearance, someone rushed off to tell the chief priest that the men they had locked in prison the day before were "standing in the temple and *teaching* the people" (5:25). The apostles were immediately taken into custody again, and in consternation the high priest said, "We gave you strict orders not to continue *teaching* in this name, and behold, you have filled Jerusalem with your *teaching*"[7] (5:28).

Perhaps the most significant observation regarding the teaching process with non-Christians in the early days of the church is that it was used primarily by the apostles. This may imply that it is a more sophisticated process than just "speaking" or "evangelizing," calling for greater skill and knowledge. Obviously, it involved more than just presenting the Gospel of Christ but rather included the presentation of the total message of Scriptures (see 5:21-22). The apostles, of course, were in a unique position to communicate this message, having spent three and a half years being trained by the greatest Teacher who ever lived. It is significant that the rulers and scribes "observed the confidence of Peter and

John, and understood that they were uneducated and untrained men." Consequently, "they were marveling, and began to recognize them as having been with Jesus" (4:13).

Note too that the apostles' teaching among non-Christians brought both positive and negative results. The positive results were conversions, first among the Jewish lay people. Consequently, the negative results came from their religious leaders. Here was one group of religious leaders against another group of religious leaders, false teachers reacting to true teachers. The apostles were presenting the truth, which laid bare the sins and false views of the priests and leaders of Israel. They became jealous and angry and fought back.

But, interestingly, we read in the chapter following this persecution that when the apostles resolved the material problems in Acts 6 and were able to maintain their priorities in teaching the Scriptures, "many of the priests" also responded to the Gospel (6:7).

Here we see the true test of effective teaching among non-Christians. The apostles not only won lay people to Christ but eventually won many religious leaders as well.

They proclaimed or preached. The word *kerusso* means to cry or proclaim as a herald. "Philip went down to the city of Samaria and began *proclaiming* Christ to them. And the multitudes with one accord were giving attention to what was said by Philip" (8:5-6).[8]

The word "proclaim" is used primarily in conjunction with the activities of certain key people in the Book of Acts, specifically, Philip the evangelist, the Apostle Peter and the Apostle Paul. Again, like "teaching," this activity among non-Christians seemed to be the responsibility of certain gifted individuals who had been chosen by God to proclaim in a special way the Gospel of Christ (see Acts 10:40-42). All Christians, of course, spoke about Christ and witnessed for Him, but not all proclaimed Christ in a formal way.

They announced. A word closely related to *kerusso* is the word *katangello*, meaning "to announce publicly," or "to proclaim and tell thoroughly." Like *kerusso*, it is used in Acts in describing the communication of apostolic leaders, particularly the ministry of Paul.[9]

In most cases this word was used to describe communication in the various Jewish synagogues. Here in these religious centers of learning and worship Paul "thoroughly announced" and "proclaimed" the Word of God.

They solemnly testified. A common word for *testify* is *martureo,* meaning "to bear witness" (1:8). However, throughout the Book of Acts some form of the verb *diamarturomai* was also used to describe the evangelistic process and is frequently translated "solemnly testified." It means to "earnestly charge and attest," and has both strong intellectual and emotional overtones. The Word of God was being presented seriously, carefully, and with determination. If *martureo* means "to bear witness," *diamarturomai* means "to bear a thorough witness."

This concept first appeared in Acts in Peter's sermon on the Day of Pentecost, when "with many other words he *solemnly testified* and kept on exhorting them, saying, 'Be saved from this perverse generation!' " (2:40) And it appeared finally in the last chapter of Acts, where we find Paul in Rome. When he arrived he was allowed to "stay by himself, with the soldier who was guarding him" (28:16). Paul called together the Jewish leaders and rehearsed the events from Jerusalem onward. The Jews appointed a day for Paul to present his total case. And on that day, "they came to him at his lodging in large numbers; and he was explaining to them by *solemnly testifying* about the kingdom of God, and trying to persuade them concerning Jesus, from both the Law of Moses and from the Prophets, from morning until evening" (28:23).[10]

As you trace this word through the Book of Acts, it takes on a strong "apologetic" syndrome. Both Peter and Paul, the two apostles whose communication was described by this word, were attempting to convince their hearers that Jesus Christ was truly the Messiah promised in the Old Testament. They were not simply presenting the Gospel but were attesting and giving evidence from the Old Testament as well as from their own personal experience that Jesus was the Christ.

They reasoned. The word *dialegomai,* meaning to "to reason, to discourse with, or to discuss," is used *only* of Paul's communication with the non-Christian world. And, also, the word does not appear in the Acts until Paul arrived in Thessalonica. Here we find him going into the synagogue and "for three Sabbaths, *reasoned* with them from the Scriptures, explaining and giving evidence that the Christ had to suffer and rise again from the dead" (17:2-3).[11]

As you look at the communication process that took place in this new dimension involving extensive dialogue and interaction, note that Paul's ministry was increasingly taking him into a pagan environment permeated with Greek and Roman thought and culture. Both Jews and Greeks were totally ignorant of what had really transpired in the land of Palestine over the last several years. To the religious Jews the promised Messiah was not a new concept, but they probably knew little about Jesus of Nazareth. What they *had* heard was no doubt colored with prejudicial interpretations. The Greeks, of course, would have known little if anything, their only source of information being the Jewish community.

Notice too that Luke began recording time factors in the context where this word was used. For example, Paul stayed on in Corinth for a year and a half (18:11) and in Ephesus for two years (19:10).

Taking into consideration the mentality of these people, their cultural backgrounds, their total ignorance regarding Christianity as well as the method of communication they were used to, the implication is obvious. Paul adopted an evangelistic methodology that could more effectively reach these people. Furthermore, he knew he had no foundation from which to build. Consequently, he settled into these strategic communities, got to know the thinking of these people, and taught the Scriptures in depth on their mental and emotional wave lengths.

EVANGELISTIC COMMUNICATION IN THE EPISTLES

As you trace through the communication process in the Book of Acts, the emphasis is naturally upon the activities and functions of first-century Christians as they *spoke* about Christ, *told* the Good News, *taught, proclaimed, testified,* and *reasoned* with unbelievers. But as you move to a study of the Epistles, activities become directives. This, of course, is what we would expect. Luke's purpose was to record the "acts" of the followers of Christ, and the Epistles were written to teach and nurture those who responded to the Gospel.

There is also a decided shift in emphasis. The Epistles add a new dimension to the way evangelism was carried out by the established churches.

It is clear that the evangelistic thrust launched in Acts was to continue in communities where local churches had been established. Paul was particularly pleased with the impact of the churches in Thessalonica and Rome (1 Thes. 1:9; Rom. 1:8). Everywhere he went, he seemed to get positive feedback regarding the testimony of these Christians.

But as you read through the Epistles with "evangelism" in mind, you soon discover that to be settled in a community calls for more than verbalization. In fact, communication must be solidly aligned with a Christian lifestyle—both at the individual and corporate levels. This Christian lifestyle must be demonstrated in the various contexts of living—the Christian's business life, his social life, his home life, his church life, and his life in general.

Business life. Paul admonished the Thessalonians particularly to conduct their business affairs in a proper manner. Some of them were using the doctrine of the second coming of Christ as an excuse for being lazy. "Attend to your own business and work with your hands," Paul exhorted (1 Thes. 4:11) and then gave the reason why—"so that you may behave properly toward *outsiders* and not be in any need" (4:12). Paul taught that for a Christian to have material needs because of laziness was to bring the Gospel and the church of Jesus Christ into ill repute. If they were to effectively evangelize their unsaved neighbors, they certainly would not be able to communicate the Gospel effectively by living irresponsible lives.

Both Paul and Peter were concerned about the fact that Christians should maintain a good testimony before unsaved masters. They were to regard them "as worthy of all honor so that the name of God and our doctrine may not be spoken against" (1 Tim. 6:1). "Be submissive to your masters," said Peter (1 Peter 2:18).

What a way to attack the evils of slavery! In many instances they won their unsaved masters to Christ as well *as winning their freedom.* To do the opposite in those days would have brought instant persecution and perhaps even death. But most of all, it would have interfered with the cause of Christ.

Regarding Paul's approach to the problem of slavery, Merrill Tenney succinctly observes:

> Nowhere in its pages is the institution attacked or is it defended. According to Paul's letters to the Asian churches, there were both slaves and slave holders who were Christians. Slaves were enjoined to obey their masters, and the masters were commanded not to be cruel to them. Such was the power of Christian fellowship, however, that the institution of slavery gradually weakened under its impact and finally disappeared.[12]

Social life. To live in a community day after day and week after week necessitates maintaining relationships. Many of the believers of the New Testament were converted out of a society that involved a lifestyle unbecoming to a Christian. With their unsaved friends in view, Paul admonished Christians to "give no offense either to Jews or to Greeks" in their social life. "Whether, then, you eat or drink or whatever you do, do all to the glory of God," in order, said Paul, "that they may be saved" (1 Cor. 10:31-33).

With the pagan Corinthian culture in view, these words are not hard to understand. The way to win people to Christ was *not* to tell them about Jesus Christ and then to participate in their immoral and anti-Christian activities either within the church or outside in the community. To do so would only offend the unbeliever and create disillusionment with the true message of Christianity.

"Keep your behavior excellent among the Gentiles," wrote Peter, "so that . . . they may . . . glorify God in the day of visitation" (1 Peter 2:12). Also, he said, "Keep a good conscience so that . . . those who revile your good behavior in Christ may be put to shame" (3:16).

Peter was not saying that all would respond to the Gospel. But he was saying that when the Holy Spirit begins His work in the heart of a man, he needs the backdrop of a Christian lifestyle to be able to evaluate objectively the claims of Christianity. Furthermore, Peter was saying that those who do not respond will be "put to shame" or silenced.

Home life. There were those in New Testament days who were married to unbelievers. Their marital partners had not yet come to Christ, particularly husbands.

Were these Christian wives to verbally bombard their unsaved husbands with the Gospel? Were they to hound them to come out to church and hear the pastor or visiting evangelist? Were they to talk about the virtues of other Christian men, particularly the leaders of the church?

Not at all! "Be submissive to your own husbands," wrote Peter, "so that even if any of them are disobedient to the Word they may be won *without a word by the behavior of their wives*" (3:1).

The apostle was stating a profound truth! It is not the piling up of words that convinces unsaved spouses that they need Christ, but rather the impact of a continuous Christlike lifestyle that reflects the reality of the indwelling Holy Spirit (3:2-7).

Church life. Very little is said in the New Testament about preaching Gospel messages when believers gathered to be edified. Rather, Christians were to devote themselves "to the apostles' teaching"; that is, to learning the Word of God. They were to devote themselves to "fellowship" with one another and with God. And in the process they were to have "favor with all the people"; that is, with the unsaved world. We see this model in the first church—the church in Jerusalem (Acts 2:42-47). And as will be demonstrated later, we see this emphasis throughout the Epistles.

The Corinthian church stands out as a *negative* example. The church meetings were chaotic. People spoke in tongues—one after the other—with no interpreter. No doubt more than one spoke at the same time, and women were obviously doing much of the talking. "If . . . unbelievers enter, will they not say you are mad?" queried Paul (1 Cor. 14:23).

This is why he put an emphasis on prophesying in church meetings and speaking the Word of God clearly and in an orderly manner. Unbelievers must understand the Word in order to be saved (1 Cor. 14:25).

The church was also to engage in another very important evangelistic ministry—that of prayer. They were to pray for all men that they may be saved (1 Tim. 2:1-4). They were also to pray for those who were called especially to preach the Gospel to regions beyond their own communities. On several occasions Paul requested prayers for his own evangelistic ministry, "that the Word of the Lord may spread rapidly and be glorified" (Eph. 6:19).

Life in General. Though the Epistles pinpoint special situations and environments in which Christians were to maintain a good testimony, they also speak to life in general. "You are our letter . . . known and read by all men," Paul said to the Corinthians (2 Cor. 3:2). "Love your neighbor as yourself," he wrote to the Romans (Rom. 13:9). "Conduct yourself with wisdom toward outsiders, making the most of the opportunity," he admonished the Colossians. "Let your speech always be with grace, seasoned, as it were, with salt, so that you may know how you should respond to each person" (Col. 4:5-6). To this Peter adds: "Being ready to make a defense to every one who asks you to give an account for the hope that is in you" (1 Peter 3:15). The Philippians were told to conduct themselves "in a manner worthy of the Gospel" (Phil. 1:27).

SUMMARY
The Book of Acts and the New Testament correspondence leave no doubt that the great evangelistic impact of a group of believers in a given community was based first of all upon an individual and corporate testimony before the unsaved world, reflecting love, unity, and godly living. This was to become the backdrop against which a vital verbal witness was to be shared with those who were influenced daily, as Christians carried on their business in the community, associated with the unsaved through social contacts, demonstrated a dynamic homelife in each particular community, reflected love, unity, and maturity as a local body of believers, and in general lived a Christian life, both in what was said and what was done.

Footnotes

[1]For an excellent study of how Jesus worked with the Twelve, see Robert E. Coleman, *The Master Plan of Evangelism,* Fleming Revell.

[2]Appendix B includes a compilation of the biblical functions and results, and directives and objectives which grow out of an inductive study of the scriptural materials outlined in chapter 2 and compiled in Appendix A.

[3]Francis A. Schaeffer, *The Church at the End of the Twentieth Century,* InterVarsity, p. 138.

[4]See also Acts 5:20, 40; 11:19-20; 14:1, 25; 16:13, 32.

[5]See also Acts 8:4, 25, 35; 11:20; 14:5, 7, 21; 16:10.

[6]See also Acts 5:41-42; 28:30-31.

[7]Frequently translated "doctrine."

[8]See also Acts 9:20; 10:39, 42; 20:25; 28:30-31.

[9]See Acts 4:2, 13:5, 38; 15:36; 17:3.

[10]See also Acts 10:42; 18:5; 20:24; 23:11.

[11]See also Acts 17:17; 18:4, 19; 19:8-10; 24:24-25.

[12]Merrill C. Tenney, *New Testament Survey,* rev. ed. Eerdmans, p. 50.

FIVE

PRINCIPLES OF NEW TESTAMENT EVANGELISM

What does a study of first-century evangelism say to the twentieth-century church, wherever it may be? What overarching principles can we glean from the study, which in turn can be established as purposes for the church today, in any culture or subculture?

Following are seven key principles which grow naturally out of the study of the evangelistic activities and functions described in the Book of Acts and the directives stated in the Epistles.

CREATE A BASIS FOR EVANGELISM

First, *every local body of believers is responsible to saturate its community with love and to demonstrate a unity and oneness that provide the basis for verbal communication; to demonstrate a Christian lifestyle in all human relationships, so as to create a basis on which to discuss the life-changing Christ.*

This principle is clear from the activities of New Testament Christians and the directives given to local groups of believers in the Epistles. They began in Jerusalem, and then, as churches were established in other communities and countries, Christians were instructed to live like Jesus Christ in every human relationship to be able to share the Gospel forcefully.

Frequently, local churches neglect their own communities. A virile foreign missions program becomes a substitute for local outreach. Missionary budgets replace "across the street" evangelism. Overseas missionaries supported by the church become a substitute for engaging in local outreach.

This ought not be! We must not neglect our own "Jerusalem." The field is the world—of course—but the world begins in our own backyard, our own hometown, our own community. This was the story of New Testament believers. They set the example for foreign missions—true—but they had a proper world view. It included "Jerusalem," "Judea," "Samaria," and then "the remotest part of the earth" (Acts 1:8).

True, one of the greatest accomplishments of evangelical Christianity has been its foreign missionary thrust. It is commendable! And it should be continued and expanded. But the words of Jesus apply at this juncture, "These are the things you should have done without neglecting the others" (Matt. 23:23).

It is important to underscore again that when Jesus Christ was on earth, people saw and heard *Him*. His miracles and lifestyle became the means by which unbelievers could evaluate His claims (John 20:20-31). But when He returned to heaven, His body, the church, became the visible means by which people could evaluate the message of Christ. (Read again John 13:13-35; 17:19-23.)

One of the challenges facing us in our ministry in the Dallas metroplex is *how* to apply this principle. We have made some attempts. First, we work hard at creating an atmosphere of warmth and love when the church meets corporately. The people leading and participating in any given service are encouraged to view the place we meet as a large, comfortable living room. This, in turn, affects our manner and approach from the platform and also influences the attitude of our people toward others—particularly newcomers. We want people to sense that we are real, that we care about one another and we care about them, though they may be new.

We've also formed a group we call a "hospitality team." Trained and encouraged to reach out to new people particularly, they nevertheless try not to neglect the regulars. Following each service, we introduce new people and ask volunteers to meet each visitor after the service and have a cup of coffee (or tea, or whatever) in a designated area for fellowship.

CORPORATE EVANGELISM BASIC

This leads us to a second New Testament principle, *corporate evangelism is basic to personal evangelism.*

In the New Testament the functioning body of Christ set the stage for individual witness. This is why Jesus said, "Love one another" so that "all men will know that you are My disciples" (John 13:34). This is why Paul said, "Love your neighbor as yourself" (Rom. 13:9), and why Peter exhorted believers to keep their "behavior excellent among the Gentiles" (1 Peter 2:12). Personal evangelism takes on unusual significance against the backdrop of a mature body of local believers—Christians who are making an impact in their communities because of their integrity (1 Thes. 4:11-12), their unselfish behavior (Rom 13:7); their orderly conduct (1 Cor. 6:1); their humility (1 Peter 2:18); and yet, their forthright testimony for Jesus Christ (3:15).

It is difficult to witness in isolation. It is often necessary, but God's general plan is that community evangelism be carried out in the context of dynamic Christianity and vigorous "body life."

United and functioning in all of its parts, the local church can make a powerful impact on a pagan community. Then it is not so much the extrovertish individuals who are often glamorized as the "most spiritual" because they witness, but it becomes a ministry of the total church in which all share the joy and reward of those who have the privilege of "drawing the net" for Christ.

Applying this principle calls for unique church structures in the twentieth-century culture. Most traditional forms do not provide the best opportunities to demonstrate love in action. True, we can create a warm, accepting atmosphere when the church meets corporately, but as the congregation grows, quickly "body life" of necessity becomes difficult to maintain.

Furthermore, many unsaved people who need to see the body functioning in love and unity will not enter a church building.

However, many will come to a meeting in a home. In that sense, we can take the "functioning body" to the world—through evangelistic home Bible studies, nonthreatening discussion meetings, and what we call in our own ministry minichurches. There is great potential in this kind of "form" for applying the New Testament principles just stated. Personally, I feel we have not even begun to implement this principle in this kind of "family setting."

EVANGELIZE IN LOVE

Third, *when possible, presenting the Gospel to the unsaved is to take place against the backdrop of a loving and unified body of Christians.*

The Scriptures do not suggest that non-Christians should be excluded from the "church gathered." Rather, the Bible teaches that unbelievers should be exposed to the church gathered as an orderly and unified body.

Again, this was the problem in Corinth. Unbelievers who might enter would misinterpret what was happening because of the lack of orderliness. But Paul also spoke of non-Christians who might enter and fall under conviction and come to Christ (1 Cor. 14:23-25).[1]

Notice in this passage that the unbeliever will be "convicted by *all*" and will be "called to account by *all*" (14:24). Here is a clear-cut reference to "body evangelism." It was the whole church functioning that was to be used by the Holy Spirit to win this person to Christ.

Note too that he would not come to Christ because of a special evangelistic message preached from the pulpit by a pastor, geared to the unsaved in the audience. Rather, he would be impressed by the believers themselves, their behavior, and the process of mutual edification.[2]

I am reminded of a non-Christian businessman who was attending a new church I was pastoring in its initial days. He asked if he might talk with me about his spiritual condition.

Later when he walked into my office, he told me how impressed he was with the love and concern expressed among the members of this new church. "I have been in many churches," he said, "and served on a number of boards—but have never experienced the kind of Christianity I have seen in this new church."

He then stated openly that he was sure he didn't know Christ personally.

Interestingly, he did not tell me how impressed he was with my sermons, though I knew he appreciated the messages. Rather, he was impressed with the "body." Yes, I had the privilege of leading him to Christ, but it was the local body of functioning believers who were used by God to bring conviction to the man.

The New Testament then presents the "church gathered" as a context in which non-Christians can view and experience the realities of Christianity—love, unity, and Christlike living. And, within this context, the Holy Spirit is able to bring conviction and a desire to worship the same God and to know the same Saviour.

Evangelism in the New Testament also took place, not only as the "church gathered," but as the church was "scattered" into the world—at work, in the communities where the believers lived, in their homes. In fact, it appears that it was in this context that non-Christians were most frequently verbally confronted with the Gospel of Jesus Christ.

AIM FOR ADULTS/FAMILIES
Fourth, *the primary target for evangelism should be adults and consequently, whole households.*

Nowhere in the New Testament are examples given of "child evangelism" as we frequently practice it today; that is, to win children to Christ out in the community apart from the family setting. But don't misunderstand. This does not mean there is not emphasis on the importance of child life and child conversion. Jesus Christ Himself set the supreme example in His attitude toward children. Also Paul wrote to Timothy reminding him of his religious heritage, "From childhood you have known the sacred writings which are able to give you the wisdom that leads to salvation through faith which is in Christ Jesus" (2 Tim. 3:15).

New Testament evidence is also buttressed by the tremendous Old Testament examples of child nurture. In fact, when the family is discussed in Scripture, more seems to be said about children— their needs and their importance—than any other aspects of family life.[3]

The New Testament pattern is clear! The target for conversion was adults. Jesus chose twelve grown men—not children. He spoke to the multitudes (children were no doubt included in the crowds), but His remarks were directed at the adults.

Similarly, in the Book of Acts, the apostles won adults to Christ first of all. They did not go after children as their primary target, hoping to use this as a means to get to parents, nor did they go after children because they were more pliable or easier to reach for Christ.

No, they reversed the process. They went after adults—knowing that parental conversion meant reaching the whole household. Dr. George Peters goes so far as to say in his excellent book *Saturation Evangelism* that "household evangelism and household salvation are the biblical ideal and norm in evangelism and salvation."[4] By this he does not mean that children become Christians because their parents believe. Nor does he mean a "covenant idea" which teaches that children of believing parents experience regeneration through "infant baptism," or that through this rite the child is related to God in some unique way that makes him a potential and actual candidate for conversion later in life.[5]

Conversion is not automatic for any human being. It is an individual matter based on an intelligent and reponsible decision—receiving Christ as personal Saviour.

Household salvation, however, refers to first reaching parents and consequently reaching the whole family for Christ. The New Testament gives several outstanding illustrations of this process. In Philippi, Paul first spoke to Lydia at the riverside. She was converted, and consequently her whole household came to Christ (Acts 16:15). Later in the same city, the Philippian jailer believed in Christ, and as a result his whole household was converted. (16:31-34).

Other examples in the New Testament include Zaccheus, and the nobleman in the Gospels (Luke 19:9; John 4:53). In Acts and the Epistles we see Cornelius (Acts 10), Crispus (18:8), Stephanas (1 Cor. 1:16), Onesiphorus (2 Tim. 1:16), and Philemon (Phile. 1). In fact, the household churches referred to frequently both in the Book of Acts and in the Epistles were no doubt the results of the conversion of whole families.

There are some very practical advantages in reaching adults for Christ and consequently, the whole family. First, it is often psychologically frustrating for a small child to become a Christian apart from the understanding and blessing of his father and mother and other members of the family. In fact, the basic need of a child is "acceptance" and "love" within the family setting, and to experience this kind of rejection can be psychologically devastating. A child is ordinarily emotionally incapable of tolerating this kind of "family persecution."

Second, parents who are also Christians become the primary means for the child's spiritual growth following conversion. If adults need nurture and help following conversion (and they do), so much more do children. The family is a natural spiritual womb for spiritual growth and development.

Third, a total family reached for Christ can create a tremendous impact in a community. Each member of the household in turn becomes an influence for Christ in winning other households.

Fourth, "family units" are the building blocks for a healthy church. Again, Dr. Peters reminds us:

> Only churches that are built out of basic social units have the true health and the potential of rapid growth and steady expansion. The decisive question in founding a church is not how many people are interested in the project but rather how many families form the foundation of the church. Churches founded by families have the potential to flourish.[6]

Let me say in conclusion, however, that this does not mean that children should not be reached for Christ before parents are reached. Though biblical examples do not support the sequence, it certainly does not eliminate this approach. The Lord *is concerned* about children and that they come to know Him personally.

But what the biblical examples *do* say is that when the child is reached for Christ through an individual Christian or through an agency of the church, every attempt should be made to reach the parents for Christ as well, and in the process to seek to keep from interfering with the family's unity and harmony. It may also mean that the church must provide in some way a "father or mother substitute" in cases where non-Christian parents are unresponsive and particularly if they are antagonistic. The very nature of the child makes this almost imperative in order to keep the traumatic experience of parental rejection from creating psychological problems that may even carry over into adult life and perhaps cause the individual eventually to turn against Christianity.

And finally, it means that Christians must not allow the difficulty of reaching adults and the fear of rejection themselves, to cause them to put all of their efforts in winning children because they are more responsive and it is easier to "secure decisions."

One reason statistics show that more children come to Christ is that we are *not efficiently winning adults.* Statistics simply reflect our failure. If whole families could be reached for Christ in the first-century pagan community, we can reach whole families in the twentieth century. The task before us is to develop the right strategy and approach that will work in pagan America.

We must realize, however, that the American culture particularly and the Western culture generally is very much different from the New Testament culture. When a father and mother come to Christ, it does not mean the children will automatically become believers, particularly if the children are older. Furthermore, if a husband comes to Christ, it does not mean the wife will respond as well—or vice versa.

I saw this cultural difference illustrated dramatically on one occasion when a Vietnamese family came to the States and came in contact with one of the members of our church. The father became a believer, told his wife, and she immediately wanted to accept Christ as well. And then all of his children who were old enough to understand automatically did the same. Here, we saw the "biblical" or "Eastern" culture at work in our Western society that so often fosters individualistic rather than corporate decisions.

Nevertheless, adult influence is far greater on children than child influence on adults—even in the Western culture. The biblical emphasis is still normative and transcends culture.

IDENTIFY MISSIONARIES

Fifth, *the church is responsible to identify those who have a desire to carry the Good News in a special way out into the community and beyond the immediate community—even to "the remotest part of the earth."*

As emphasized earlier, the unique nature of the church, with its potential for mutal love and unity, gives unlimited opportunities for an "apologetic" ministry among the unsaved. But within the body are certain people who sense a special burden for evangelistic work. These people must be encouraged to use their talents and represent the local body in a special ministry of evangelism.

Yet they must not become substitutes for the other members

of the body but rather function as those who are able in a special way to present Christ to various individuals and groups. We see this principle demonstrated clearly in the Book of Acts. Many believers "spoke" the message of Christ, and all believers seemed to have a part in "telling the Good News," but it was the apostles especially who engaged in evangelistic *teaching* and *preaching*. It was Peter and particularly Paul who engaged in an evangelistic ministry characterized by "solemnly testifying" and "reasoning" with unbelievers.

The church is further responsible to pray God's blessing upon those individuals and in some cases to suppport them financially as they engage in a part-time or full-time ministry of evangelism and missionary work. This principle is illustrated by the church at Antioch when it set apart Barnabas and Saul and commissioned them for an evangelistic ministry (Acts 13:1-2).

But the church must be careful at this point! Its tendency is to look beyond its immediate community and overlook those within the whole group of believers who are *not* led to leave the community and sail the seven seas. There are those who should be encouraged, trained, and used in a special way to reach out into the community surrounding the church and to lead people to Christ. Yet it should not be done as a work involving "a few individuals" alone but in a way that the whole body assists by saturating the community with the realities of Christianity and the message of the Gospel. Not all may be able to "draw the net" with ease, but all have the capacity to love people and to "sow the seed" and to prepare the way for those who can.

One way we have discovered which creates a desire for evangelism and missions is to encourage young people to participate in overseas ministries, particularly on a short-term basis. Teen Missions,[7] provides an outstanding opportunity for both young people and the church. Youth can spend a summer assisting veteran missionaries and the church can support them financially.

I've seen the effects of this oportunity in my own family. My son spent two summers with Teen Missions, one summer in Sweden and the other in Switzerland. Both times he served on a work team but had opportunities to be involved in evangelism. The impact on his life was enormous.

INTEGRATE NEW BELIEVERS
Sixth, *new believers as soon as possible should be integrated into the life of the local church.*

What it means to be a part of the church will be discussed in more detail later, but at this juncture it is important to emphasize—and to emphasize emphatically—that outside of the context of the church and the experience of drawing upon other members of the body, a new babe in Christ will not grow into a mature responsible disciple of Jesus Christ. He cannot, for he is not involved in basic experiences which God has designed as absolutely essential for spiritual growth.

There are some who will interpret these ideas as criticisms of parachurch organizations and agencies. Let me clarify! I believe God has raised up many organizations, first, to supplement the work of the local church, and, second, to do what, in many cases, the churches have failed to do. But I firmly believe that these organizations must not ignore biblical examples and principles; for if they do, God's richest blessings will not rest on them ultimately. The most obvious example and principle is that God ordained the local church as the primary place where believers are to be nurtured and edified. Each new Christian needs the body of Christ in order to be built up in the Christian life.

Every parachurch organization should seriously consider its relationship to the local church. It must teach this biblical doctrine, promote it as basic to Christian nuture, and strive in a loving and tactful way to correct both the church's theological and functional errors. It must not become a substitute for the local church nor antagonistic to the local church. It must in every way cooperate in furthering the ministry and outreach of this God-ordained plan.

DEVELOP NEW METHODS
Seventh, *the twentieth-century church must develop its own contemporary forms and approaches to evangelism, using the principles just stated as biblical guidelines.*

One thing becomes clear from the study of the functions of the New Testament church. *What* they said is consistent; the *way* they said it and *how* they went about evangelizing varies from situation to situation. They considered the directives as *absolute*. But their methods were *relative* and merely served as means to accomplish divine ends.

This is the genius of the Scriptures. They set men free to create unique approaches and devise methods that are workable in any culture and at any time in history.

Whether you study the structure of Peter's sermons, or follow Paul as he moved out from the Jewish community into the Gentile world, one thing is certain! These men were not locked into *one* approach or a single way of presenting the divine message. They varied their methodology, depending on the circumstances. As a result, as we have noted, as Paul entered the pagan world and moved farther and farther away from the environment that had been previously saturated with the teachings of Jesus Christ, he changed his methods of communication. What had been previously a "proclaiming" type approach became one that was characterized by dialogue and interaction. In Paul's initial work, he could at least assume a basic belief in God and divine revelation, but in the pagan world he could assume neither. It called for a distinct, apologetic approach to evangelism.

Thus the new culture, the new mentality, the difference in awareness—all of these things—served to help Paul determine what methods he should use to reach these people with the Gospel of Christ. True, he always communicated the "simple Gospel" and did so "with humility," but this has to do with message and attitude, not methods.

One of the key problems with the evangelical church in the twentieth century is that we have allowed nonabsolutes to become absolute. We have permitted "ways of doing things" to become normative.

On the one hand we have taken biblical patterns (which vary considerably throughout the Bible) and fixated on the one we feel is the right one—perhaps the one with which we feel the most comfortable. Rather than viewing *all biblical* examples as divine resources which yield absolute principles and guidelines, we develop tunnel vision and allow ourselves to get locked into a single method.

Furthermore, we have allowed purely human patterns and forms which have been developed in the last fifty to one hundred years to become absolute. We actually believe some of the ways we do things now are biblical norms.

A typical example of allowing a purely human approach to become absolute is our thinking regarding the Sunday night evangelistic service (or for that matter any other evangelistic service in the church). Many believers actually believe this is the way the church in the New Testament functioned, whereas we don't have a single example of this approach, nor is it alluded to. In fact, as already pointed out, all church meetings illustrated in the New Testament were designed to build up believers, not to "preach at" unbelievers.

Is it wrong, then, to have a Sunday night evangelistic service? Of course not. The New Testament certainly allows this freedom. But let's remember that this approach was developed in America around the turn of the century, and it worked effectively because of a completely different cultural situation and religious mentality. In many places in America today, the Sunday night evangelistic service is a total failure, for unbelievers no longer come out to church. And yet, some pastors keep preaching their Sunday night evangelistic sermons to a crowd of believers and actually feel guilty if they even consider changing the format and thrust of the service.

The evangelical church *cannot* and *must not* allow itself to get locked into forms and patterns—either first-century or twentieth-century—that have been designed as a means to biblical ends. Every church in every culture and subculture needs to develop its own unique approaches to community evangelism. Under the creative leadership of the Holy Spirit, and using all of the human resources available, we need to develop dynamic twentieth-century churches that are creating contemporary evangelistic strategies that are built on New Testament principles and guidelines.

SUMMARY

Why the church exists in the world is clear! God is calling out a people to be His very own. Someday Christ will return to take the church to be with Himself.

But *why* has He not returned? This question was asked even by the skeptics in the first century (2 Peter 3:4). Notice Peter's answer! "The Lord is not slow about His promise, as some count slowness, but is patient toward you, not wishing for any to perish but for all to come to repentance" (3:9).

How well is your church reaching people for Jesus Christ—*first* in your "own Jerusalem" and *then* in "all Judea and Samaria, and even to the remotest part of the earth"?

The following New Testament principles will guide you in carrying out this aspect of the Great Commission:

1. Every body of believers must be responsible for its own community first.
2. Corporate evangelism is basic to personal evangelism.
3. When possible, presenting the Gospel to the unsaved is to take place against the backdrop of a loving and unified body of Christians.
4. The primary target for evangelism should be adults and consequently, whole households.
5. The church is responsible to identify those who have a desire to carry the Good News in a special way out into the community and beyond the immediate community, even to "the remotest part of the earth."
6. New believers as soon as possible should be integrated into the life of the church.
7. The twentieth-century church must develop its own contemporary forms and approaches to evangelism using the principles and purposes just stated as biblical guidelines.

Footnotes

[1]Note that this is the only specific illustration in the New Testament of evangelism "in the church."

[2]This does not mean it is "wrong" to preach an evangelistic message in a church service. God has used and continues to use this aproach. It *does* mean, however, that the New Testament does not model this approach for carrying out local church evanglism.

[3]See Gene A. Getz, *The Measure of a Family,* Regal Books.

[4]George W. Peters, *Saturation Evangelism,* Zondervan, p. 160. Dr. Peters, Professor Emeritus of World Missions at Dallas Theological Seminary, discusses this idea in depth in his book on pages 147-167.

[5]Ibid., pp. 148-149.
[6]Ibid. p. 155.
[7]P.O. Box 1056, Merrit Island, FL 32952

SIX

BUILDING THE CHURCH

Disciples were to be taught! This is the second great task spelled out in Christ's commission. Believers were to meet as a "gathered community" in order to become a mature organism.

Just as there are a variety of words used to describe the activities of the disciples as they went about "evangelizing," there are also a number of different words used to recount their ministry of "edification." They, of course, *baptized* and *taught* the new believers as Jesus had commanded in the Great Commission. But this process of growth and development also involved *fellowshiping* with one another, *breaking bread*, uniting their hearts in *prayer*, and *praising God*. They were *encouraged, strengthened, implored, exhorted, admonished*, and *established* in the faith.

They also received oral reports which *described* the results of evangelistic effort in other parts of the world. They also received a number of letters (the Epistles) instructing them *how* to live the Christian life.

On occasion, too, there was *dissension* and *debate* as the apostles and leaders confronted other Christians who were guilty of causing confusion among the brethren through false and incorrect teaching. The results of this activity are described in the Book of Acts as causing disciples to "be of one mind," to "be of one heart and soul," and to "be built up." We read that "the churches were being strengthened in the faith," and "the Word of the Lord was growing mightily and prevailing." They also experienced "gladness," and "sincerity of heart," and "great joy." For example, when the disciples in Antioch received the letter from Jerusalem, "they rejoiced because of its encouragement" (Acts 15:31).

As you move from the study of the *functions* and *results* among believers in the Book of Acts to an analysis of the Epistles, once again, *functions* often become *directives,* and *results* often become *objectives.* "Encourage one another," "build up one another," "admonish the unruly," "encourage the fainthearted," "help the weak," "seek after that which is good for one another" are all examples of Pauline directives to the local church (1 Thes. 5:11-15). All believers were to be involved in the edification process, ministering to each other. They were to always abound "in the work of the Lord" (1 Cor. 15:58) and to "teach and admonish one another with psalms and hymns and spiritual songs" (Eph. 5:19).

Timothy, as a young pastor, was also given specific directives: "Prescribe and teach theses things," "give attention to public reading of the Scriptures, to exhortation, to teaching." He was to "preach the word," "be ready in season and out of season," "and to reprove, rebuke," and "exhort." In turn, Titus was to "set in order what remains," "appoint elders," and "speak the things which are fitting for sound doctrine."

Elders were to "shepherd the flock of God," and all believers were to "contend earnestly for the faith which was once for all delivered to the saints." Husbands were to "love their wives" and wives were "to submit to their husbands." Fathers were instructed not to "provoke their children to wrath," and not to "exasperate" them lest "they lose heart." Rather, they were to bring up their children "in the discipline and instruction of the Lord."

Frequently *directives* regarding edification in the Epistles were followed *immediately* with a statement of "expected results" or *objectives,* just as in the area of evangelism. Paul wrote to the Corinthians that he, along with Timothy and Silas, had exhorted and encouraged and implored them so that they might "walk in a manner worthy of the God" who had called them. Later he said that they constantly prayed that they might see the Thessalonians again so as to "complete" what was lacking in their faith. Paul urged the Roman Christians to present themselves to God to be able to "prove what the will of God is." He prayed for the Ephesians that they might be "filled up to all the fullness of God." He instructed the Colossians to "bear fruit in every good work." "Let us press on to maturity," said the writer to the Hebrews.

Why then does the church exist as a gathered community? The answer to this question is clear-cut in the New Testament. *The church is to become a mature organism through the process of edification* to honor and glorify God, and in the process become a dynamic witness in the world.

Luke recorded that "the church throughout all Judea and Galilee and Samaria enjoyed peace, being *built up* [that is edified]" (Acts 9:31). Paul informed us that gifted leaders were given to the church to equip all Christians for service so that the body of Christ would be *built up* [edified] (Eph. 4:11-12, 16). "*Build-up* one another," he exhorted the Thessalonians (1 Thes. 5:11).

Some form of the word "edification" appears more times in Paul's letter to the Corinthians (particularly in his first Epistle) than in any other New Testament book (1 Cor. 8:1; 10:23; 14:4-5, 12, 17, 26; 2 Cor. 12:19). This, of course, is not surprising, for of all the churches in the New Testament world, this church was the most carnal and immature and in need of spiritual growth and development (1 Cor. 3:1-3).

Edification should lead to *maturity* or *completeness* in Christ. "And we proclaim Him," wrote Paul to the Colossians, "admonishing every man and teaching every man with all wisdom, that we may present every man complete [mature] in Christ" (Col. 1:28). The apostle's primary concern for the body of Christ was that we "all attain to the unity of the faith, and the knowledge of the Son of God, to a mature man, to the measure of the stature which belongs to the fullness of Christ" (Eph. 4:13).

A MATURE CHURCH—WHAT IS IT?
How can we recognize a mature church? By what criteria can we measure ourselves as a local body to see if we have arrived at a degree of completeness? Again, the New Testament is explicit. "But now abide *faith, hope, love,* these three; but the greatest of these is love" (1 Cor. 13:13). Maturity in the body of Christ can be identified by the enduring virtues. The degree of completeness

can be measured by the degree to which the church manifests faith, hope, and love. This is quite clear from Paul's writings, since he frequently used these three virtues to measure the maturity level of the New Testament churches.[1] Notice these introductory paragraphs in his letters to various churches.

THE FIRST THESSALONIAN LETTER

We give thanks to God always for all of you, making mention of you in our prayers, constantly bearing in mind your work of **FAITH** and labor of **LOVE** and steadfastness of **HOPE** in our Lord Jesus Christ in the presence of our God and Father (1 Thes. 1:2-3).

THE SECOND THESSALONIAN LETTER

We ought always to give thanks to God for you, brethren, as is only fitting because your **FAITH** is greatly enlarged, and the **LOVE** of each of you all toward one another grows even greater; therefore, we ourselves speak proudly of you among the churches of God for your perseverence and **FAITH** in the midst of all your persecutions and afflictions which you endure (2 Thes. 1:3-4).

THE COLOSSIAN LETTER

We give thanks to God, the Father of our Lord Jesus Christ, praying always for you, since we heard of your **FAITH** in Christ Jesus and the **LOVE** which you have for all the saints; because of the **HOPE** laid up for you in heaven, of which you previously heard in the word of truth, the Gospel (Col. 1:3-5).

THE EPHESIAN LETTER

For this reason I too, having heard of the **FAITH** in the Lord Jesus which exists among you, and your **LOVE** for all the saints, do not cease giving thanks for you, while making mention of you in my prayers; that the God of our Lord Jesus Christ, the Father of glory, may give to you a spirit of wisdom and of revelation in the knowledge of Him. I pray that the eyes of your heart may be enlightened, so that you may know what is the **HOPE** of His calling, what are the riches of the glory of His inheritance in the saints (Eph. 1:15-18).

THE FIRST LETTER TO TIMOTHY

But the goal of our instruction is **LOVE** from a pure heart and a good conscience and a sincere **FAITH** (1 Tim. 1:5).

Peter, too, makes reference to this trilogy:

For He was foreknown before the foundation of the world, but has appeared in these last times for the sake of you who through Him are believers in God, who raised Him from the dead and gave Him glory, so that your **FAITH** and **HOPE** are in God. Since you have in obedience to the truth purified your souls for a sincere **LOVE** of the brethren, fervently **LOVE** one another from the heart (1 Peter 1:20-22).

THE LETTER TO THE HEBREWS:
Let us draw near with a sincere heart in full assurance of **FAITH** .... Let us hold fast the confessions of our **HOPE**.... Let us consider how to stimulate one another to **LOVE** and good deeds (Heb. 10:22-24).

It is clear what the New Testament criteria is for determining the maturity level of a local body of believers. First of all, is there *love* manifested toward other members of the body of Christ? Second, is there a strong and vital *faith?* Third, is there a demonstration of *hope?* But these words can be merely theological concepts. What do they mean? It is only as we reinforce these words with meaning and content that we get the complete picture. Once again the New Testament speaks articulately.

LOVE
"The greatest of these is love," concludes Paul (1 Cor. 13:13). The apostle consistently drives home this truth in his correspondence with the churches, which corresponds to Christ's exhortation recorded in John 13:34, to "love one another."

THE COLOSSIAN LETTER
And so, as those who have been chosen of God, holy and beloved, put on a heart of compassion, kindness, humility, gentleness, and patience; bearing with one another, and forgiving each other, whoever has a complaint against any one; just as the Lord forgave you, so also should you. *And beyond all these things put on* **LOVE**, which is the perfect bond of unity (Col. 3:12-14).

THE FIRST THESSALONIAN LETTER
Now may our God and Father Himself and Jesus our Lord direct our way to you; and may the Lord cause you *to increase and abound in* **LOVE** for one another, and for all men, just as we also do for you (1 Thes. 3:11-12).

THE PHILIPPIAN LETTER

And this I pray, that your **LOVE** *may abound still more and more* in real knowledge and all discernment, so that you may approve the things that are excellent, in order to be sincere and blameless until the day of Christ (Phil. 1:9-10).

THE EPHESIAN LETTER

As a result, we are no longer to be children, tossed here and there by waves, and carried about by every wind of doctrine, by the trickery of men, by craftiness in deceitful scheming; but *speaking the truth in* **LOVE**, we are to grow up in all aspects into Him, who is the head, even Christ, from whom the whole body, being fitted and held together by that which every joint supplies, according to the proper working of each individual part, *causes the growth of the body for the building up of itself in* **LOVE** (Eph. 4:14-16).

The Apostle Peter also elevates love to the "greatest level" when he says, "*Above all, keep fervent in your* **LOVE** for one another, because love covers a multitude of sins" (1 Peter 4:8). And there is no question as to John's concern, for in his first epistle alone, he states four times that believers are to "love one another" (1 John 3:11, 23; 4:7, 11).

But what is *love?* How is it manifested? How can it be recognized in the body of Christ? The most prominent passage portraying the particular aspects of love is, of course, 1 Corinthians 13. Here Paul spells out for the *immature* Corinthian church exactly *what love is*—how it is to be manifested by the body of Christ. Unfortunately, this "great love chapter" is often lifted out of context and used in isolation. To get the full meaning and impact of Paul's words, you must see his description of love in the light of the whole Corinthian epistle, and you must interpret his definitions in the light of the Corinthian carnality. Then too we must observe Paul's words in 1 Corinthians 13 in relationship to the *body* of Christ, not just to individual Christians.

First, note that the Corinthians were "not lacking in any gift" (1 Cor. 1:7). Yet, they were an immature church. Paul classified them as "babes in Christ" (3:1), carnal and fleshly (3:3). Obviously, the manifestation of spiritual gifts in a local church is not synonymous with spirituality and maturity. It certainly was not true with the Corinthians.

This is Paul's major assertion in 1 Corinthians 13. No doubt there were more individuals in the Corinthian church who spoke in tongues than in any other New Testament church; yet there was a lack of love and, consequently, they were like a "noisy gong or a clanging cymbal" (13:1).

These Corinthians also had the gifts of prophecy, wisdom, knowledge, and faith, but they did not have love and, therefore, Paul implied, they were "nothing" (13:2).

Some of these believers at Corinth no doubt had the gift of "giving" and were even willing to physically sacrifice their lives in acts of martyrdom, but said Paul, without love this type of behavior is totally unprofitable (13:3).

In contrast to the operation of spiritual gifts, Paul then described how to recognize love in the body of Christ:

- *Love is patient* (13:4). In other words, it is the opposite of what the Corinthians were demonstrating. They were *impatient* with one another, and there were disagreements and divisions among them (1:10).

- *Love is kind and is not jealous* (13:4). Earlier in his letter Paul had written about the "jealousy and strife" among the Corinthians (3:3).

- *Love does not brag and is not arrogant* (13:4). Paul had to warn the Corinthians against false boasting (1:29). "If any man among you thinks that he is wise in this age, let him become foolish that he may become wise. . . . Let no one boast in men. . . . What do you have that you did not receive? But if you did receive it, why do you boast as if you had not received it?" (3:18, 21; 4:7).

- *Love . . . does not act unbecomingly* (13:5). There was immorality in the church at Corinth and, said Paul, "immorality of such a kind as does not exist even among the Gentiles" (5:1; 6:15-20). Furthermore, they were acting in a most unbecoming manner at the Lord's table—some even overeating and overdrinking—even to the point of drunkenness (11:20-21).

- *Love . . . does not seek its own, is not provoked, does not take into account a wrong suffered* (13:5). Here were believers who were taking each other to court (6:1-7). They were wronging and defrauding each other (6:8). They were also insensitive to the weaker members of the body of Christ and some allowed their liberty in Christ to become a "stumbling block to the weak" (8:9). Some, in fact, were actually participating in idolatry (10:14).

• *Love . . . does not rejoice in unrighteousness but rejoices with the truth* (13:6). It is hard to conceive of such gifted Christians bragging about the immorality in the church, but Paul states emphatically, "You have become arrogant [about this immorality], and have not mourned instead" (5:2).

After defining love and contrasting its ingredients with what the Corinthians so glaringly lacked, Paul gave some positive statements about love (13:7). It "bears all things" (that is, it suffers and bears up under pressure). It "believes all things" (that is, it is "always eager to believe the best," Moffatt). It "hopes all things" (that is, it demonstrates a forward look, not hopeless pessimism). It "endures all things" (that is, it is steadfast and enables a Christian to continue on in the thick of battle).

The Corinthians, of course, were guilty of failure on every count. They were not bearing with one another; they were eager to believe falsehoods, even about the Apostle Paul (4:3-5; 9:1-3); they were negative in their attitudes; and they were succumbing to the pressures of the world and its system.

Now as we approach verses 8-12 in 1 Corinthians 13, some aspects of Paul's statements are somewhat difficult to understand. But in context, certain truths become very obvious. Paul naturally and logically concludes that "love never fails" (13:8). Gifts are temporal, but love goes on forever (13:8).

"For," says Paul, "we know in part, and we prophesy in part; but when the perfect comes, the partial will be done away" (13:9-10).

What is Paul referring to? Notice the contrasting words and phrases he used in these verses just quoted and the ones to follow (that is, in verses 9-12):

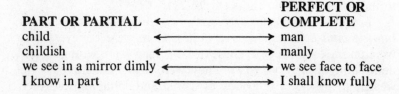

PART OR PARTIAL	PERFECT OR COMPLETE
child	man
childish	manly
we see in a mirror dimly	we see face to face
I know in part	I shall know fully

Looking at the whole of 1 Corinthians and comparing it with the Epistles Paul wrote to other churches, several conclusions stand out. These believers had not reached the degree of maturity and completeness or perfection that other New Testament churches had reached. They were still *babes* or *infants*. They were *childish* in their behavior. They had made very little progress in becoming conformed to the image of Jesus Christ.[2] They had not yet reached the place in their spiritual development where Paul could write to them as he did to the Thessalonians, the Colossians, the Ephesians, and the Philippians and thank God for their *faith, hope,* and *love*. Rather, it seems they were almost void of these virtures as a local body of believers. They were living in a state of "partiality," "childishness," and "dimness" in their spiritual life.[3] In order to correct the situation, Paul admonished them to refocus their priorities. First, he told them to strive for the "more excellent way"; they were to "pursue love" (12:31; 14:1); and then, "earnestly desire" for the body "the greater gifts" (12:31).[4]

FAITH AND HOPE

Faith and *hope*, the other two virtues set forth as standards by which we can measure the maturity level of the local church, are also uniquely described in the New Testament. Though there is no central passage describing these virtues such as 1 Corinthians does for love, there are a number of descriptive words and phrases used by the New Testament writers to add significant meaning and content to these words. Following are some of these phrases:

FAITH

Work of faith (1 Thes. 1:3)
Breastplate of faith (1 Thes. 5:8)
Faith in Jesus Christ (Col. 1:4)
Faith in the Lord Jesus (Eph. 1:15)
Faith in God (1 Peter 1:21)
Faith greatly enlarged (2 Thes. 1:3)
Faith without hypocrisy (1 Tim. 1:5)
Faith toward the Lord Jesus and toward all the saints (Phile. 5)

HOPE

Steadfastness of hope (1 Thes. 1:3)
Hope of salvation (1 Thes. 5:8)
Hope laid up for you (Col. 1:5)
That you may know what is the hope of His calling (Eph. 1:18)
Hope in God (1 Peter 1:21)
Hold fast the confession of our hope without wavering (Heb. 10:23)
Christ Jesus who is our hope (1 Tim. 1:1)

Full assurance of faith (Heb. 10:22)

We fixed our hope on the living God (1 Tim. 4:10)

Not to fix our hope on the uncertainty of riches but on God (1 Tim. 6:17)

Hope of eternal life (Titus 1:2)

Looking for the blessed hope (Titus 2:13)

Born again to a living hope (1 Peter 1:3)

Fix your hope completely on the grace to be brought to you at the revelation of Jesus Christ (1 Peter 1:3)

Even a casual reading of this list reveals that *faith* and *hope* are closely aligned in meaning and significance. The writer of Hebrews clarifies this relationship when he says, "*Faith* is the assurance of things *hoped* for, the conviction of things not seen" (Heb. 11:1). Faith has to do with Christians themselves—their personalities—that is, their minds, their attitudes, their wills. It involves inner convictions and assurance. The primary object of our faith is God the Father and His Son Jesus Christ, but it also includes faith in our fellow Christians (1 Cor. 13:7; Phile. 5).

Hope on the other hand, though linked to faith, has to do with the object and content of faith. It is most frequently used to refer to salvation and ultimate deliverance from this world into the presence of Jesus Christ when He comes again.

The word *hope* is also used to describe the state of Christians. It is used in conjunction with such words and phrases as "steadfastness" (1 Thes. 1:3), "without wavering" (Heb. 10:23), and "fixed" (1 Tim. 4:10; 6:17; 1 Peter 1:13). It is used to describe "certainty" and "stability."

In conclusion it is obvious why Paul refers to *faith, hope* and *love* as the primary virtues by which we may measure the maturity level of a local church. *Love* has to do with Christlike relationships among members of the body and toward all men—an attitude that creates unity and one-mindedness.

Faith has to do with the confidence that the body of Christ has in its Head—the Lord Jesus Christ. There is that unified conviction and assurance that God is, that He answers prayer, and that He is our divine source of life and existence.

The presence of *hope* is manifested in stability, steadfastness, and certainty, and particularly looks beyond the present to that day when Jesus Christ shall come again for the church, and in turn, to set up His eternal kingdom.

SUMMARY

Why then does the church exist as a gathered community? The church is to become a mature organism through the process of edification, and this maturity is reflected, first of all by the degree of love that exists in the body of Christ, and second, by the degree of corporate faith and hope that is manifested.

"Be careful how you build!" warned Paul. A church can be weak and immature—constructed of wood, hay, and stubble. Or it can be strong and mature—composed of gold, silver, and precious stones (1 Cor. 3:10-15). If it is immature, if reflects impatience, jealousy, strife, divisions, pride, arrogance, and unbecoming behavior. If it is mature, it reflects a growing love, a unity of faith, and a steadfast hope.

Footnotes

[1]For an in-depth study of the concepts of faith, hope, and love, see Gene A. Getz, *The Measure of a Church* (Regal, 1975).

[2]Note that Paul utilizes the same literary technique throughout this chapter. He uses personal pronouns and applies these statements to himself: "If I speak . . . I have become . . . If I have the gift . . . I am nothing . . . And if I give . . . it profits me nothing . . . . When I was a child, I used to speak as a child . . . . When I became a man, I did away with childish things . . . . Now I know in part, but then I shall know fully." In the light of the context it is obvious he is speaking of the deep spiritual needs of the Corinthians, but he illustrates these truths by referring to his own life. The Corinthians had no problem in getting the point.

[3]Compare the Letter to the Hebrews with the Letter to the Corinthians and note the similarities (Heb. 5:1—6:2).

[4]The concept of the "greater gifts" is developed at length in chapter 7.

SEVEN

VITAL NEW TESTAMENT EXPERIENCES

When attempting to formulate guidelines for the twentieth-century church and to establish purposes and principles that grow out of the New Testament, we must look closely at experiences of first-century Christians. Though there are a variety of such experiences recorded in the Book of Acts and additional instruction given in the Epistles regarding these experiences, they seem to fall into three basic categories: vital learning experiences with the Word of God, vital relational experiences with God and with one another, and vital witnessing experiences with the non-Christian world.

VITAL LEARNING EXPERIENCES
The Great Commission of our Lord is emphatic about the importance of teaching new believers the Word of God. "Make disciples," exhorted Jesus, and then "teach" these disciples.

And this the apostles did, for the new believers in Jerusalem were "continually devoting themselves to the apostles' teaching" (Acts 2:42). There was the immediate intake of biblical truth and doctrine. "Like newborn babes," wrote Peter, "long for the pure milk of the word, that by it you may grow in respect to salvation" (1 Peter 2:2).

Though there are a number of words used for "teaching" in the Greek New Testament, the form used in Matthew 28:20 is the most common. There are about one hundred occurrences of the verb *didasko,* and its use is about evenly distributed in each Gospel, the Book of Acts, and in the Epistles. Interestingly, the word is used about half the time in Acts to describe the teaching-learning process among non-Christians, and about half the time with Christians.[1]

No one can deny the importance of "data input" in the process of edification. A church that does not provide good Bible teaching cannot be classified as practicing New Testament principles of church life. The form that this teaching took, however, varied greatly. There are no absolute guidelines or stereotype patterns. The methods and approaches—whether used by Jesus, the apostles, or other members of the body of Christ—varied according to the situation. Sometimes the group was large; sometimes it was small. Sometimes teaching was done by one person; other times it was done by two or more. Sometimes the presentation was lengthy; sometimes it was brief. Sometimes it took place spontaneously; at other times it was planned. Sometimes it was basically a lecture; sometimes it involved the people in interaction and discussion. Sometimes it was verbalized; sometimes it was visualized. Sometimes it involved mostly transmission of truth; sometimes it involved interaction. But there was always one objective in view (when it took place among Christians), their edification. Methods and approaches were means to this divine end.

VITAL RELATIONAL EXPERIENCES

The New Testament is filled with illustrations and instructions regarding relational type experiences that believers had with one another and with God. Furthermore, these two relationships are so closely interwoven and linked together, it is difficult to separate the two even when writing about them.

For example, the new believers in Jerusalem, in addition to being instructed in doctrine, were "continually devoting themselves to fellowship [*koinonia*], to the breaking of bread and to prayer" (Acts 2:42). As they ate together and prayed together, they experienced dynamic fellowship with one another and with God. In this peculiar set of circumstances, they were no doubt literally sharing their food with each other—and at the same time remembering the Lord's broken body and shed blood. As they prayed for one another, they worshiped God in praise and thanksgiving.

John recognized the interrelatedness of these two experiences when he wrote: "What we have seen and heard we proclaim to you also, that you also may have *fellowship with us;* and indeed our *fellowship is with the Father, and with His Son Jesus Christ"* (1 John 1:3).

CORPORATE PRAYER

At the time the church was born, one of the most predominant experiences of those who were waiting in the Upper Room was corporate prayer. In the spirit of unity and "one-mindedness," the 120 believers "were continually devoting themselves to prayer" (Acts 1:14) as they waited for the Holy Spirit to come as Jesus had promised.

When the Holy Spirit came on the Day of Pentecost, Peter, hereafter a frequent spokesman for the believers in Jerusalem, interpreted this marvelous manifestation to the multitudes. And as he preached the Gospel with power and conviction, immediately the 120 believers swelled to over 3,000 (2:41). We then are told that these new Christians, within the context of teaching and fellowship, were "continually devoting themselves . . . *to prayer"* (2:42).

In many of the Epistles, the church was instructed to engage in corporate prayer.[2] Paul told the Christians in Rome and Colossae to devote themselves to prayer (Rom. 12:12; Col. 4:2). He exhorted the believers at Ephesus and Thessalonica to "pray at all times" and "without ceasing" (Eph. 6:18; 1 Thes. 5:17). To the Philippians he wrote, "Be anxious for nothing, but in everything by prayer and supplication with thanksgiving let your requests be made known to God" (Phil. 4:6). James admonished believers to "pray for one another" (James 5:16), and Paul told Timothy to "urge that entreaties and prayers, petitions, and thanksgivings be made on behalf of all men" (1 Tim. 2:1).

Interestingly, many of these references to prayer appear in a context that seems to imply "body life" and *koinonia.* For example, note the context of prayer in each of the passages which follow, giving special attention to the term *one another.*

Be devoted to *one another* in brotherly love; give preference to *one another* in honor; not lagging behind in diligence, fervent in spirit, serving the Lord; rejoicing in hope, persevering in tribulation, (devoted to prayer,) contributing to the needs of the saints, practicing hospitality (Rom. 12:10-13).

And we urge you, brethren, admonish the unruly, encourage the fainthearted, help the weak, be patient with all men. See that no one repays another with evil for evil, but always seek after that which is good for *one another* and for all men. Rejoice always; (pray without ceasing;) in everything give thanks; for this is God's will for you in Christ Jesus (1 Thes. 5:14-18).

Is anyone among you suffering? Let him (pray.) Is anyone cheerful? Let him (sing) praises. Is anyone among you sick? Let him call for the elders of the church, and let them (pray) over him, anointing him with oil in the name of the Lord; and the (prayer) offered in faith will restore the one who is sick, and the Lord will raise him up, and if he has committed sins, they will be forgiven him. Therefore, confess your sins to *one another*, and (pray) for *one another*, so that you may be healed. The effective (prayer) of a righteous man can accomplish much (James 5:13-16).

The end of all things is at hand; therefore, be of sound judgment and sober spirit for the purpose of (prayer.) Above all, keep fervent in your love for *one another*, because love covers a multitude of sins. Be hospitable to *one another* without complaint. As each one has received a special gift, employ it in serving *one another*, as good stewards of the manifold grace of God (1 Peter 4:7-10).

Notice also how frequently corporate prayer is put in the context of being thankful (Eph. 5:20; Phil. 4:6; Col. 4:2; 1 Thes. 5:17-18; 1 Tim. 2:1). Though it was to include petition and request for personal needs, prayer was not to be oriented toward "selfish behavior" but to flow out of hearts overflowing with "thanksgiving to God."

On several occasions Paul requested prayer for himself (2 Thes. 3:1; Eph. 6:19), particularly that the Word of the Lord would spread rapidly and be glorified (2 Thes. 3:1) and that he might be able to speak out boldly in presenting the "mystery of the Gospel" (Eph. 6:19). In turn, Paul frequently reminded believers of his personal prayers for them (Rom. 1:8; Eph. 1:16; 3:14; Phil. 1:9-10).

These were the characteristics of a New Testament "prayer meeting." These prayer experiences did not seem to be only "periods of prayer," or a "time," or an "evening," or a "day" set aside for prayer, though it certainly included this. On special occasions they met for prayer, particularly when there were special needs (Acts 12:12). More frequently, however, prayer seemed to be interwoven into a variety of experiences believers participated in as they met together to be edified. And as they prayed, they prayed for each other's needs. They prayed for those carrying the Gospel to others, and they prayed for *all* men.[3]

CORPORATE SINGING

Music has always been a part of the life of the people of God. The Old Testament is filled with illustrations of various types of musical expression, particularly singing. David, of course, is the outstanding example of a man who used his voice both for song and as an instrument to praise God.

In the New Testament, Jesus exemplified the place of singing, for after He had eaten the Last Supper with His disciples and just before "they went out to the Mount of Olives," they sang a hymn (Mark 14:26).

Paul particularly made reference to singing, "Speaking to one another in psalms and hymns and spiritual songs," he wrote in the Ephesian letter, "singing and making melody with your heart to the Lord" (Eph. 5:19).

To the Colossians, he said, "Let the word of Christ richly dwell within you; with all wisdom teaching and admonishing one another with psalms and hymns and ... singing with thankfulness in your hearts to God" (Col. 3:16).

Notice again the context of "corporate singing" and especially its purpose. They were to minister to *one another*—to "teach" and "admonish" *one another*. It was to edify the body of Christ. It was also to flow out of a heart of "thankfulness" to God. Just as with corporate prayer, corporate singing was to be a natural and spontaneous expression and a specific experience that was vitally related to the basic experience of body life and *koinonia*.

Notice too that Paul relates corporate singing to the basic experience of *learning biblical truth*. In fact, singing actually was to be a means whereby believers "teach" and "admonish" one another and whereby the "word of Christ" can "richly dwell" within them (3:16).

Regarding this concept, Herbert Carson suggests the following:

> Their experience of the Word is not merely an individual one, for it is in the context of a fellowship of the church that they are to learn its truths. Thus there must be a mutual sharing of the Word. It is from the indwelling Word that they will learn the wisdom of God, and that wisdom will then become the atmosphere in which they move as they seek to build one another up in knowledge. The worship of the church is here viewed from the standpoint of the edification of the believers . . . such singing will not be of mere form of release, but will be a means of instruction.[4]

This is a direct correlation between the purpose of corporate singing and the content Paul refers to, both in Ephesians and Colossians. These believers were to teach and admonish one another with "psalms, and hymns, and spiritual songs" (3:16; Eph. 5:19).

Some believe the apostle may have been referring to the Old Testament psalter when he used the word "psalms." If so, no further comment is necessary to emphasize the quality of this content. Nothing can surpass the very "words of God" as a basis for edification.

The term *hymn* refers to "praise psalms"—poetic composition, probably uninspired from the standpoint of biblical revelation, but very much "inspired" in terms of the human spirit. Though of human origin, these hymns were to be used to teach one another and to glorify God.

"Spiritual songs" may be called "spiritual odes." The term *ode* used by itself is broad in meaning and refers to any poetry, sacred or secular. Believers, however, were to make melody in their hearts with *spiritual* odes—songs that expressed their attitudes and feelings toward the Lord and each other.

Be careful, however, that you do not interpret Paul's words here through a traditional grid of various Christian approaches to "musical expression" over the years. Paul was not speaking here of musical *forms*—that is, tempo, rhythm, melody, or harmony. The "words" or the "poetic expression" become the focal point. The words used are to be, said Paul, first, the very words of God (as the psalms); second, words of praise to God (those written by believers); and third, words that express true Christian experiences.

The *way* the New Testament church expressed itself musically would be hardly identifiable if compared with the typical hymnbook used in the evangelical church today.

But the *way* that it was expressed is not the important matter— *what* was expressed *is!* As will be developed at length later, the Bible allows a great deal of freedom when it comes to musical form, but it is specific when it comes to content and purpose. Here Paul was speaking of one element of Christian experience— music. Tempo, rhythm, melody, and the means used to express this music are all relative factors. They are culturally related. But the purpose of Christian music—edification—is absolute. And the Bible is clear that Christians need to sing together in order to build up one another. The kinds of musical expressions really don't matter provided they create dynamic relational Christianity and help believers to learn the Word of God.

CORPORATE GIVING

The story of the church in the New Testament is a story of a group of people who "cared about others," particularly other believers. "Let us do good to all men," but, Paul added, "especially to those who are of the household of the faith" (Gal. 6:10; 1 Thes. 5). Writing to the Christians at Rome, he exhorted them to contribute to the needs of the saints and to practice hospitality (Rom. 12:13).

Corporate sharing and giving is exemplified by believers right from the very beginning of the church in Jerusalem. Because of the socioeconomic factors at that time, they "had all things in common." The Christians sold their "property and possessions ... sharing them with all, as anyone might have need" (Acts 2:44-45).

But as the disciples were scattered and as the Word was proclaimed and taught throughout Judea and Samaria and all over the New Testament world, the concept of corporate giving and sharing was never lost. Even though socioeconomic conditions were different—people had their own homes, their own particular jobs, and they made their own livings—they still demonstrated care for other believers in need.

When Paul wrote to the church at Philippi, he thanked God for their "participation *[koinonia]* in the Gospel from the first day until now" (Phil. 1:5). No doubt, he was referring to the fact that these Christians had "more than once" sent material gifts to care for his material needs (4:14-16).

Writing to the Corinthians and urging them to get involved in the "gracious work" of corporate giving, Paul used the church in Macedonia as an example. "For I testify," he said, "that according to their ability, and beyond their ability they gave of their own accord, begging us with much entreaty for the favor of participation in the support of the saints" (2 Cor. 8:3-4).

Paul believed and taught that corporate giving was an essential experience for all believers. "You will be enriched in everything for all liberality," he wrote to the Corinthians (9:11). But he went on to explain that corporate giving will be an experience bringing mutual edification. "For the ministry of this service is not only fully supplying the needs of the saints, but is also overflowing through many thanksgivings to God. Because of the proof given by this ministry they [the recipients of the gifts] will glorify God for your obedience to your confession of the Gospel of Christ, and for the liberality of your contribution to them and to all, while they also, by prayer on your behalf, yearn for you because of the surpassing grace of God in you" (9:12-14).

This Corinthian passage (chaps. 8—9) in itself provides a fascinating study in relational Christianity. It demonstrates the importance of caring for the needs of other members of the body of Christ; it emphasizes the spiritual growth that results in the life of those who share; it refers to not only the physical benefits to those who receive the gifts but also the spiritual benefits; it illustrates the development of mutual care, not only in giving, but in praying for each other (9:14).

Furthermore, the implication is clear (as it was in Jerusalem in the early days of the church), that nonbelievers took cognizance of the body of Christ at work caring for itself, not only in local geographical settings, but all over the New Testament world. This in itself became a backdrop against which the Gospel of Christ, as it was preached to the pagan world, took on meaning and true theological significance. No activity like sharing material blessings can demonstrate so well the concepts of "true Christian love," "unity," and "the reality of the Christian faith." Verbal appreciation and concern are inexpensive and relatively easy acts of kindness. But tangibly sharing what is "yours" with others "costs," and it is an experience all mankind (saved and unsaved) can identify with. How easy it is to "love ourselves"—but how difficult it is to "love" our neighbors as we love ourselves.

Unbelievers who saw these sacrificial acts of kindness could not but be impressed with the supernatural qualities of life in Christ. This was against nature! This was the opposite of what man *wants* to do! This was a demonstration of unusual qualities that came from a supernatural source—the indwelling Christ—the One who was being proclaimed as the Son of God.

CORPORATE EATING

It is impossible to read the New Testament carefully without concluding that "corporate eating" *was* a significant experience for first-century Christians. It was, of course, a *regular* experience for the disciples of Jesus—particularly the Twelve—as they traveled with Him during His ministry on earth. But their meal together, just prior to the time Christ was taken captive, took on special significance. It was during this meal that "Jesus took some bread, and after a blessing, He broke it and gave it to the disciples, and said, 'Take, eat; this is My body' " (Matt. 26:26).

Next, the Lord "took a cup and gave thanks, and gave it to them, saying, 'Drink from it, all of you; for this is My blood of the covenant, which is to be shed on behalf of many for forgiveness of sins' " (26:27-28).

No doubt the new Christians in Jerusalem in the early days of the church emulated this experience the Twelve had with Christ. Luke records that "they were continually devoting themselves . . . to the breaking of bread and prayer. . . . And day by day continuing with one mind in the temple, and breaking bread from house to house, they were taking their meals together with gladness and sincerity of heart, praising God, and having favor with all the people" (Acts 2:42, 46-47b).

These meals were not just ordinary meals for these new believers. No doubt they often broke bread and partook of the cup, and in so doing proclaimed the death of Christ. Some feel that in those early days they remembered the Lord in this way on a daily basis.

Religious meals were not an uncommon practice in those days, even among the pagans and other religious sects. The Jews, of course, had historically kept the Passover. It was, therefore, not a totally new experience for these Jewish Christians to participate in a religious meal. What *was* new, however, was that a part of the meal now became a special means to remember the sacrificial death of Jesus Christ.

When Paul wrote to the Christians in Corinth, he had to correct the misuse of this religious meal (1 Cor. 11:28-34). Some were coming and eating early; some were not getting any food and were still hungry; some were actually overeating and overdrinking. In general, they were selfishly using this meal for their own behalf and not for its original purpose.

Paul had to remind them of the Lord's example, how that during the Last Supper He had broken the bread as a reminder of His broken body, and after supper He had shared the cup with His disciples as "the new covenant" in His blood. The Corinthians were partaking of these elements in an "unworthy manner" (11:27). They were ignoring the original purpose and meaning of this sacred experience.

The most important aspect of this religious meal was the breaking of bread and the sharing of the cup. Thus, these two elements have been shared by Christians down through the years as a token meal and has been designed as holy communion.

There is no biblical reason, however, to reject the concept of the religious meal as being "out of order" or improper in the church of the twentieth century. In fact, Zane Hodges, Professor of New Testament literature and exegesis at Dallas Theological Seminary, believes that the religious meal should be a definite part of Christian worship and experience today. He argues his position by referring to the Lord's example with the disciples, plus the obvious practice of the Corinthians and Paul's instructions in

1 Corinthians 11:20-24. He feels to reject the "religious meal" concept on the basis of its misuse by the Corinthians is not adequate grounds for abandoning this total experience and replacing it with a token meal.

The crucial aspect, he believes, is the breaking of bread and partaking of the cup. He believes, however, that these elements are only part of the Lord's Supper, and that the meal proper provides opportunity for Christian fellowship and mutual edification as the Word of God is informally discussed. He believes further that this experience helps to create a family environment for the body of Christ, and if done with reverence and respect, adds a great deal to the process of mutual Christian growth.

It cannot be denied that "corporate eating" is a concept in the New Testament. Whether it should be practiced in the same way as in the early days of the church is, in my opinion, a matter of interpretation. No one who reads the Scriptures objectively can deny the necessity of remembering the Lord by means of Communion. Paul said, "For as often as you eat this bread and drink the cup, you proclaim the Lord's death until He comes" (11:26). Obviously, Paul believed and taught that this aspect of the meal should continue until Jesus Christ returns again.

Many factors in the twentieth-century culture are naturally different today from those in the first century, particularly in Jerusalem where the communal life of the church made the Lord's Supper a frequent and natural experience. However, even if the religious meal is not a normative pattern for the church today, is there not inherent in these biblical examples a principle—that of utilizing "corporate eating" as a vital experience for Christians? Leon Morris reminds us in his commentary on 1 Corinthians that "there is a marked stress throughout this whole passage on the corporate nature of the rite and on the responsibility to all."[5]

Much was stated earlier regarding relational Christianity. What better environment can be used to create this kind of experience when a group of dedicated Christians gather about a table eating together. Whether it is related to Communion or not, it should and can always be a spiritual experience with "one another" and "with God." For, said Paul on another occasion, "whether, then, you eat or drink or whatever you do, do all to the glory of God" (10:31).

All close-knit families will testify that there is no experience that equals the intimate fellowship of gathering about a table and eating together. Are not all Christians brothers and sisters in Christ? Are not believers members of the family of God? Are not we *one* body? Is the church today utilizing the experience of "corporate eating" in its most vital way to contribute to the building up of the body of Christ?

VITAL WITNESSING EXPERIENCES
There is another dimension to the edification process which can be easily overlooked—and is in many churches—especially among those who attempt to duplicate the New Testament pattern. A church can become so intent on fulfilling its purpose as a "gathered community" that, without actually being aware of what is happening, it is becoming an "inward-oriented group" rather than an "outward-oriented group."

The church exists for two basic purposes—remember?—"to make disciples" and "to teach them." An "inward-oriented" church becomes an end in itself. It grows "stale" and "self-centered" and "lifeless." The basic experiences of learning biblical truth can become purely academic and relational experiences can become very superficial.

Only as a church, both as a body and as individual members within that body, reaches out and touches the lost world will it maintain the fresh flow of life and power that keeps "learning biblical truth" and "relational Christianity" dynamic and fresh.

The churches mentioned in the Book of Acts are excellent examples of this! Following the persecution which was initiated in Jerusalem, the believers "enjoyed peace." But we read that they were "being built up" (edified); and, "going on in the fear of the Lord and in the comfort of the Holy Spirit, it [the church] continued to increase [to grow numerically]" (Acts 9:31).[6]

The record in Acts and the Epistles of the total impact of the church on the world is clear. Extrabiblical history also records the continuing influence the church had upon the world. Christians helped to change the total culture. They affected and infected the total community. In addition to the Scriptural record, history reports "that in the Greek and Roman world the cry went out, 'behold, how they love one another.' "[7]

The Thessalonians are probably one of the most outstanding examples of a witnessing church. "For," said Paul, "the Word of the Lord has sounded forth from you, not only in Macedonia and Achaia, but also in every place your faith toward God has gone forth, so that we have no need to say anything" (1 Thes. 1:8). To the Roman Christians, he also wrote, "First, I thank my God through Jesus Christ for you all, because your faith is being proclaimed throughout the whole world" (Rom. 1:8).

Note too that Christian witness in the New Testament church was both "corporate" and "individual." The functioning body became the backdrop against which effective personal witness took place.

At this juncture, it is important to remind ourselves again of Jesus' words to His disciples and of His words to the Father in His high priestly prayer. "By this," said Jesus, "all men will know that you are My disciples, if you have love for one another" (John 13:35). And to His Father He prayed that His disciples might "be one . . . that they may be perfected in unity," in order, "that the world may know that Thou didst send Me" (17:21, 23).

SUMMARY

What then is edification in the New Testament sense of the word? It seems to be that ongoing experience where biblical truth (doctrine) is learned within the context of "relational Christianity" and "dynamic Christian witness." All three experiences are needed to create a mature body of believers. To neglect any one of these facets of New Testament life is to interfere with the God-ordained plan for edification in the local church. Without these three experiences, a church will not grow to reflect the three marks of corporate maturity—*faith, hope,* and *love.*[8]

Footnotes

[1]For an excellent treatment of the Greek words for "teach," see Roy B. Zuck, "Greek Words for Teach," *Bibliotheca Sacra* 122 April-June 1965: 158-68.

[2]Not all of these references would be limited to corporate prayer. It would also apply to the believer's personal prayer life. However, the context in which most of these injunctions to prayer are given strongly suggest the idea of corporate prayer.

[3]For a more in-depth study of corporate prayer, see Gene A. Getz, *Praying for One Another,* Victor Books.

[4]Herbert M. Carson, *The Epistles of Paul to the Colossians and to Philemon,* Eerdmans, p. 90.

[5]Leon Morris, *The First Epistle of Paul to the Corinthians* Eerdmans, p. 164.

[6]In this verse the term for church is seemingly used to refer to the universal church; however, the total context implies that there were many local congregations scattered throughout Judea, Galilee, and Samaria. This general growth was reflected through the growth of individual local assemblies.

[7]Francis A. Schaeffer, *The Church at the End of the Twentieth Century,* p. 71.

[8]For a basic exposition of Acts 2:42-47 which outlines the three vital experiences as reflected in the Jerusalem church. See Gene A. Getz, *The Measure of a Church,* Regal, chapter 12, pp. 145-146.

EIGHT

PRINCIPLES OF NEW TESTAMENT EDIFICATION

In order for a local church to become a mature body of believers reflecting *faith, hope,* and *love,* there are certain New Testament principles that must be applied. These principles grow naturally out of our study of the activities and functions of New Testament Christians and the directives that were given to them in the Epistles.

THE WHOLE BODY, A MATURE ORGANISM
First, *keep the local church in focus as the primary means by which edification is to take place.* Paul's ultimate concern was that the *whole* body—the universal church—become a mature organism (Eph. 4:11-13), but he demonstrated unequivocably in his own ministry that the way to achieve this goal was to establish local churches and then to help these "microcosms" of the universal church to become mature entities and independent units. He, with his co-workers, made disciples, taught and encouraged them, and helped each group to become a dynamic *koinonia.*

Part of his teaching, of course, was to help them recognize their relationship to the universal church—that they were part of the whole. This was even more difficult to achieve in New Testament times, since these local groups were much more geographically cut off from one another. Their primary means of relationship with other local bodies of believers was through oral reports from traveling representatives and through correspondence. But even with a limited means for communication, it is obvious that strong ties and relationships developed between local groups, even when they had never met personally (2 Cor. 8:1-6).

At this juncture no attempt will be made to exhaust the various ideas regarding what must be present to have a local church. There is a variety of opinions. I personally tend toward a simple view. Seemingly, a body of *believers* can be classified as a church whenever and wherever that group meets on a regular basis for the purpose of mutual edification. *Why* a group meets is more significant, it seems, than coming up with a list of norms or specifics which must be present to have, in actuality, a church. Yet it must be added that any group so described may be an *infant church.* It must grow and develop, taking on certain norms and practices to be a full-grown, mature, and dynamic church. These basic norms are quite clear in Scripture. The most foundational of these has already been stated: that the church is a body of *believers*—born-again people; second, they must meet *regularly.* Also the Bible clearly states that there should eventually be *qualified leaders,*[1] and a form of discipline for those who claim to be believers but violate scriptural teachings regarding living the Christian life. Certainly there must also be *teaching* of the Word, *prayer,* practice of *baptism,* and sharing of the *Lord's Supper.* All of these factors point to a church that has the potential for maturity. But it must be emphatically emphasized that many of these practices can be present and still there may be a dead, sterile, immature church. It takes true life and vitality to give meaning to these experiences. It is God's plan that as these norms are established, they contribute to edification.

In conclusion then, this first New Testament principle for edification must be reemphasized and amplified. It is simply this: Any of us who wish to have spiritual success in our ministries and have the full blessing of God upon our efforts must work toward either the establishment of local churches as new converts are won to Christ, or if we are serving with a parachurch agency, we must channel new Christians into an already established church. It is there that they can be nurtured into full-grown Christians as they become a part of a local body of believers, drawing strength from other members of the body as well as contributing to the growth of the church.

One of my most encouraging experiences in sharing principles of New Testament church life in a transcultural setting took place in Brazil. There I met with a number of national Christian leaders who had come to Christ through the ministry of The Navigators. Jim Pederson, Latin American director, invited me to share with this dynamic group what the Bible teaches regarding the process of edification. Jim recognizes that if the people they are reaching for Christ are to grow spiritually, they must have the experiences God ordained in the context of a "local church."

These Christian leaders have a problem, however. There are no "traditional" local churches that can absorb these new believers. For one thing, it would interfere with their unique strategy to continue reaching people like themselves—people who are totally secularized. Therefore, they must face this problem creatively— which they have! More later regarding their solution. Suffice it to say at this juncture, Jim agrees with this New Testament principle. The "local church" must be kept in focus as a primary means whereby edification is to take place. However, the *way* the church is identified in this culture is another story.

GET BELIEVERS INTO THE WORD

Second, *provide believers with a basic knowledge of the Word of God.* This is why Paul spent an entire year in Antioch teaching the disciples and why Paul and Barnabas returned to Lystra and Iconium and Antioch "strengthening the souls of the disciples, encouraging them to continue in the faith." This is why Paul said on another occasion, "Let us return and visit the brethren in every city in which we proclaimed the Word of the Lord and see how they are." This is why Paul also spent a year and a half in Corinth and three years in Ephesus teaching and admonishing believers.

Paul also went beyond a personal ministry among his converts. While in Athens he sent Timothy back to Thessalonica "to strengthen and encourage" the believers in their faith (1 Thes. 3:2). Likewise, Paul sent Timothy back to Corinth to teach them the doctrines that he was teaching "everywhere in every church" (1 Cor. 4:17). Titus remained in Crete to "speak the things which are fitting for sound doctrine" (Titus 2:1). Beyond doubt, Paul was vitally concerned that believers be instructed in basic doctrine.

It is the Word of God that is foundational to spiritual growth. "Like newborn babes," said Peter, "long for the pure milk of the Word, that by it you may grow in respect to salvation" (1 Peter 2:2). Unfortunately, there are individuals in the twentieth-century church who have been Christians for years but who have never been taught even the most elementary Bible doctrines. It is here we must begin in the edification process, whether we are ministering to "new babes" or "old ones."

PROVIDE IN-DEPTH TEACHING
Third, *provide believers with an in-depth knowledge of the Word of God.* Teaching his new converts face to face and sending others to instruct and lead them was not sufficient follow-up in Paul's opinion. His next step involved correspondence—letters to the Thessalonians, the Corinthians, the Galatians, the Ephesians, and the Philippians. All of these Epistles were written to provide these believers, not just with a basic knowledge of the Word of God, but with a deeper knowledge of God's truth. And of no little significance, he put this instruction in permanent form, so that it could be rehearsed again and again, studied, and circulated among other churches. On occasions they wrote back to him about what he meant, and he, in turn, wrote another letter to elaborate on his previous correspondence. (For example, 1 and 2 Corinthians.) Ultimately, of course, he was providing us with a large portion of the written Word of God, which we have at our disposal today to use in the same way it was intended to be used in the first century—to provide Christians with a comprehensive knowledge of God's message to man.

DEVELOP CAPACITIES BEYOND KNOWLEDGE
Fourth, *provide believers with opportunities to develop capacities that go beyond knowledge*—to include wisdom, enlightenment, appreciation, and an awareness and sensitivity to the Spirit of God. That is why Paul prayed for the Ephesians the way he did! Probably no other Christians had the opportunity to be exposed to Paul's teaching as those in Ephesus. They had the wonderful

privilege of listening to him teach month after month; and remember too that it was in Ephesus that Paul lectured daily for two years in the school of Tyrannus. This helps to explain the depth of the Ephesian letter. These people were beyond the "infant" stage!

But notice what Paul prays for these well-fed Christians: that they may gain a "spirit of wisdom," that the eyes of their "heart may be enlightened," that they may truly *know* what it means to be called, that they may really know how *rich* they are, and how much power was demonstrated toward them in saving their souls. Paul further prays that they might be strengthened with power through the Spirit in the *inner man,* so that they may "be able to comprehend with all the saints what is the breadth and length and height and depth, and to know the love of Christ which surpasses knowledge," in order that they "may be filled up to all the fullness of God" (Eph. 1:16-19; 3:14-19).

Note carefully: Paul wanted them to know the love of Christ which *goes beyond* knowledge! The greatest danger today in the edification process is that Christians learn the deep truths of the Word of God but never move to the level of behavior that demonstrates wisdom, appreciation, deep awareness, and sensitivity to their position in Christ.

We must lead Christians beyond the realm of *knowing* in a merely superficial sense. Experience has demonstrated beyond doubt that *knowing* does not automatically lead to doing. "Association psychology" is a dead theory. It simply does not work. A Christian can know many things about God without sensing His greatness, His power, His riches, and His grace, without being moved by the marvel and wonder of it all. It is possible to know every jot and tittle in the Scriptures and still lack the conviction and motivation to live out one iota of its truth. In short, it is possible to have doctrine and truth "coming out of our ears" without being mature disciples of Jesus Christ.[2]

We have established that knowledge, however, is *basic* to arriving at maturity. What, then, is the means by which Christians go beyond the knowledge level? The answer lies in another New Testament principle.

PROVIDE BEYOND-KNOWLEDGE EXPERIENCE

Fifth, *provide believers with the sum total of experiences which will help them to get beyond the knowledge level.*

This begins with *teaching-learning experiences,* but it is far more inclusive than a transmissive-receiving type process. It must go beyond mere dissemination of scriptural content and even beyond interaction with that content by those who are being taught.

This learning process must be in the context of *relational Christianity*—fellowshiping with God and with one another. It must also be in the context of dynamic *Christian witness* and outreach. If believers are merely recipients of truth without the opportunity to truly worship God, minister to one another, and to win others to Christ, they will not get beyond the knowledge level.

The great problem in many evangelical churches has been in maintaining a balance in all three vital New Testament experiences. In fact, churches can almost be classified by these emphases.

There is the church that has a strong emphasis on Christian witness. (See figure 13 for churches structured around "evange-

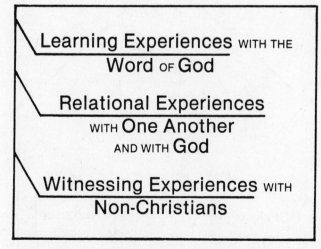

Figure 12. Three Vital Experiences

lism.") Most of the time the believers hear evangelistic messages from the pulpit, and the Bible teaching they get is often superficial. For those who are sensitive to the Lord, they yearn for solid Bible teaching and good exposition. Many who become dissatisfied eventually leave and find a good Bible-teaching church. (See figure 13 for churches structured around "Bible teaching.") Here the Word is faithfully taught every Sunday morning and every Sunday night and several times during the week. For a while their hearts are thrilled and their souls are fed. But eventually the excitement of hearing the Word taught begins to disappear. Taking notes and underscoring scriptural truths in their Bibles becomes purely an academic routine. Again, those who are sensitive to the Lord begin asking the question, "What's wrong with my Christian life?"

Then there are those who are starved for fellowship and long for intimate relationships within the body of Christ. They seek out a church where there is sharing and discussion and informality and warm fellowship. (See figure 13 for churches structured around "relationships.") They have small-group involvement and an emphasis on "honesty" and "openness." There is body life.

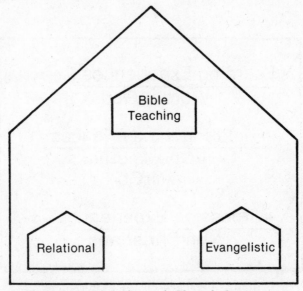

Figure 13. Unbalanced Church Structures

Individual members of the church function. For a while the vacuum is filled in their lives. They are excited and thrilled with their new relationships. But gradually these experiences seem to become mechanical and routine, and even superficial. In some cases relationships are spawned that degenerate into behavior that is questionable and have led at times even to immoral activities.

What is the problem? Believers need *all three vital experiences* to grow into mature Christians. They need good Bible teaching that will give them theological and spiritual stability; they need deep and satisfying relationships, both with each other and with Jesus Christ; and they need to experience seeing people come to Jesus Christ as a result of corporate and individual witness to the non-Christian world. (See "Three Vital Experiences" in figure 12 on page 113.)

And they need *all* three! Not just one or two will do. Any combination other than the three in proper balance will not produce New Testament results. It is therefore the task of every church leader to determine and plan a structure for the twentieth-century church that will allow Christians to have these vital experiences which were also the experiences of the first-century Christians.

EQUIP FOR SERVICE

Sixth, *equip believers for Christian service.* Note again: this involves *all believers.*

This is the primary thrust of Ephesians 4:

"And He gave some as apostles and some as prophets, and some as evangelists, and some as pastors and teachers, *for the equipping of the saints for the work of service,* to the building up of the body of Christ ... but speaking the truth in love, we are to grow up in all aspects into Him, who is the head, even Christ, from whom the whole body, being fitted and held together by that which *every joint supplies,* according to the proper working of *each individual part,* causes the growth of the body for the building up of itself in love" (Eph. 4:11-12, 15-16).

The church is a unique organism. It is edified and becomes mature as every member functions. God never intended for members of the body of Christ to depend on one leader to do "the work of the ministry." As will be shown in more detail later, God did not even intend for *several leaders* to do the work of the ministry. Rather, He intended for the *whole* church to do this work. It is a responsibility of church leaders to "equip the saints" to serve one another. Then—and only then—can a local body of believers grow and develop into a mature church.

DEVELOP FAMILY LIFE

Seventh, *help believers develop qualitative family life.* Husbands and wives must grow in their own relationship even as the church grows in its relationship to Christ (Eph. 5:24-33). Fathers and mothers must be assisted in rearing their children in the discipline and instruction of the Lord (6:1-4).

The family unit has a central place in the Bible. It antedates the church, being a basic unit throughout the Old Testament. And in the New Testament it is to form the "building blocks" of the church. Strong Christian families make strong churches, both in terms of evangelism and edification. And in turn, strong churches create strong families. In fact, the New Testament presents the family as the "church in miniature."

Deuteronomy 6:6-9 is a classic biblical example of how a home should function according to God's pattern. This message was delivered to the Children of Israel before they entered the Promised Land. They had been wandering in the wilderness as a result of their disobedience. Now as they are ready to take the final step securing for themselves the land God had promised, they were given these instructions: "And these words, which I am commanding you today, shall be on your heart; and you shall teach them diligently to your sons and shall talk of them when you sit in your house and when you walk by the way and when you lie down and when you rise up" (Deut. 6:6-7).

These instructions were followed by a warning. Be careful, Moses said, for when you get into the land your tendency will be to "forget the Lord." When you inherit "houses full of good things" and "cisterns" and "vineyards and olive trees," then "watch yourself, lest you forget the Lord who brought you from the land of Egypt, out of the house of slavery" (6:11-12).

Unfortunately, when they arrived in the land they *did* forget

God. When they had "eaten" and were "satisfied," when their "herds" and their "flocks" and their "silver and gold" multiplied (8:12-13), they said in their hearts, "My power and the strength of my hand made me this wealth" (8:17).

Most tragic of all, they forgot to instruct and teach their children by precept and example. The instructions in Deuteronomy 6 became only a memory, so far removed from their consciousness that they were no doubt unaware of their existence. The result was pitiful! Consequently, "there arose another generation after them who did not know the Lord, nor yet the work which He had done for Israel" (Jud. 2:10).

The rest of the story can be simply told. The family unit failed and so did the nation, for a strong nation is no stronger than its family units. The same is true of the Christian community or the church. If the family unit fails to function, if husbands and wives do not experience true *koinonia,* if members of the family as a whole cannot relate to each other, how can we expect dynamic fellowship at the church level? It is virtually impossible!

Then we must—I repeat—assist husbands and wives to develop in their mutual life, and churches must help fathers and mothers rear their children in the discipline and instruction of the Lord. We must help them develop qualitative Christian families that will serve as solid building blocks within the local church and also serve as dynamic examples in their individual communities. This is particularly true at a time in our own nation when we are beginning to experience disintegration. Interestingly, many sociologists agree that disintegration is distinctly related to the breakdown at the family level. Thus the church can have a dual role in bolstering the family: it can help build dynamic and thriving churches and also help preserve the strength of the nation.[3]

DEVELOP CONTEMPORARY FORMS AND STRUCTURES

Eighth, *the twentieth-century church must develop its own contemporary forms and structures for applying the biblical principles just outlined.*

One thing is clear from a careful study of the New Testament: Forms and structures in Scriptures are presented as a means to biblical ends. In themselves they are not absolute. This is a danger area for evangelicals because we think in terms of absolutes. We believe in a God who has spoken through the inspired Word and who has given us propositional truth that is *absolute* and "never changing." We believe in a God who is *eternal* and a Saviour who is the same "yesterday, today, and forever" (Heb. 13:8). Consequently, it is easy for us to allow forms and patterns and ways of doing things to become just as sacred as our theology.

The twentieth-century church *must* be creative in the areas where God intended it to be free. For example, the Bible does not dictate how *frequently* believers should meet together, nor does it dictate *when.* We are not told what *kinds* of meetings to have, nor are we locked into certain *formats* or *patterns* which should characterize these meetings. Furthermore, the Bible doesn't dictate *where* we should meet. Actually, the Bible doesn't even "lock us in" to nomenclature in describing the church. All of these are areas of freedom.

Back to my experience in Brazil. As stated earlier in this chapter, the Christian leaders I ministered to face unusual challenges. The vast majority have come to Christ out of a totally secular society. They are doctors, lawyers, dentists, architects, teachers, and other professional people. They grew up secularized, having rejected the institutional church as they know it in their culture. Though they as Christians now understand more fully that the church as they experienced it in their preconversion days is not a true reflection of the church as God designed it to be, they are still concerned about reaching others who are still like they *were* —totally "turned off" to any mention of the church and its leadership.

Therefore, understanding freedom in form, they meet in groups to be edified. But they do not call themselves a "church." Rather, they use the word *turma,* which means "group" in Portuguese. They do not use the word *pastor.* Rather, they use the word *mestre,* which means "teacher." And they have not built church buildings since this too creates a barrier to those they are trying to reach. In summary, these Brazilian Christians are applying New Testament principles of church life, but they are using the freedom God has given them to do His work in a supracultural situation.

In conclusion, the important fact is that whatever terminology we use, and whatever structures we develop, we must make sure they are helping Christians become a mature body of believers, and they are not causing us to violate the biblical principles for edification just outlined. And above all, whatever forms and structures the twentieth-century church develops, and in whatever culture, they must never be allowed to become absolute or an end in themselves. If we do, we will fall into the same subtle trap that the church has fallen into again and again throughout church history.

SUMMARY
1. The local church must be kept in focus as the primary means by which edification is to take place.
2. Believers must be provided with a basic knowledge of the Word of God.
3. Believers must be provided with an in-depth knowledge of the Word of God.
4. Believers must be provided with opportunities to develop capacities that go beyond knowledge.
5. Believers must be provided with the sum total of experiences which will help them get beyond the knowledge level—vital learning experiences with the Word, vital relational experiences with one another and with God, and vital witnessing experiences, both individually and corporately.
6. All believers must be equipped for Christian service.
7. Believers must be helped to develop qualitative family life.
8. The twentieth-century church must develop its own contemporary forms and structures for applying the biblical principles just outlined.

Footnotes

[1]Note in Acts 14:21-23 that the text seems to indicate that elders were appointed in Lystra, Iconium, and Antioch *after* the groups of believers were designated as churches. In other words, it was not necessary to have elders before a group of believers were called a church. It is my personal opinion that there were no elders in the Corinthian church, particularly when Paul wrote his first letter, because there was not a man mature enough to be one. (See 1 Cor. 6:5).

[2]Association psychology was a prominent theory in the nineteenth century which advocated that knowing automatically resulted in feeling and willing and doing. The totality of ideas constituted the will. Ideas once in the mind keep seeking to return and similar ideas tend to reinforce each other. On the other hand, dissimilar ideas tend to repel each other.

Even a brief reflection upon our own personal experience is ample reason as to why this theory has been discredited. Yet there are many Christians who seem to believe that if you store the mind with Bible truth and doctrine, it will automatically become a part of life.

[3]See Gene A. Getz, *The Measure of a Marriage,* Regal Books; see also *The Measure of a Family.*

NINE

LEADERSHIP IN THE NEW TESTAMENT CHURCH —PHASE ONE

The study of leadership in the New Testament church must be classified into two phases. They are overlapping phases, and yet each one is distinctive.

The first one has to do with early days of the church, and particularly the *universal church*. Phase two grows naturally out of phase one, and has to do with leadership in each *local church*.

HISTORICAL BACKGROUND

In order to understand the need for the two phases in God's plan for church leadership, it is necessary to gain some historical perspective.

As the followers of Christ began to carry out the Great Commission and to "make disciples," their only Bible was the Old Testament, which was used primarily to convince people that Jesus Christ was the promised Messiah.[1] But they had no New Testament literature from which to instruct these new Christians. After Pentecost, this literature as we know it today did not even begin to come into existence for approximately another fifteen or twenty years.[2]

As churches were founded, the Epistles were gradually written—particularly the Pauline letters to the churches. They were composed during the decade leading up to A.D. 60, nearly thirty years after Pentecost.[3] The Pastoral Epistles were written still later, during the early part of the 60s, and John did not complete his Epistles until sometime in the 80s.

It was actually during the period of A.D. 60 to 100 that the New Testament churches began to experience cohesiveness. Commenting on this development, Merrill Tenney states:

> The survey of the literature will show that in the last third of the first century the church was rapidly consolidating into a recognized institution. From being a scattered collection of isolated bands of believers, each with its own problems and with its own standards, it was beginning to acquire social and doctrinal solidarity and to be regarded as a potent factor in society.[4]

Obviously, the task of edifying the church during the first thirty to fifty years of its existence carried with it some unusual problems. Humanly speaking, without a body of literature there could be no systematized set of doctrines. But God had a plan whereby the church could be equipped and stabilized.

THE GREATER GIFTS

In recent years Ephesians 4:4-16 has become the basis for many discussions, lectures, sermons, articles, and even books—particularly as it relates to church leadership.

In the Ephesian passage we read that God gave certain gifts to some (not all), to equip *all* members of the body for service and ministry. A corollary passage is found in 1 Corinthians 12:28-31. Significantly, the passage in Ephesians refers primarily to the *universal church,* whereas the Corinthian passage also refers to the universal church with a more specific application to the *local church.* Notice the similarities:

EPHESIANS	1 CORINTHIANS
4:11 And He gave some *as* apostles, and some *as* prophets, and some *as* evangelists, and some *as* pastors and teachers,	12:28 And God has appointed in the church first apostles, second prophets, third teachers, then miracles,
4:12 for the equipping of the saints for the work of service, to the building up of the body of Christ;	then gifts of healing, helps, administrations, various kinds of tongues.

12:29 All are not (apostles,) are
         they?
         All are not (prophets,) are
         they?
         All are not (teachers,) are
         they?
         All are not workers of
         miracles, are they?
12:30 All do not have gifts of
         healings, do they?
         All do not speak with
         tongues, do they?
         All do not interpret, do
         they?
12:31 But earnestly desire *the
         greater gifts.*
         And I show you a still
         more excellent way.

When you compare these two passages several things become clear:

1. Paul in the Corinthian passage classified apostles, prophets, and teachers as the "greater gifts" and instructed the church—as a group—to desire that the greater gifts be active in the local body (1 Cor. 12:31).[5]

2. The Ephesian passage lists only the greater gifts, whereas the Corinthian passage lists the lesser gifts as well.

3. There is a similarity but yet a lack of conformity in the listing of the greater gifts in the two passages. The sequence is basically the same, but *evangelists* are added in the Ephesian passage and the *pastor* gift is combined with the *teaching* gift.

Why is there a lack of conformity in these two lists of "greater gifts"?

To answer this question, consider the individuals who had these greater gifts in the New Testament. Who were these people and how were these gifts manifested?

APOSTLES

The term *apostle* almost without exception is used in the New Testament in a very distinct sense. The word refers primarily to the twelve men Jesus Christ selected out of the larger group of disciples and "named as apostles" (Luke 6:13; see also Matt.

10:1-4). The Greek word *apostolos* means literally, "a delegate, a messenger or one sent forth with orders." When Judas turned his back on the Lord and later took his own life, he was replaced by Matthias, who was "numbered with the eleven apostles" (Acts 1:26). Paul also classifies himself as an apostle who was "untimely born." He describes himself as one who was called to be an apostle, but who was "not fit to be called an apostle" because he "persecuted the church of God" (1 Cor. 15:8-9).[6] Luke's record in the Book of Acts verifies Paul's claim and testimony without question. He is presented as the great apostle to the Gentiles, who in a special way left the ranks of Judiasm and penetrated the pagan world with the Gospel of Jesus Christ.

There is a secondary sense, however, in which the word *apostle* is used in the New Testament. Luke called Barnabas an apostle when referring to his "ministry" with Paul (Acts 14:4-14).[7] Also Paul seemingly classified Silas and Timothy as fellow apostles (1 Thes. 2:6-7), and it is also possible that he may have used the same description of Andronicus and Junias, who he said were "outstanding among the apostles" (Rom. 16:7). But it is quite clear from the Scriptures that these descriptions are used in a secondary sense. On the one hand they were messengers and delegates sent forth by Jesus Christ as any missionary or Christian leader involved in proclaiming the Gospel of Christ. But in a primary sense, apostles were those men who were eyewitnesses of Jesus Christ and who were taught by Him personally and particularly selected for an initial ministry in bringing into being the body of Christ—His church.

Dr. George Peters in his own study of the role of these men recognized and has written about their unique calling. He states: "The unique position of the apostles in the beginning ministries of the church is recognized throughout the New Testament—only they are known as the *apostles of Jesus Christ,* while others are known simply as apostles or as apostles of the church."[8]

Luke verified this particular apostolic role in the Book of Acts when he recorded their work. The apostles of Jesus Christ "solemnly testified" and "exhorted" (Acts 2:40); they taught (2:42), worked signs and miracles (2:43; 5:12), and gave witness to the resurrection of Jesus Christ (4:33).

The apostles also helped organize the rapidly developing church in Jerusalem but did not allow themselves to get bogged down with administrative detail. Rather, they devoted themelves to prayer and the ministry of the Word (6:1-7). A majority of the apostles spent most of their time in Jerusalem in the early days of the church. Even when persecution drove many disciples out of Jerusalem, the apostles stayed (8:1), perhaps because they felt it was their duty. F. F. Bruce speculates also that the persecution at that time may not have been so much directed at them but at the Hellenists in the church.[9]

An exception to their staying on location in Jerusalem is noted by Luke when Peter and John left Jerusalem to go to Samaria to help establish the new believers there, and to use their apostolic authority and power to lay hands on these new believers so that they might receive the Holy Spirit (8:14-17).

It is clear, however, that God had a divine purpose in planning that the apostles stay in Jerusalem. It was here that they, with the elders, hammered out the theological and practical problems of the new and growing church. Luke devoted a lengthy section in his narrative to describe the leadership of the apostles and elders in resolving the Jewish-Gentile problems, particularly as they related to the teachings of law and grace. After much debate and discussion (15:7), the apostles and elders composed and sent a letter to Antioch, clarifying some of these issues (15:22-29).

After Acts 15, the apostles are mentioned only once, and in this instance Luke recorded the ministry of Paul and Timothy as they traveled from city to city "delivering the decrees, which had been decided upon by the apostles and elders who were in Jerusalem" (16:4).

Hereafter, the ministry of the Apostle Paul received primary attention in the Lukean account. Clearly, Paul had a unique apostolic ministry compared with the other apostles who remained in Jerusalem. He was called in a special way to be a church planter. He was a multigifted man. He "was appointed a preacher and an apostle and a teacher" (2 Tim. 1:11; see also 1 Tim. 2:7). He demonstrated "the sign of a true apostle . . . signs, and wonders, and miracles" (2 Cor. 12:12). And to him, above all the apostles, was revealed in a most detailed manner the mystery of the church (Eph. 3:1-12; Col. 1:24-28).

The apostles' work then was foundational, as described by Paul:

> So then you are no longer strangers and aliens, but you are fellow-citizens with the saints, and are of God's household, having been built upon the *foundation of the apostles* and prophets, Christ Jesus Himself being the cornerstone; in whom the whole building, being fitted together is growing into a holy temple in the Lord; in whom you also are being built together into a dwelling of God in the Spirit (Eph. 2:19-22).

Therefore, when Paul placed apostles at the top of the list in both 1 Corinthians 12:28 and Ephesians 4:11, he was no doubt using the word *apostles* in a primary sense. He was not just describing an "apostolic ministry or work," but he was talking about a specific calling and appointment made by God to specific men who were to have a unique ministry of evangelism and edification in the early days of the church.

PROPHETS

The second of the "greater gifts" listed in Ephesians 4 and 1 Corinthians 12 is prophecy. To prophesy literally means "to speak forth" or "to speak out"; hence, a prophet was a person who "spoke forth."

As used in both the Old and New Testaments, however, a "prophet" had a distinct function. This person was not just an ordinary preacher or teacher. Rather he had access to information by means of a supernatural gift from God. By means of divine inspiration, he was able to communicate information related to future events. This is abundantly illustrated in the New Testament.

Some, if not all, of the apostles were also prophets. They not only demonstrated this in their apostolic ministry as recorded in the Book of Acts, but Peter, James, John, Matthew, and Paul all left us with a sizable portion of the New Testament, which certainly includes information that was communicated by means of the prophetic gift.

But there were also individuals in New Testament days who were not apostles in the primary sense but who were given the gift of prophecy. The first reference to a New Testament prophet other than the apostles appears in Acts 11. Several came to Antioch from Jerusalem. Luke identified one of them as Agabus, who "stood up and began to indicate by the Spirit that there would certainly be a great famine all over the world" (Acts 11:28). As a result of this declaration, the church prepared for this future event, and believers were able to help Christians in other parts of the country who were in need (11:29-30).

Agabus appeared later in the Book of Acts and once more demonstrated his gift of prophecy when he warned Paul regarding the problems and persecution the apostle would encounter in Jerusalem (21:10-14).

There were other individuals identified by name in the Book of Acts who had this same divine ability as Agabus. In the church at Antioch, Barnabas, Simeon, Lucius, Manean, and Saul were classified as prophets (13:1).

Judas and Silas, who were "leading men among the brethren" in the Jerusalem church (15:22), are also identified as having this prophetic gift. Upon coming to Antioch to assist in delivering the Jerusalem letter, we read that they "also being *prophets* themselves, encouraged and strengthened the brethren with a lengthy message" (15:32).

This special prophetic gift was not limited to men. Philip, one of the seven men appointed in Acts 6 to care for the distribution of food, had four daughters, all of whom were "prophetesses" (21:9). Thus women too were recipients of these divine abilities. This also was no doubt true in the church at Corinth (1 Cor. 14:27-35).

Certainly, Luke and Mark and Jude also had the gift of prophecy, though it is not specifically mentioned. Rather they demonstrated this gift in their prophetic revelations embodied in their New Testament writings.

On the basis of the biblical evidence, we can conclude that the gift of prophecy mentioned in 1 Corinthians 12 and Ephesians 4 referred to a special group of individuals in New Testament days who were given special revelations from God in order to help the new and infant church grow and develop into a mature organism. As with the gift of apostleship, it was also a "foundational" gift. You have been "built upon the *foundation of the apostles and prophets,*" wrote Paul to the Ephesians.

EVANGELISTS

The gift of evangelism is mentioned in the Ephesian passage but not in the Corinthian passage. It was no doubt also classified as a "greater gift" because of its inclusion in the Ephesian list. The word *evangelist* literally means a "bringer of good tidings." In the New Testament, these individuals brought the good tidings of the Gospel—the Good News of Jesus Christ's coming, death, and resurrection. Yet, of all the gifts listed as the "greater gifts," evangelizing is the most difficult to associate with particular individuals in the New Testament. There is only one clear-cut reference to an "evangelist" per se, and that is Philip, one of the seven and father of the four prophetesses (Acts 21:9). His gift is abundantly demonstrated, however, in his ministry in Samaria (8:5-13) and particularly in his encounter with the Ethiopian eunuch (8:26-30).

Philip was no ordinary man in the body of Christ. His gift of evangelism set him apart. He, like the apostles and prophets, was especially gifted with unusual and supernatural abilities. He cast out unclean spirits and healed the lame and paralyzed (8:7). He received a direct revelation from the Lord regarding the Ethiopian (8:29) and after he led the eunuch to Christ, "the Spirit of the Lord snatched Philip away" (8:39). The word "snatched" is a strong word, meaning to be caught up or seized. Evidently, the Lord removed Philip bodily from this place and, miraculously, Philip found himself in a different location and continued with his evangelistic work—that of "preaching the Gospel" (8:40).

Though there are few references to "evangelists" per se in the New Testament, there are other ways to recognize those with this gift. For example, there were the "men of Cyprus and Cyrene who came to Antioch and began speaking to the Greeks also, preaching the Lord Jesus" (11:20). The phrase "preaching the Lord Jesus" actually identifies their evangelistic ministry, for the phrase actually meant "to evangelize." We see the results of their evangelistic work for "a large number . . . turned to the Lord" (11:21).

The apostles, and particularly Paul, also demonstrated the gift of evangelism. In fact, all of these New Testament pioneers were multigifted men. This gives us a significant clue as to why the list of "greater gifts" is not exactly parallel as listed in the Corinthian-Ephesian passages. This will become more obvious when we look at the gift of teaching mentioned next in the list.

TEACHERS AND PASTOR-TEACHERS

The *didaskalos,* or teacher, was used in the New Testament to describe a person who, in a more comprehensive sense, taught basic Christian doctrines. The term *pastor* (*poimen*) means shepherd and includes the concept of "teaching." It would be impossible to be a good shepherd without "feeding the flock of God."

The apostles also had the gift of teaching (4:2; 5:21, 25, 28). Of their ministry in those early days in Jerusalem, we read, "And every day, in the temple and from house to house, they [the apostles] kept right on *teaching* and *preaching* Jesus as the Christ" (5:42).

Some of the New Testament prophets who were not apostles in the primary sense also had the gift of teaching. Barnabas, Simeon, Lucius, and Manaen are called *prophets* and *teachers* (13:1). Saul (or later Paul) was also included in this list, probably before his apostolic calling was made clear to him. We see Barnabas and Saul using their teaching gifts in Antioch. Luke tells us "that for an entire year they met with the church, and *taught* considerable numbers" (11:26).

This leads us to observe more carefully why Paul, in categorizing the "greater gifts," specifies only "teachers" in the Corinthian passage and lists "pastors and teachers" together in the Ephesian list. In reality, he is doing the same thing as Luke in Acts 13:1, when he identified these four men as prophets *and* teachers. In other words this is why we see similarity but also variance in the two lists. As we have already demonstrated, some men during the initial days of the church were apostles-prophets-evangelists-pastors-teachers. Paul, it appears, had all five gifts. Others, however, were prophets-teachers. And again some were only classified as prophets. Still others seemed to have been evangelists-teachers. Apollos fits this category. He was an "eloquent man" and "mighty in the Scriptures" (18:24). While in Achaia, "he helped greatly those who had believed through grace; for he powerfully refuted the Jews in public, demonstrating by the Scriptures that Jesus was the Christ" (18:27-28).

Here we seem to see a combination ministry of apologetic evangelism and teaching. Paul also made reference to this combination ministry in Corinth when he asked the questions: "What then is

Apollos? And what is Paul?" He then answered these questions in this manner: "Servants through whom you believed. . . . I planted, Apollos watered, but God was causing the growth" (1 Cor. 3:5-6). Notice that evidently the Corinthians had come to know Jesus Christ through the evangelistic ministry of both Apollos *and* Paul, for they came to "believe" through the ministry of these men. But note also that both of these men had an edification ministry among these people in that Paul planted the seed and Apollos followed Paul's ministry by watering the seed.

Timothy is the outstanding New Testament example of a pastor-teacher. Paul frequently used him in this capacity, leaving him to help a new and struggling church to get on its feet spiritually. He sent him back to Thessalonica "to strengthen and encourage" these Christians in their faith (1 Thes. 3:2). Likewise, he asked him to go to Corinth to teach them the doctrines that he himself was teaching "everywhere in every church" (1 Cor. 4:17). He asked him to "remain on at Ephesus" so that he might "instruct certain men not to teach strange doctrines" (1 Tim. 1:3).

Later Paul wrote to Timothy, "And the things which you have heard from me in the presence of many witnesses, these entrust to faithful men, who will be able to teach others also" (2 Tim. 2:2). Perhaps Paul was referring to the pastor-teacher gifts in his two letters to this young man. There seems to be some evidence for this conclusion. Notice the context in which Paul makes reference to Timothy's gift.

> *Prescribe* and *teach* these things. Let no one look down on your youthfulness, but rather in speech, conduct, love, faith, and purity, show yourself an *example* of those who believe. Until I come, give attention to the *public reading* of Scripture, to *exhortation* and *teaching.* Do not neglect the *spiritual gift* within you, which was bestowed upon you through prophetic utterance with the laying on of hands by the presbytery. Take pains with these things; be absorbed in them, so that your progress may be evident to all. Pay close attention to yourself and to your *teaching;* preserve in these things; for as you do this you will ensure salvation both for yourself and for those who hear you (1 Tim. 4:11-16).

Note too that Paul in his second letter warned Timothy not to be timid, but "to kindle afresh the gift of God" (2 Tim. 1:6). Undoubtedly, he had been criticized for his youthfulness (1 Tim. 4:12). His sensitive pastoral heart may have caused him to withdraw and neglect his responsibilities. It is logical that Paul would encourage him not to withdraw, but to continue his pastoral-teaching ministry with boldness.

Titus too was probably a New Testament pastor-teacher. He, like Timothy, was closely associated with Paul in his missionary travels (2 Cor. 2:13; 7:6-7, 13-14). Paul identified him as his "true child in a common faith" (Titus 1:4) and as his "partner and fellow worker" (2 Cor. 8:23). Paul left Titus in Crete to carry out a pastoral-teacing ministry, to set things in order and to "appoint elders in every city" (Titus 1:5). While there, he was to "speak the things which are fitting for sound doctrine" (2:1), and to "exhort and reprove with all authority" (2:15).

There may have been other men who were closely associated with Paul who were pastor-teachers like Timothy and Titus. Luke was left behind to help establish the new church in Philippi. And Paul made reference to Gaius, Aristarchus, and Erastus, who may have functioned in a similar role.

In conclusion, we see a number of different gift combinations functioning in the Book of Acts. This is why Paul was not concerned about complete uniformity, even in listing the greater gifts. There is a natural sequence, however, which is clear in both passages, going from the foundational gifts (apostles, prophets and evangelists) to those that were used more specifically in founding and establishing churches (pastors and teachers). In view of all of the combinations, it would have been awkward to attempt to come up with a uniform list. This is seemingly why Paul spoke of "pastors and teachers." Not all had this combination of gifts. While Apollos had the gift of teaching, he probably did not have the gift of pastor or shepherd. Silas may have been a prophet *and* pastor *and* teacher. He is definitely identified as a prophet (Acts 15:32), and he certainly engaged in a teaching ministry in his travels with Paul (15:40-41). And furthermore, he obviously engaged in a shepherding ministry while in Thessalonica (1 Thes. 1:1; 2 Thes. 1:1).

It is important to note once again that Paul exhorted the Corinthian church to emphasize the "greater gifts." As a body, they were to desire the assistance of those individuals with these gifts. In order to be edified and to grow up and mature, they were to encourage those who were apostles, prophets, and teachers to have a ministry among them.[10]

SUMMARY

A study of the Book of Acts, particularly, leaves little doubt as to what is meant by those who had the greater gifts. In the most part they were gifted men who were used of God to found and establish the church. The *apostles* were those who were especially called, appointed, and trained by Christ to form a small nucleus that would bring the church into being.

Prophets, also classified as having a foundational ministry, were given access to information from God by direct revelation, and were able to predict future events in order to assist the body of Christ in its growth and development. Most of the apostles were also prophets.

Evangelists were given special abilities in preaching the Gospel. Thus most of the primary apostles were also evangelists.

Teachers were those who communicated God's truth in a comprehensive way. The gift was used both in evangelism and edification.

In the early days of the church before the completion of the canon, those with the gift of teaching seemingly had access to doctrinal truth by direct revelation from God. The apostles particularly were able to recall by means of the Holy Spirit what they had learned from Jesus Christ. While with them, He said: "These things I have spoken to you, while abiding with you. But the Helper, the Holy Spirit, whom the Father will send in My name, He will teach you all things, and bring to your remembrance all that I said to you" (John 14:25-26).

Pastors or shepherds were those who gave special help to new churches. In the most part they were also *teachers* who helped both in the organization of the church as well as in its growth through the process of instruction.[11] In the first-century church, they had a foundational ministry, along with the others who had the greater gifts. They went from church to church assisting in the appointment of local leadership and making sure the church learned the basic doctrines of Christianity.

It seems, therefore, that these greater gifts mentioned in 1 Corinthians 12 and Ephesians 4 were, in a *primary sense,* designed by God for "a church-planting" ministry in the early days of Christianity, and were directly related to the universal church. These were special gifts given prior to the writing of the New Testament. These early Christian leaders were given supernatural capacities and abilities, including both knowledge and skill, in order to "equip the saints for the work of the ministry." Wherever local churches were founded, and as people came to Christ and formed these groups of believers in specific geographical locations, God instituted His second phase or plan for church leadership—a plan that clearly relates to the *local church.* As will be shown, this new phenomenon called for church leaders who, though they are not classified as individuals possessing the greater gifts, were in a *secondary sense* to have a ministry that included a *similar function* as those who actually possessed these greater gifts.

Footnotes

[1] It is an enlightening study to trace in the Book of Acts the way the apostles used the Old Testament in winning people to Christ.

[2] Many scholars believe that James and Galatians represent some of the earliest New Testament Epistles, probably written between A.D. 45 and A.D. 50.

[3] Approximate dates: 1 and 2 Thessalonians and 1 Corinthians (A.D. 52); 2 Corinthians (A.D. 54); Romans (A.D. 55); Colossians, Ephesians, and Philemon (A.D. 56); Philippians (A.D. 60).

[4] Merrill C. Tenney, *New Testament Survey,* p. 319.

[5] The conclusion that Paul is classifying *apostles, prophets,* and *teachers* as the "greater gifts" is based on several observations. (1) Paul gave a definite order of importance where he said, "*first* apostles, *second* prophets, *third* teachers." (2) He further placed these three gifts in a distinct category when he followed this sequential listing by saying "*then* miracles, *then* gifts of healings, helps, administrations, various kinds of tongues" (italics added). (3) Note also that Paul was not instructing these believers as *individuals* to seek for these gifts. Rather, he used the second personal plural in the Greek language, which clearly implies that the Corinthians, as a *group,* should desire that the greater gifts be used in the church rather than the lesser gifts. The larger context also verifies this observation.

134 / **Sharpening the Focus of the Church**

[6]See also Gal. 1:1, 11-12; 2:8; 1 Cor. 9:1-2; 2 Cor. 12:11-12; 1 Tim. 2:7; 2 Tim. 1:11.

[7]Though Barnabas is described as an apostle (that is, as one who is engaged in an apostolic work), he seemingly recognized that there was a special group of men who were designated as apostles of which he was not a part (Acts 9:27).

[8]George W. Peters, *A Theology of Church Growth,* Zondervan Publishing House, p. 17.

[9]F. F. Bruce, *The Book of Acts,* Eerdmans, p. 175.

[10]Some of the Corinthians were rejecting Paul's apostolic ministry in favor of others who were exercising the lesser gifts.

[11]It is also possible that the gift of pastor was synonymous with the gift of teaching. The gift of pastor is never referred to apart from the teaching gift. Furthermore, as we'll demonstrate in the next chapter, the *function* of "pastoring" always includes "teaching."

TEN

LEADERSHIP IN THE NEW TESTAMENT CHURCH —PHASE TWO

As pointed out in the previous chapter, New Testament church leaders faced some unusual problems during the early years of the church's existence. They had no inspired literature from which to teach doctrine which was distinctly New Testament. It is conceivable that some Christians even at the end of the first century had not yet been exposed to all of the Gospels, Paul's letters, and the other Epistles.[1]

God had a plan, however, which enabled the apostles, prophets, evangelists, pastors, and teachers to "equip the saints for the work of service"—even apart from having the New Testament literature. He bestowed upon these individuals supernatural capacities and abilities—involving both knowledge and skill—to enable them to edify the church (Eph. 4:7-12).[2]

But as churches were founded and established in the faith, a new plan for church leadership unfolded—one which, for practical reasons, is designated as phase two.

LOCAL CHURCH LEADERSHIP

The Book of Acts as well as some material in the Epistles clearly demonstrate that, in the most part, those individuals who possessed the "greater gifts"—that of apostle, prophet, evangelist, pastor, and teacher—had a ministry at large. They "made disciples," founded churches, and moved from one group of believers to another, helping them become established in the faith.

135

The primary responsibiity of the first-century pastor-teacher was to help the new and struggling church to get organized and to grow spiritually. As mentioned previously, Timothy was one of the most prominent pastor-teachers in the New Testament. When the church at Corinth was struggling in its carnality and immaturity, Paul sent Timothy to teach them (1 Cor. 4:17). Paul also indicated his plans to send him to Philippi to have a ministry among the Christians there (Phil. 2:19-20). He left him in Ephesus to instruct and guide the believers (1 Tim. 1:3). On his second missionary journey, he left Timothy in Berea along with Silas (Acts 17:14), apparently to help establish the church. On the same journey, after starting the church in Thessalonica, Paul sent Timothy back to this church "to strengthen and encourage" them (1 Thes. 3:1-2).

Timothy and other men like him, such as Titus, served the New Testament church as God's plan for church leadership moved from phase one to phase two. They instituted the second phase as soon as there were believers in the local congregation who were mature enough to be appointed as elders. Paul and Barnabas demonstrated this as they retraced their steps and went back to the cities in which they had previously "made many disciples" and then "appointed elders . . . in every church" (Acts 14:21-23).

ELDERS OR BISHOPS?

Following are several important observations regarding this process:

1. *These local church leaders are identified in Scripture with two basic titles.*

The two words used to describe these spiritual leaders were "bishop" (*episkopos*) and "elder" (*presbuteros*). The terms were used interchangeably, particularly by Paul.[3]

The word *bishop* actually means "an overseer." This word was used as an official title among the Greeks, and Lightfoot reminds us that "in Athenian language it was used especially to designate commissioners appointed to regulate a new colony or acquisition."[4] Synonyms for the word *bishop* might be overseer, curator, guardian, or superintendent.

The word *elder,* though used in the literature of many societies, is found most frequently in the writings which describe the activities of God's chosen people. Again, Lightfoot has made some significant observations:

> In the lifetime of the lawgiver, in the days of the judges, throughout the monarchy, during the Captivity, after the return, and under Roman domination, the "elders" appear as an integral part of the governing body of the country.... Over every Jewish synagogue ... a council of "elders" presided. It was not unnatural, therefore, when the Christian synagogue took its place by the side of the Jewish, a similar organization should be adopted with such modifications as circumstances required; and thus the name familiar under the old dispensation was retained under the new.[5]

Moreover, the word *elder* appears in the New Testament more frequently than the word *bishop,* and especially in the Book of Acts. Luke used the word to refer to the "elders of Israel,"[6] and after the church was established in Jerusalem and in other parts of the world, it was used to refer to the "elders of the church."[7] Reference to being a bishop appears only once in Acts, and that is where Paul is addressing the Ephesian elders (20:28). The rest of the time it appears in the Pauline epistles, and as just mentioned, is used interchangeably with the word *elder.*

Some have suggested that the term *bishop* is used to refer to the office and the word *elder* has to do with the man or person. It seems there is a more accurate explanation. Since Paul had a special ministry to the Gentiles, and since he used the word *bishop* more frequently than other New Testament writers, it appears he did so to communicate more effectively to the mixture of converted Jews and Gentiles in the New Testament church. Note that the word is used in writing to the *Philippians* (Phil. 1:1), to Timothy who was stationed at *Ephesus* (1 Tim. 3:1-2), and to Titus who was in *Crete* (Titus 1:7). All of these churches were founded in a pagan world and were composed of both Jew and Gentile converts. If this is true, it indicates Paul's sensitivity to culture and how important it is to communicate in the language of the people. He wanted to bring both groups together in oneness, to show them there was no barrier or "dividing wall" but rather "one new man." Christ has reconciled "them both in one body to God" (Eph. 2:14-16). They were no longer Jews and Greeks but the "church of God" (1 Cor. 10:32).[8]

So whether we call them elders (a term well known to Jews) or bishops (a term well known to Greeks), it matters not, implied Paul. The important issue is what characterized their lives and what they did. The title was secondary, their qualifications and functions were primary.[9]

2. *These spiritual leaders were to manage and shepherd God's people.*

There are also two words used to describe the overall responsibility of elders. They were to *manage* and to *pastor* or *shepherd*.[10] "Managing" is the more technical term, whereas "pastoring" and "shepherding" are more colorful and illustrative concepts.

Managing the Church. Paul first used the word "manage" in his writings when listing the qualifications for elders. Note that he did so by referring to the role of the father in a family setting. An elder "must be one who *manages* his own household well," wrote Paul (1 Tim. 3:4). He then correlated this observation with leadership in a local church. "If a man does not know how to *manage* his own household, how will he take care of the church of God?" (3:5)

This is a very significant observation. *First,* it demonstrates a relationship in Paul's thinking between a "family unit" and the "local church." A single household was often the church in miniature. The father was to lead his family just as elders were to lead the church. In fact, in some instances the father was probably *both* father *and* elder.

Second, it is important to note that Paul's illustration gives us a functional definition of the word *manage.* It is an all inclusive concept. There is nothing that is not included in this task. It involves total and complete oversight of the family or the church. Put another way, God holds the father responsible for the overall leadership in a home, and He holds the elders responsible for the overall leadership in a church.

Third, this relationship between the family and the church also demonstrates the importance of not attempting to form a philosophy of ministry for either the church or the home without understanding this relationship. In other words, God has not ordained one set of principles for the church and another for the family. The same can be said regarding the husband-wife relationship as well as how an individual believer orders his life within the body of Christ.[11]

Fourth, this family-church relationship as described by Paul leads to a very practical question. It is clear from Scripture that God never intended the home to function with more than one primary leader—the husband and father. Does this imply, particularly in Paul's reference to family and church management, that local churches also need one primary leader? We need to address this question particularly in view of the various opinions that exist on this subject in contemporary churches. But first, we need more biblical data.

Pastoring the Flock. The words *pastoring* and *shepherding* are used more frequently in Scripture to describe the overall leadership responsibility of an elder than the words *manage* and *rule*.[12] This concept would be meaningful to first-century Christians who understood experientially a relationship between a shepherd and his sheep. Unfortunately, many twentieth-century Christians do not grasp the full meaning of this kind of analogy, as pointed out by Phillip Keller in his delightful and informative book *A Shepherd Looks at Psalm 23.* He states: "Many who either read or study the Scriptures in the twentieth century come from an urban man-made environment. City people, especially, are often unfamiliar with such subjects as livestock, crops, land, food, or wildlife. They miss much of the truth taught in God's Word because they are not familiar with such things as sheep, wheat, soil, or grapes."[13]

The Apostle Peter used this analogy more graphically than any other New Testament writer. In his first Epistle, he exhorted the elders to "shepherd the flock of God." They were to do it with freedom ("not under compulsion") and with pure motives ("not for sorted gain"). Furthermore, they were not to approach this task in an authoritarian manner, lording it over those allotted to "their charge." Rather, they were to "be examples to the flock" (1 Peter 5:1-3). Peter then ended this paragraph on pastoral leadership by referring to the greatest Shepherd who ever walked the face of the earth—Jesus Christ Himself. "And when the Chief Shepherd appears," he wrote, "you will receive the unfading crown of glory" (5:4).

As with the term *manage, shepherding* is an all inclusive term. A shepherd is responsible for the total welfare of his sheep. He is to "guard" them from "savage wolves"—false teachers (Acts 20:28-29). He is to feed them by declaring and teaching the "whole purpose of God" (20:27; Titus 1:9). He is to care for them and pray for them when they are ill (James 5:14).

Psalm 23 illustrates the shepherding responsibility more completely than any other passage of Scripture. David's description of God's care for him personally provides a powerful model for men who serve as shepherds of God's people:

Psalm 23

"I shall not want."	*He meets my spiritual needs.*
"He makes me lie down in green patures."	*He makes me feel secure and restful.*
"He leads me beside quiet waters."	*He cares for my spiritual thirst.*
"He restores my soul."	*He builds me up when I have failed and am discouraged.*
"He guides me in the paths of righteousness."	*He leads me into the will of God.*
"Even though I walk through the valley of the shadow of death, I fear no evil, for Thou art with me."	*He stays beside me in times of difficulty and danger.*
"Thy rod and Thy staff, they comfort me."	*He lovingly disciplines me when I go astray from God's will.*
"Thou dost prepare a table before me in the presence of my enemies."	*He provides spiritual food in the midst of a world feasting on worldly knowledge.*
"Thou hast anointed my head with oil."	*He provides healing for my hurts and wounds.*

Just so, an elder shepherds and manages his people by

- Meeting their spiritual needs
- Making them feel secure and restful
- Caring for their spiritual thirst
- Building them up when they fail and are discouraged

- Leading them into the will of God
- Staying beside them in times of difficulty and danger
- Lovingly disciplining them when they go astray
- Providing spiritual food
- Providing healing for their hurts and wounds

"Managing" and "shepherding" then describe synonymous functions. They are overarching concepts which include more specific functions, such as exemplifying Christlikeness, preaching the Gospel, exhorting and warning Christians against inappropriate behavior, teaching the truth of God, and praying for those who are sick. This is what is meant by the observation—these leaders were to manage or shepherd God's people.

3. *Some of these leaders were to be remunerated for their ministry.*

Paul made specific reference to this congregational responsibility in his first letter to Timothy. He wrote that "the elders who rule well be considered worthy of double honor, especially those who work hard at preaching and teaching" (1 Tim. 5:17). This is clear from the context. Paul followed this exhortation with quotations from the Old Testament—"For the Scripture says, 'You shall not muzzle the ox while he is threshing,' and 'The laborer is worthy of his wages' " (5:18).

This is the biblical basis for spiritual leaders who are identified today as *staff pastors.* When an individual gives a large portion of time to the ministry, that person usually doesn't have time left over to work at a regular job in order to provide for his family. If a body of believers encourages and accepts this kind of effort, then that church is responsible to remunerate that person for his efforts.

Note that this is the verse used by some to establish two roles for elders—"ruling elders" and "teaching elders." I do not believe this passage is teaching this dichotomy nor do other New Testament references to elder function. Paul is simply saying that there will be those elders—when they carry out their "ruling" or "managing" role—who will work particularly hard in the areas of "preaching and teaching." Anyone who has served as a staff pastor with this primary responsibility can verify that these are the most time-consuming aspects of managing or shepherding—that is, if "preaching and teaching" are to be done in a qualitative manner.

4. *New Testament churches evidently had more than one elder or bishop.*

At this juncture the New Testament record becomes somewhat unclear. The reason is that we cannot draw accurate conclusions regarding the exact forms and patterns in New Testament churches. And unless we understand their structures, it is difficult to state dogmatically how elders carried out their functions.

MULTIPLE ELDERSHIP

What can we say for sure relative to multiple eldership in a given church?

First, it is true that the Bible always speaks of the "elders" of the church; that is, the term is pluralized. The only exception is when an individual elder is referred to (see 1 Tim. 3:1-2), but again this kind of reference is always in the context of plurality.

Second, the term *church,* as it is used to speak of local churches in specific geographical settings, was used by scriptural writers to refer to *all* the believers in a particular area, whether they met together regularly or not. For example, Luke referred to the "church in Jerusalem" (Acts 8:1). But we know from the biblical record that believers were not able to continue to meet in one place. There was not a building large enough, nor would they have been allowed to do so if there had been. The fact is that they initially met in the temple (2:46a). On one occasion shortly after the church was founded, they gathered in the portico of Solomon to hear Peter preach. As a result, both Peter and John were arrested (3:11; 4:1-3). Eventually, the persecution spread to the whole church and Luke recorded that "they were all scattered throughout the region of Judea and Samaria, except the apostles" (8:1). Until that happened, the normal meeting place in Jerusalem was in homes. They met "from house to house" (1:46b).

The church in Ephesus gives us another illustration. Luke referred to "the *elders* of the *church*" in that city (20:17). Here the term *elder* is pluralized in conjunction with the single, local church, just as it was in Jerusalem (21:18). But again, this does not refer to the fact that the church had a permanent or even a temporary meeting place as we usually do in our twentieth-century American culture. True, Paul met with believers (and probably unbelievers) daily in the school of Tyrannus for a period of two years (19:9-10). But it is clear from the context that this was not the regular meeting place for the church to fellowship, worship, and be taught. Rather, they also no doubt met in homes.

The facts are that we cannot find any record of church buildings as we think of them in terms of our culture until sometime in the third century. In fact, one of the first buildings used primarily as a regular place for Christian meetings was discovered by archeologists in the ruins of the ancient city Dura-Europus in the Syrian desert. It was used as a private home by a well-to-do person. The date of construction was the year A.D. 232-233.[14]

Before drawing any firm conclusions, consider one more New Testament example. Paul left Titus in Crete to help these new churches get organized. The process was to "appoint elders in *every city*" (Titus 1:5). Again, we have the term *elder* pluralized. But we also have reference to more than one city. Therefore, we can conclude only one thing: Titus was to appoint more than one elder in each city.

Assuming that "house churches" were the normative meeting place for the churches in Crete as they were in other places in the New Testament world, we can now raise some interesting questions (see fig. 14).

1. Was there one elder for every house church? If so, this would in no way be in contradiction to the previous reference to plurality of elders in Jerusalem or Ephesus. It would simply mean there was more than one house church in each city.

2. Was there more than one elder in each house church? Perhaps, but probably not unless the house church was unusually large. This is a possibility, however, since they have discovered homes that were used for the church to meet in that had rooms that could seat up to 500 people. Practically speaking, it would probably take more than one elder to adequately manage and shepherd this size church.

From these biblical examples we can safely conclude that there was more than one elder in the churches in Jerusalem, Ephesus, and the cities in Crete. The same would be true in Lystra, Icon-

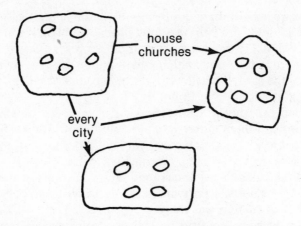

Figure 14. New Testament Structures

ium, and Pisidian Antioch since we are told that in these cities, Paul and Barnabas "appointed *elders* for them in every *church*" (Acts 14:23). But beyond this we cannot go! There is not sufficient biblical data regarding church structure to explain more fully the concept of plurality of elders and how this actually worked out in a given locality. There are, however, some pragmatic considerations we can bring to bear upon the observation that New Testament churches seemingly had more than one elder or bishop. But more about that later.

5. *These spiritual leaders were to delegate responsibility to other qualified men and women to care for the cultural needs of the church.*

Elders were not the only leaders appointed in New Testament days to direct the affairs of the local church. The Bible also refers to deacons and deaconesses.

In Paul's letter to Timothy, who was stationed at the time in Ephesus, he specified, first of all, the qualifications for elders (1 Tim. 3:1-7). He then specified the qualifications for deacons, *men* in serving roles (3:8-10, 12), and deaconesses, *women* in serving roles (3:11).[15]

Functions of Deacons and Deaconesses. What were these people supposed to do in the church? To some it may be surprising that

LEADERS	QUALIFICATIONS	FUNCTIONS
Elders or Overseers	Specified	Pastor and Teacher (Supracultural)
Deacons and/or Deaconesses	Specified	Vary (Cultural)

Figure 15. Leadership Comparison

biblical writers did not specify functions for these church leaders as they did for elders. Rather, the Scriptures specify qualifications for both positions, but they leave the deacon's and deaconesses' roles open-ended. (See figure 15.)

Why is this true? Once again, we see the importance of understanding culture. The role of elders is supracultural. No matter what their societal background, Christians will always need to be managed, pastored, taught the Word of God, and ministered to in other spiritual ways. On the other hand, cultural needs vary from society to society and from time to time even in the same community.

This is illustrated in the church in Jerusalem. When the Hellinistic widows were being neglected in the daily distribution of food (Acts 6:1-7), the apostles appointed seven men to make sure the women's needs were cared for. Though they were not directly identified as deacons, it is clear they were functioning as deacons should.[16] Later, when the church was scattered, these men no longer were needed for this task. In fact, we know that at least two, Stephen and Philip, became evangelists (Acts 7—8).

Note one other observation. When Paul instructed Titus to "appoint elders in every city" in Crete (Titus 1:5), he said nothing about deacons. However, when Timothy was in Ephesus, he gave instructions regarding elders, *plus* deacons as well as deaconesses. The question is why? From a study of all passages that deal with local church leadership, the reason seems to be related to cultural needs. The church in Ephesus had already become established and operative for sometime. As the church grew, cultural needs had developed over the process of time. However, the churches in Crete were new. The first step was to appoint elders to meet spiritual needs, just as Paul and Barnabas had done in Lystra, Iconium, and Pisidian Antioch (Acts 14:21-23). The implication is clear. Deacons were to be appointed in Crete when the need arose.

6. *These spiritual leaders were to be appointed on the basis of spiritual qualification.*

There are two passages that specify elder qualifications (1 Tim. 3:1-13; Titus 1:5-9). Paul's letter to Timothy includes qualifications for elders, deacons, and deaconesses. His letter to Titus includes only qualifications for elders.

Though each "maturity profile" for elders is self-contained and in essence is qualitatively the same as the other, it is helpful to combine them for a more thorough perspective on what God expects spiritual leaders to reflect with their lives. This combined list is as follows:[17]

1. *Above reproach* (1 Tim. 3:2; Titus 2:7): that is, blameless or of good report. There was to be no grounds of accusing this man of improper Christian behavior. In essence, this means to have a good reputation. It is the overarching qualification, appearing at the top of each list.

2. *Husband of one wife* (1 Tim. 3:2; Titus 1:6): that is, not involved with more than one woman. In a culture where men frequently had more than one woman in their lives, Paul made it clear that an elder in the church was to be a "one-woman man"—loyal to his wife and to her alone.

Thus, Paul does not seem to be referring to polygamy, since having *more than one wife* was illegal in the Roman Empire. Neither does he seem to be referring to divorce and remarriage. Paul seemingly is stating a simple fact—in a culture where married men were frequently involved sexually with women other than their legal wives, a Christian man was to be a "one-woman man." And since some of these new Christians did not change their lifestyles immediately, Paul made it clear that a man who still violated this moral standard should never be put in a leadership role in the church.[18]

3. *Temperate* (1 Tim. 3:2; Titus 1:8): that is, self-controlled. He must not be a man who is in bondage to himself and to the desires of the flesh. Furthermore, he should not be given to tangents. He has a clear focus on where history is going. He realizes that his one main concern is to carry out the Lord's Great Commission, no matter what his profession. Thus, he doesn't allow moral, political, material, or social concerns to divert him from his primary purpose in life.[19]

4. He must be *prudent* (1 Tim. 3:2; Titus 1:8): that is, sensible, wise, and balanced in judgment. He must not be given to quick and superficial decisions based on immature thinking. Nor does he "think more highly of himself than he ought to think." Rather, he thinks "so as to have *sound judgment*."[20]

5. *Respectable* (1 Tim. 3:2): that is, he must have an orderly life. He must demonstrate good behavior. The word *respectable* comes from the Greek word *cosmios* from which we get our English word "cosmetics." The verb *kosmeo* is often translated "to adorn."

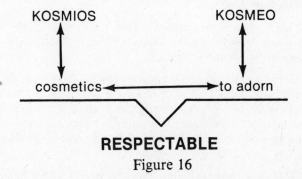

RESPECTABLE
Figure 16

Thus we can see Paul's play on words. A Christian who is respectable "adorns the Gospel of God." His life is like "cosmetics" to the Gospel. A *respectable* lifestyle makes the message of Christ attractive to others, as cosmetics properly used make a person attractive to other people.

6. He must be *hospitable* (1 Tim. 3:2; Titus 1:8): that is, he must be unselfish and willing to share his material blessings with others. His home life and personal life must be characterized by "hospitality."

7. *Able to teach* (1 Tim. 3:2; Titus 1:9): that is, able to communicate the truth of God to others and "to exhort sound doctrine" in a nonargumentative, nondefensive and sensitive way (2 Tim. 2:24-26).[21]

8. *Not addicted to wine* (1 Tim. 3:3; Titus 1:7): that is, he must not be in bondage to wine. It is important to understand that Paul was not teaching total abstinence with this statement. Total abstinence may be a standard some Christians should practice, particularly in some cultural situations, but to set it up as a biblical absolute on the basis of this qualification for eldership is not accurate biblical interpretation. A case for total abstinence can better be built from the "stumbling block principle" in Romans 14, 15, and 1 Corinthians 8.

9. *Not pugnacious but gentle* (1 Tim. 3:3; Titus 1:7): that is, he must not be a "striker" or a person given to physical or verbal violence, but one who is characterized by forebearance and tenderness.

10. *Uncontentious* (1 Tim. 3:3): that is, not given to quarreling and selfish argumentation.

11. *Free from the love of money* (1 Tim. 3:3; Titus 1:7; 1 Peter 5:2): that is, not "greedy of filthy lucre," or "fond of sordid gain," or stingy with his material blessings.

12. *One who manages his own household well,* keeping his children under control with all dignity (1 Tim. 3:4; Titus 1:6): that is, he must have the respect of his family and be recognized as the leader of the household. Paul adds, "But if a man does not know how to manage his own household, how will he take care of the church of God?" (1 Tim. 3:5)

13. *Not a new convert* (1 Tim. 3:6): that is, one who is not a new Christian and a babe in Christ. He must be a mature believer and obviously one who has been a Christian for a period of time—at least long enough to demonstrate the reality of his conversion and the depth of his spirituality.

14. *A good reputation with those outside the church* (1 Tim. 3:7): that is, unbelievers must also respect his character and integrity.

15. *Not self-willed* (Titus 1:7): that is, not stubborn and one who always tries to have his own way. He must not be an insensitive person, forcing his own ideas and opinions on other people.

16. *Not quick tempered* (Titus 1:7): that is, one who gets angry quickly and "flies off the handle." He must be in control of his own spirit. When he *does* get angry (and we all do), he must not sin and let the sun go down on his anger (Eph. 4:26).

17. *Love what is good* (Titus 1:8): that is, he must not follow after and desire those things which are evil and sinful. He must be the kind of person who desires to do the will of God in everything (1 Peter 5:2).

18. *Just* (Titus 1:8): that is, he must be fair and impartial. He must be one who can make objective judgments based on righteous and holy principles.

19. *Devout* (Titus 1:8): that is, holy and separated from sin.

20. *Hold fast the faithful word* (Titus 1:9): that is, he must be stable in his faith and obedient to the Word of God in all respects. He must not be hypocritical, teaching one thing and living another.

Paul also included a list of qualities for deacons and deaconesses in 1 Timothy 3. Notice the similarity to the qualifications for elders:

DEACONS
1. Men of dignity (1 Tim. 3:8)
2. Not double tongued (3:8)
3. Not addicted to much wine (3:8)
4. Not fond of sordid gain (3:8)
5. Holding to the mystery of the faith with a clear conscience (3:9)
6. Beyond reproach (3:10)
7. Husbands of only one wife (3:12)
8. Good managers of their children and their own households (3:12)

DEACONESSES
1. Dignified (3:11)
2. Not malicious gossips (3:11)
3. Temperate (3:11)
4. Faithful in all things (3:11)

7. *The specific forms for elder and deacon functions are seldom described in Scripture.*

When it comes to describing *how* spiritual leaders (elders particularly) did their work, we are told less by Scripture writers than any other area of New Testament church life. For example, elders' functions are clear and the qualities that are to grace their daily lifestyles are spelled out in detail. But the following "form questions" are not answered in the Bible:

1. How old should these leaders be?
2. How should these leaders be selected?
3. How many leaders should there be in a single church?
4. How long should these leaders serve?
5. What is the best way for these leaders to carry out their functions?
6. When there is more than one spiritual leader, who takes primary leadership?

SUMMARY

What have we learned about phase two in God's plan for leadership in the New Testament church?

1. God does not lock us into specific titles for our spiritual leaders in the church.
2. Spiritual leaders should manage and shepherd the people of God.
3. Spiritual leaders who spend a lot of time in the ministry should be cared for financially.
4. When possible, churches should have more than one spiritual leader to serve as godly models.
5. When necessary, spiritual leaders should delegate responsibility to other qualified leaders to care for cultural needs.
6. All church leaders should be spiritually and psychologically qualified to lead.
7. Adequate forms should be developed in particular cultures for church leaders to carry out their funtions in the best possible way.

Footnote

[1]Regarding the canon of the New Testament, Tenney notes: ". . .It is evident that not all of the present books of the New Testament were known or accepted by all the churches in the east and in the west during the first four centuries of the Christian era." (Merrill C. Tenney, *New Testament Survey,* p. 411.)

[2]All members of Christ's body were recipients of spiritual gifts. However, as we've seen in the previous chapter, the "Greater Gifts" were important in God's plan "to prepare God's people for works of service" and their expression was to be given priority in local churches.

[3]Compare Acts 20:17 and 28; Titus 1:5 and 7; 1 Tim. 3:1-2 and 1 Tim. 5:17, 19.

[4]J.P. Lightfoot, *Saint Paul: The Epistle to the Philippians*, McMillan, p. 95.

[5]Ibid., p. 96.

[6]See Acts 4:5, 8, 23; 6:12; 23:14; 24:1; 25:15.

[7]Note that when used to refer to the "elders of the church" it is used to refer most frequently to elders in the church at Jerusalem, which was made up primarily of Jewish Christians. (See Acts 11:30; 14:23; 15:2, 4, 6, 22, 23; 16:4; 20:17; 21:18). There are also numerous references to "elders" in Revelation.

[8]There are three basic passages which make reference to elders and bishops: 1 Timothy 3:1-7; Titus 1:5-10; 1 Peter 5:1-5. James 5:14 also makes reference to the function of elders.

[9]The only other author of Scripture who recorded the word "bishop" interchangeably with the word *elder* was Luke. Significantly, he used the term to describe the spiritual leaders in Ephesus (Acts 20:17), and then quoted Paul who addressed these leaders as "bishops" (20:28). It is also interesting to note that Luke was a Gentile convert and would understand this cultural adaptation.

[10]Since the title "elder" is used more frequently in our culture, hereafter it will be used in this book to describe spiritual leaders in the local church. In actuality the term *bishop* is often used differently from what it was in the New Testament. Today it often refers to an individual who has the oversight of a group of churches and/or pastors. The word *elder*, however, has continued to be used in similar ways as it was used in the New Testament. Consequently, the word *elder* is more acceptable to many evangelical Christians.

[11]See once again the introductory section of this book on pages 25-30 where this interrelationship is described more fully under the topic "biblical renewal."

[12]The word *rule* which comes from the same basic Greek word translated "manage" is also used in Paul's letter to Timothy to describe those elders who are remunerated financially for their efforts (1 Tim. 5:17).

[13]Phillip Keller, *A Shepherd Looks at Psalm 23*, Zondervan, p. 9.

[14]Jack Finegan, *Light From the Ancient Past*, vol. 2, Princeton University Press, pp. 495-499.

[15]Though there is some ambiguity regarding the role of deaconesses, it appears that the "women" Paul referred to in 1 Timothy 3:11 were those who served as deaconesses (3:8). It seems Paul was outlining the qualifications for men and then very naturally inserted the statement that "women [who are in a serving role] must likewise" have certain qualifications. Otherwise, the flow of Paul's thoughts is interrupted with a totally different idea—the "qualifications of Christian women *in general.*" If this is true, and in view of the context, it is legitimate to ask— "Qualifications for what position?" The only logical answer to this question seems to be "deaconesses." It should be noted that some believe Paul was referring to "deacons' wives." But, if so, why didn't Paul specify qualifications for "elders' wives"? In view of an elder's function in the church, it woud seem more important to include qualifications for their wives, orat least to include them too.

[16]These men were appointed to "serve tables" and the word *deacon* comes from the word *serve.* In this sense we can legitimately call these men "deacons."

[17]For a more in-depth study of these qualities see Gene A. Getz, *The Measure of a Man* published by Regal Books.

[18]See Robert L. Saucy, "The Husband of One Wife," *Bibliothecasacra,* vol. 131, no. 523, pp. 229-240.

[19]See 1 Thessalonians 5:1-11 for a rather descriptive commentary on this quality, which is translated to be "sober" in the *New American Standard.*

[20]See Romans 12:3 which describes a "prudent" Christian.

[21]See page 162 for a comprehensive definition of what it means to "be able to teach."

ELEVEN

THE FUNCTIONING BODY

We cannot formulate leadership principles without looking carefully at another important dimension of New Testament churches—*total body function.* The church is a unique entity. Even in its local expression, it is much more than an organization. Every localized group of believers is composed of individual members who are to function and be a part of the whole. The church is to be a dynamic organism.

There are several figures of speech used to describe the church but none so graphic as the term *soma* or "body."[1] Though exclusively a Pauline analogy, the word appears approximately thirty times to illustrate and describe the functioning body of Christ. Approximately half the time Paul used the word literally to refer to the physical body. The rest of the times he applied the word to the "church" and called God's people the *body of Christ.* He described the church as being "many members" yet "one body." However, "all the members" did not "have the same function" (Rom. 12:4). All had gifts that differed "according to the grace given" by Christ (12:6). One member of the body could not say to the other, "I have no need of you" (1 Cor. 12:21). Since the church was "many members but one body" (12:20), all members were to contribute to the growth of the body. Anything that interferred with the "functioning body" interferred with the process of edification.

This means, first and foremost, that every member of the body of Christ is important! In a sense, every member is a leader, called of God to help other members of the body to grow and mature. Every "joint" must function and every "individual part" is to make its contribution to the life of the church. When this happens, the body of Christ will build itself up in love (Eph. 4:16).

SPIRITUAL GIFTS

In studying the concepts of the "functioning body" in the New Testament, you cannot bypass reference to "spiritual gifts." Furthermore, there is a renewed interest on this subject in the twentieth-century church. This is understandable, for the evangelical church in general has for years neglected the importance of body function and relational Christianity. We have come to rely on the "preacher" and the "pastor" to do "the work of the ministry."

What does the Bible actually teach about spiritual gifts? Many have attempted to answer this question. For years some evangelical Christians have taught that all of the gifts are present in the church today. They form a large segment of the body of Christ and identify themselves as "charismatic Christians."[2] There's also a large segment of Christians who classify themselves as "noncharismatic." In turn, some noncharasmatics believe that some gifts are present but not all. Generally speaking, they contend that there were "sign gifts" which have ceased—such as the gift of tongues, prophesy, healing, etc. On the other hand, they believe that there are nonsign gifts which continue to be present in the church—such as the gifts of pastoring, teaching, evangelism, administration, etc.

There is a third category of evangelical Christians who believe that all gifts have ceased. They teach that the original gifts were all sign gifts to demonstrate the validity of the Gospel and were also given to assist the body of Christ in functioning until a corpus of Christian truth was revealed to enable Christians to function in the body of Christ.

It should be added that within each of these general viewpoints are varied opinions regarding what these gifts are, their purposes, how they should be used in the church, and how Christians discover their gifts.

In view of so many different viewpoints, is it possible to discover what the Bible actually teaches on this subject? Several years ago I decided to face that question as objectively as possible. As much as it was humanly possible, I attempted to lay aside my own presuppositions regarding this subject and once again study through the New Testament noting every reference to spiritual gifts and the context in which they appeared, in order to try to discover what scriptural writers were actually saying. As a result of this process I made the following observations:

1. *The number and kinds of gifts varied significantly from church to church in the New Testament world.*

This observation is based on the list of gifts mentioned in the letters written to various churches. Note the following:

THE LETTER TO THE CORINTHIANS

(1 Cor. 12:8-10)	(1 Cor. 12:23)
word of wisdom	apostles
word of knowledge	prophets
faith	teachers
healing	miracles
miracles	healing
prophecy	helps
distinguishing of spirits	administrations
tongues	tongues
interpretation of tongues	

THE LETTER TO THE ROMANS
(Rom. 12:6-8)

prophesies
serving
teaching
exhortation
giving
leading
mercy

THE LETTER TO THE EPHESIANS
(Eph. 4:11)

apostles
prophets
evangelists
pastors
teachers

PETER'S LETTER TO VARIOUS CHURCHES
(1 Peter 4:11)

speaking
serving

Why is this variation significant? The Corinthian church had more gifts manifested than any other New Testament church. Paul affirmed this in his introductory remarks in his first letter when he wrote that they were gifted "in all speech and all knowledge . . . *not lacking in any gift*" (1 Cor. 1:5, 7).

The Roman church was also a gifted church. But note that only two of the gifts mentioned in the Roman list (prophecy and teaching) are mentioned in the Corinthian list. Likewise, the "Ephesian list," though shorter, includes two additional gifts (evangelists and pastors) not included in the Corinthian letters *or* the Roman list.

What this seems to indicate is that there was a significant difference in the kinds of gifts manifested from church to church in the New Testament. Furthermore, some of them had many gifts; others had fewer. Therefore, as twentieth-century Christians, we must be careful not to total the gift list in the New Testament and conclude that it is God's will and plan for this "totl list" to be present in every twentieth-century church. If it were not so in the New Testament churches, it is only logical it would not be true in churches today.

2. *The passages where gifts are referred to most extensively are written to correct the improper use of spiritual gifts.*

The Corinthian Church. The Corinthians, who represent the most gifted church mentioned in the New Testament, were definitely misusing their gifts. It was not a matter of knowing what their gifts were. Rather, they were using their gifts inappropriately.

First, some were evidently using their gifts to "build themselves up" while "putting others down." They were guilty of spiritual pride. If not, why would Paul spend most of chapter 12 emphasizing that "one part of the body" should not say to "another part of the body" that it had no need for the other? (1 Cor. 12:21) Note the following key statements that emphasize this point:

- "If the foot should say, 'Because I'm not a hand, I'm not a part of the body,' it is not for this reason any the less a part of the body" (12:15).
- "And if the ear should say, 'Because I'm not an eye, I'm not part of the body,' it is not for this reason any the less a part of the body" (12:16).
- "If the whole body were an eye, where would the hearing be? If the whole were hearing, where would the sense of smell be?" (12:17)
- "And if they were all one member, where would the body be?" (12:19)
- "And the eye cannot say to the hand, 'I have no need of you'; or again the head to the feet, 'I have no need of you'" (12:21).
- "On the contrary, members of the body which seem to be weaker are necessary; and those members of the body which we deem less honorable, on those we bestow more abundant honor, and our unseemly members come to have more abundant seemliness, whereas our seemly members have no need of it. But God has so composed the body giving more abundant honor to that member which lacks, that there should be no division in the body, but that the members should have the same care for one another" (12:22-25).

Second, the Corinthians were giving attention to the "lesser gifts" while neglecting the "greater gifts."

Paul clearly stated what the greater gifts were *"first, apostles; second,* prophets; *third,* teachers." He then listed the "lesser gifts" — miracles and gifts of healing, helps, administrations, various kinds of tongues (12:28). He then made his point. The Corinthians should "earnestly desire the greater gifts" (12:31). The context clearly indicates that they were giving attention primarily to the lesser gifts (see chapter 14).

Third, the Corinthians were not only giving priority to the "lesser gifts," but they were misusing them in the church. (Again, carefully read chapter 14.) There was disorder and confusion. Thus, Paul ended chapter 14 with this exhortation: "But let all things be done properly and in an orderly manner" (14:40).

The Roman Church. The Roman church evidently did not have as many problems as the Corinthians relative to the way in which they were using their spiritual gifts. However, one problem seems to be the same—*the presence of spiritual pride.* This is the context in which Paul discussed their gifts and emphasized humility. Thus, before listing the gifts, he wrote: "For just as we have many members in one body and all the members do not have the same function, so we, who are many are one body in Christ and individually members one of another" (Rom. 12:4-5).

Furthermore, before emphasizing unity in the body, and prior to listing the gifts he warned against pride and emphasized humility. Thus we read: "For through the grace given to me, I say to every man among you *not to think more highly of himself than he ought to think; but to think so as to have sound judgment, as God has allotted to each a measure of faith"* (12:3).

The Ephesian Church. We see the same emphasis in the Ephesian letter. Before listing the gifts, he wrote: "Walk in a manner worthy of the calling with which you have been called, *with all humility* . . . being diligent to preserve the unity of the spirit in the bond of peace. . . . But to each one of us grace was given according to the measure of Christ's gift" (Eph. 4:1-3, 7).

These are important observations. Frequently, we use these passages to teach the importance of gifts and that every believer should try to discover his gift or gifts. This is not Paul's point in these three letters. If anything, Paul was trying to temper the use of gifts and, most important, he was exhorting all believers not to use their gifts to elevate themselves in the local assembly and thus destroy unity in the church. *Striving for oneness and unity through humility is the primary theme in all of the spiritual gift passages in Scripture.*[3]

3. *Nowhere in the Bible does it say we are, as individuals, to search for or to try to discover our spiritual gifts.*

This is also an important observation—one that I personally found difficult to acknowledge and accept. The reason is that I had been emphasizing the opposite, just as many Christians today emphasize looking for and discovering gifts. Furthermore, we use the passages just outlined in the previous section to make that point. As just illustrated, that is definitely not the thrust of these passages. These people clearly knew what their gifts were. They weren't searching for them. Rather, they were *misusing* the gifts that were so obvious among them.

What about 1 Corinthians 12:31 and 14:1? This is a very legitimate question. We need to look at these verses which may appear to contradict this third observation. After Paul outlined the greater and lesser gifts in the Corinthian letter (1 Cor. 12:28-30), he then exhorted, "But earnestly desire the greater gifts" (12:31). And then at the beginning of chapter 14, he wrote, "Desire earnestly spiritual gifts" (14:1).

A careful evaluation of these specific texts, as well as the contexts, demonstrates that Paul was not encouraging *individual* Christians in Corinth to seek to be apostles, prophets, and teachers (the greater gifts—12:28). Rather, he was exhorting these Christians to give priority to those with these greater gifts. Thus he used the second person plural in the Greek text. We can legitimately paraphrase his statement in 12:31 as follows: "But, *you as a church,* desire that the greater gifts be manifested rather than the lesser gifts." In 14:1 he broadened his statement. Again we can paraphrase: "As a body of believers pursue love, yet as a body desire earnestly that spiritual gifts be manifested, but give particular attention to the prophets rather than the tongue-speakers" (see 14:2-4).

We see a similar emphasis when Paul wrote to the Romans and told them he longed to see them so that he might "impart some spiritual gift to them" (Rom. 1:11). When we realize that Paul had never been to Rome and when we look at the context of this statement in verse 11, we can see more clearly what Paul meant. The gift he wanted to impart was his own unique contribution to their spiritual growth. Since Paul possessed all of the greater gifts (1 Tim. 2:7; Acts 13:1), he would be able to help them in a special way. Furthermore, he wanted to be ministered to by them through a mutual relationship (Rom. 1:12).

Thus we must conclude from the whole of Scripture that individual Christians are never instructed to search for or to try to discover spiritual gifts. To do so would be to emphaize something that the Bible doesn't emphasize. Paul particularly implied that if a person is gifted in some special way, that individual will know it and other Christians will know it too. It has nothing to do with human effort, for God has chosen to sovereignly bestow these gifts apart from any searching or even asking (Acts 2:1-4; 10:44-48; 1 Cor. 1:4-7; 2 Tim. 1:6). Thus we read in the Hebrew letter that God bore witness to the message of the Gospel, "both by signs and wonders and by various miracles and *by gifts of the Holy Spirit according to His own will*" (Heb. 2:4).

4. *The Scriptures emphasize that there is a more excellent way than an emphasis on the gifts of the Spirit.*

We've already seen this to be true in our study of what the Bible defines as a mature church (see pages 85-93). After Paul told the Corinthians to earnestly desire the greater gifts rather than the lesser gifts (1 Cor. 12:28-31a), he went on to say, "And I show you a still *more excellent way*" (12:31b). Paul then made it clear that a Christian may have the gift of tongues (13:1), the gifts of prophecy, knowledge, and faith (13:2), as well as the gift of giving (13:3), and yet lack love, the most important quality in Christian living. If so, we are "nothing" (13:2); all of these gifts "profit nothing" (13:3).

The Corinthians lacked love, and yet again as far as we know they were the most gifted church in the New Testament. And because they were carnal and immature, Paul urged them to do away with "childish things" (13:11). Though he did not forbid them to desire that spiritual gifts be used (14:1), he exhorted them to make it a priority to pursue love, for without this quality, all of their gifts were basically meaningless.

5. *When local church leaders were to be appointed, Paul did not instruct Timothy and Titus to look for spiritual gifts; rather, he instructed them to look for spiritual qualifications and maturity.*

This is one of the most significant observations regarding spiritual gifts. When I noticed this, several questions went through my mind. Why didn't Paul tell Timothy and Titus to look for the gifts of administration and leading? After all, these men were to manage the church (1 Tim. 5:17). Why didn't Paul instruct them to look for the gift of pastor? Of teacher? Again, this was to be their

The Functioning Body / 161

responsibility (1 Peter 5:2; Acts 20:28; Titus 1:9). And since they were to pray for the sick (James 5:14), wouldn't they need the gift of healing?

Though these elder functions were definitely outlined in Scripture, Paul said nothing about selecting these men on the basis of the spiritual gifts that related to these functions. Again, the question is why?

We see the same approach in the appointment of deacons and deaconesses. Since these people were to be involved in "serving" roles, why didn't Paul specify that they were to be selected if they had the gift of serving? And what about the gifts of helps and mercy? And certainly their cultural responsibilities would require that they be good organizers. And yet there is nothing stated about the gift of administration and leading. And again, we must ask why?

Some have pointed out that Paul does mention the requirement to "be able to teach" (1 Tim. 3:2). Is this not the gift of teaching? First of all, it would be strange that Paul would refer to this gift and say nothing about the gifts of managing and pastoring when these were to be the primary functions of an elder. The facts are that Paul is very pragmatic about the ability to manage, using the family as a basic criteria in determining a man's ability in this area. Thus, he said, "If a man does not know how to manage his own household, how will he take care of the church of God?" (3:5) With this requirement, Paul was implying that every Christian father was responsible to be a good manager of his household. He could not use the excuse that he was not especially gifted in this area.

Regarding being "able to teach," Paul illustrates beautifully what this concept means in his second letter to Timothy. Here Paul used this quality in the context of a number of other spiritual characteristics. Writing to Timothy, he said, "And the Lord's bond-servant must not be quarrelsome, but be kind to all, *able to teach,* patient when wronged, with gentleness correcting those who are in opposition, if perhaps God may grant them repentance leading to the knowledge of the truth" (2 Tim. 2:24-25).

Notice the cluster of words surrounding the quality of being "able to teach." (See Figure 17.) It is clear from these characteris-

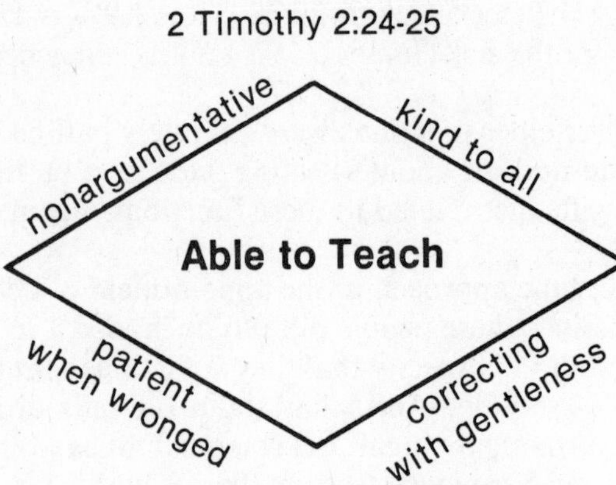

2 Timothy 2:24-25

Figure 17. "Able to Teach"

tics that Paul is dealing with a quality of life that demonstrates an even temper, kindness, patience, and gentleness. In essence, Paul was saying that when a spiritual leader faces people who oppose what he is teaching, if he is "able to teach" he will respond in a nondefensive and nonthreatening way. Though he will be firm in what he believes, he will not respond in a quarrelsome, negative, and insensitive way. This, Paul was saying, is very important in being able to communicate with those who are initially unresponsive to the Word of God.

It is difficult to explain satisfactorily why Paul bypassed any reference to the gifts of the Spirit when he listed the qualifications for spiritual leaders. However, it is not necessary to have a clear-cut answer when we realize that this observation correlates with an earlier observation; that is, that nowhere in the Bible does it say we are as individuals to search for or try to discover our spiritual gifts before we can function in the body of Christ. And this leads us to a final observation, which is perhaps the most interesting of all.

7. *Body function is not dependent on spiritual gifts, but rather on biblical teaching and a love and concern for one another.*

The Greek word *allelon* frequently translated "one another" is used approximately sixty times in the New Testament, excluding the Gospels. Paul leads the list for frequency, having used the word forty times. And just as basic doctrines are repeated from letter to letter in the New Testament, so are many of these "one another" injunctions. This is understandable, since these letters were originally designed to be self-contained for particular churches.

PAUL'S "ONE ANOTHER" PROFILE

Paul's letter to the Romans includes the most extensive "one another" profile. There are seven basic "one another" statements in chapters 12 to 16—the part of this letter that we call the practical section. The first 11 chapters are doctrinal and outline great truths of salvation. Chapters 12 to 16 outline how Christians are to live in view of their position in Christ.

The seven "one another" statements are as follows:

1. We are "members of one another" (Rom. 12:5).

2. We are to "be devoted to one another in brotherly love" (12:10a)

3. We are to "give preference to one another in honor" (12:10c).

4. We are to "be of the same mind with one another" (12:16a)

5. We are to "accept one another, just as Christ also accepted us" (15:7).

6. We are to "admonish one another" (15:14).

7. We are to "greet one another" (16:16).

Several other New Testament letters include some unique "one anothers," though somewhat similar in meaning to those in Romans. They are as follows:

- "Serve one another" (Gal. 5:13).
- "Bear one another's burdens" (6:2).
- Show "forbearance to one another" (Eph. 4:2).
- Be "subject to one another" (5:21).
- Encourage one another (1 Thes. 5:11).[4]

As you study the "one another" injunctions just outlined and compare them with the total number of "one another" injunctions listed in the New Testament (approximately sixty), you will note the following:

1. The first seven "one anothers" which appear in Paul's letter to the Romans form a basic profile which in essence includes all of the other "one another" injunctions in the New Testament.

This is not surprising when we understand the basic purpose and content of the Roman letter. It is a very comprehensive Epistle. The first 11 chapters include all of the major doctrines of Christianity. And chapters 12 to 16 (where the "one anothers" appear), include all the major concepts regarding how members of the body of Christ should live and function.

2. These "one another" functions are to be carried out by *all* members of the body of Christ—not just by Christians who are specially gifted. This means that *all believers* are to be devoted to one another, to honor one another, to accept one another, to teach and admonish one another, to greet one another, to serve one another, to bear one another's burdens, to submit to one another, and to encourage one another.

SUMMARY

A functioning body is absolutely essential for growth and maturity to take place in any given church. The very nature of the body of Christ makes it important for every member to function and contribute to the process of edification. Christians cannot grow effectively in isolation. They need to experience each other. In fact, the words *to edify* and *edification* are used most frequently in the context of the functioning body.

It is also true that the Bible describes spiritual gifts in conjunction with body function and mutual edification. However, the Scriptures do *not* emphasize searching for or trying to discover one's spiritual gifts. Rather, they emphasize again and again the importance of becoming mature in Christ, both as individual believers and as a corporate body. Furthermore, New Testament Christians were not given the choice of whether or not they wanted to function. As we've seen from our study of the "one another" injunctions, they were told to help "one another" in many ways. This process was not dependent on whether or not they were gifted in these areas.

Furthermore, if a person desired to be a spiritual leader in the church—"Which," wrote Paul, "is a fine work"—he should be primarily concerned about manifesting the qualifications of maturity specified in the New Testament, rather than being able to identify his spiritual gifts.

Footnotes

[1]Following are some additional metaphors and figures of speech used by scriptural writers to describe the church: The household of God (Eph. 2:19); the building of God (1 Cor. 3:9; Eph. 2:20-22); the flock of God (Acts 20:28; 1 Peter 5:2); the bride of Christ (2 Cor. 11:2; Eph. 5:22-32); the temple of God (1 Cor. 3:16-17; Eph. 2:20-22).

[2]The word *charismatic* is derived from the Greek word *charisma* which was used frequently to refer to the gifts of the Holy Spirit.

[3]Note that the same is true in the context of 1 Peter 4:11.

[4]For an in-depth study of the "one another" injunctions in the New Testament, see the following books written by Gene A. Getz and published by Victor Books: *Building Up One Another, Loving One Another, Encouraging One Another, Praying for One Another,* and *Serving One Another.*

TWELVE

PRINCIPLES OF NEW TESTAMENT LEADERSHIP

A study of leadership in the New Testament yields some clear-cut principles for the twentieth-century church. These principles can serve as guidelines and objectives for starting new churches in our contemporary culture—wherever that might be—and can also provide established churches with a criteria for evaluating their own philosophy and practice of church leadership.

DISTINGUISH BETWEEN LEADERSHIP PHASES

1. *In discerning and practicing God's plan for leadership in the church today, we must carefully distinguish between the two leadership phases in the New Testament, but yet understand the applicability of both an "apostolic" ministry and a local church ministry in carrying out the Great Commission in the twentieth-century world.*

Even a brief study and casual reflection regarding the context in which the church came into existence reveals some unique problems we do not face today. *First,* the Jewish religious world into which Christ came had become thoroughly institutionalized. Its leaders had become self-serving and manipulative. They had twisted God's laws to benefit themselves. Jesus' strongest barbs were directed at the leaders in Israel. "Woe to you, scribes and Pharisees, hypocrites!" He said. "For you are like whitewashed tombs which on the outside appear beautiful, but inside they are full of dead men's bones and all uncleanness" (Matt. 23:27). Jesus then applied this illustration more specifically. "Even so," He continued, "you too outwardly appear righteous to men, but inwardly you are full of hypocrisy and lawlessness" (23:28).

Second, Jesus came to launch the church, a completely new phenomenon. Though Israel represented the people of God on earth, the church was to be uniquely different. It would be composed of both Jews and Gentiles, born-again people indwelt by the Holy Spirit. Paul summarized it well when he wrote to the Ephesians speaking specifically to the Gentiles and reminded them that they were "no longer strangers and aliens, but ... fellow citizens with the saints." They were "of God's household, having been built upon the foundation of the apostles and prophets, Christ Jesus Himself being the cornerstone, in whom the whole building, being fitted together is growing into a holy temple in the Lord, in whom," Paul said, "you also are being built together into a dwelling of God in the Spirit" (Eph. 2:19-22).

Third, when Jesus returned to heaven, His followers had no body of literature to guide them in this new mission. Though the Old Testament recorded the laws of God and the history of Israel, it did not contain the doctrines and teachings they would need to equip the members of Christ's body for ministry.

Fourth, the world Christ's followers faced was hostile. The message of Christ itself challenged the Jewish leaders who rejected His messiahship. And the pagan world viewed Christianity as another fanatical religion that deserved little attention.

The first challenge facing the apostles particularly was to launch this new movement in spite of the problems just outlined. Armed with Christ's promise that He would guide them into all truth and teach them what to say by means of the indwelling Holy Spirit (John 14—16), they did just that. The church was born. Furthermore, God bore witness to their message, "both by signs and wonders and by various miracles and by gifts of the Holy Spirit according to His own will" (Heb. 2:4). God bestowed upon the apostles particularly, but not exclusively, the "greater gifts" (1 Cor. 12:28-31) to enable them to carry out the Great Commission. Through this process, local churches came into existence, which led first to the appointment of elders and later to deacons and deaconesses. The truth revealed primarily to the apostles by direct revelation and inspiration of the Holy Spirit was transmitted to local church leaders who in turn taught others. Thus Paul wrote to Timothy, "And the things which you have heard from me in the presence of many witnesses, these entrust to faithful men, who will be able to teach others also" (2 Tim. 2:2). In this sense the saints were equipped for ministry, and every joint was able to supply in causing the body of Christ to build itself up in love (Eph. 4:11-16).

Today we face a similar world. However, we have at our disposal the written Word of God in its *entirety*. The apostles and a few selected individuals first spoke the message under the leadership of the Holy Spirit but eventually recorded it for us as sacred Scripture. Armed with God's truth, we can face both a hostile religious and pagan world. Led by the Holy Spirit who dwells within us, we can speak God's truth with divine authority. Furthermore, we can demonstrate the reality of Christianity by means of visible local churches. And when those churches are unified in love, it provides the evidence that verifies that the message of Christ is true (John 13:34-35; 17:20-23).

God's two leadership phases are still necessary today. There's a need for those who will fulfill an *apostolic, prophetic,* and *teaching* ministry by evangelizing the unsaved and establishing churches—just as Paul, Barnabas, Silas, Timothy, and Titus did in New Testament days. Though twentieth-century missionaries may not be *gifted* with the same miraculous powers as the original leaders in New Testament days, they are in many respects to *function* in a similar way. Though God's power may be revealed differently, these spiritual pioneers still have the same divine message, but in completed form and the same basic authority that was given by Christ when He uttered the Great Commission.[1]

Phase two in God's leadership plan is *directly* ongoing and has been since New Testament days. Men must be equipped to be elders and appointed to manage and shepherd local churches. This leads us to a second New Testament principle of leadership.

APPOINT QUALIFIED LEADERS
2. *The first step in assisting local churches in their spiritual growth*

is to appoint spiritually qualified people to lead these churches. These leaders must be first of all selected on the basis of spiritual qualifications—not gifts, talents, and abilities.

Qualities vs. Abilities. Out of the twenty specific qualifications listed by Paul in 1 Timothy 3 and Titus 1, almost all of them have to do with a man's reputation, ethics, morality, temperament, habits, and spiritual and psychological maturity. Today we need to refocus our thinking in this area. People become qualified for a local church ministry by measuring up to the criteria set forth in the New Testament. Unfortunately, we frequently look at the obvious *abilities, talents,* and *gifts* and not at the more basic and fundamental *qualities.*

Once you get to know a person well, the qualifications for eldership listed by Paul are clearly discernible. This does not mean that this individual is perfect. Far from it. It *does* mean that the direction of his life is clear.

However, it must be noted that you cannot make accurate judgments regarding a person's qualifications without some careful and long-range evaluation by those who have lived in close proximity to that individual. This is why a church who calls a "pastor" on the basis of hearing "him preach" may make some serious errors in judgment. The person may be able to sway the people with his oratory and yet be woefully lacking in the qualifications spelled out so clearly in the New Testament.

Furthermore, in twentieth-century churches we often appoint men to church boards who are successful businessmen. They have built large organizations in the secular world. In these instances we at times make judgments based on financial acumen and administrative abilities. In the selection process, these talents may take precedence over the basic qualifications listed by Paul. For example, many men are successful in the business world but fail woefully as managers of their own households. If we overlook this very important qualification for spiritual leadership, the church is headed for serious trouble.

This same basic mistake is also made in our theological seminaries and other schools designed to prepare men and women for vocational Christian service. In most instances, graduates are evaluated for graduation and recommended for various ministries, not on the basis of the spiritual qualifications outlined in Scripture, but on the basis of academic success and communication skills. True, most schools give "lip service" to spiritual qualifications, but in reality academic success is still the "bottom line." Furthermore, it is easy to hide spiritual weaknesses in our lives, especially if we are talented with unusual intellectual abilities and social graces. Furthermore, most academic environments are not structured to surface these inconsistencies.

Age and Experience. Another factor that is significant in selecting elders who are qualified is age and experience. It is not accidental that the word *elder* in itself refers to age.

This poses problems, however, for several reasons. *First,* the Bible does not give a specific age for elders. *Second,* being an older person does not guarantee maturity. *Third,* some younger men are mature for their age—more so than some older individuals.

However, the fact remains that there are only certain things that can be learned over the process of time. Age and experience produce wisdom in Christians who are truly seeking to follow the will of God. For all of us can learn as much from our mistakes as our successes.

As a person involved in church planting, I have concluded that most major problems in the churches I've helped start were caused by the appointment of men to leadership who were too young— both as staff pastors and nonstaff pastors. They lacked experience and wisdom. Furthermore, some were threatened by older, more experienced leaders. Some became ego involved, which in turn sent them into a tragic identity crisis and in some instances led to failure in the ministry.

On the other hand, there are younger men who excel in major leadership positions in the church. Usually, however, they succeed because they have a good self-image, are teachable, and seek to learn from older and more experienced spiritual leaders. They do not react defensively to those who may disagree with them but attempt to learn in the process.

Timothy, of course, stands out as a unique example of a young man who had a heavy leadership responsibility. He was not only responsible to help establish churches but to appoint elders to lead those churches. In most instances these men were probably older than Timothy.

We must realize, however, that Timothy was probably at least thirty years old when he began his ministry. In that sense he was older and more experienced than many men who become leaders in our churches today. Furthermore, he brought himself under the authority of the Apostle Paul, who was able to guide him and lead him through the difficult aspects of the ministry. When he was discouraged, Paul encouraged him. Furthermore, Paul built bridges for Timothy. He not only encouraged Timothy to live a life that would win respect, but he encouraged Christians in various churches to accept Timothy even though he was young (1 Cor. 16:10-11). In this sense Timothy serves as an excellent role model for younger men who are entering the ministry.

I often face the question regarding "age" since many men graduate from seminary in the mid-twenties. Are they qualified to lead a church? This is a difficult question since the answer depends on several factors. How mature is the person in spite of his chronological age? How large is the church? What is the expectation level in the community and in the church?

Generally, I recommend that young men (particularly under thirty) seek an associate position for several years, assisting an older and more experienced spiritual leader. This can be done even though you may not agree totally with a particular leader's philosophy of ministry. However, the object must be to learn—not to change the senior pastor and the direction of the church. Though this may be a difficult assignment, it can yield unusual opportunities to mature and grow spiritually, psychologically, and in many areas involving management skills.

MANAGERS AND PASTORS

3. *Spiritual leaders must function as managers and pastors and not merely as administrators and decision makers.*

Unfortunately, many twentieth-century church leaders have superimposed a modern-day definition of management on the biblical concept of being a manager of God's people. As is noted in our study of New Testament leadership in a previous chapter, "Elder Management" is functionally synonymous with the concept of "pastoring." Thus, a man who serves as an elder must be a shepherd.

The greatest example of a shepherd is the Lord Jesus Christ Himself. On one occasion, He said:

> I am the Good Shepherd; the Good Shepherd lays down His life for the sheep. He who is a hireling and not a shepherd, who is not the owner of the sheep, beholds the wolf coming, and leaves the sheep and flees, and the wolf snatches them, and scatters them. He flees because he is a hireling, and is not concerned about the sheep. I am the Good Shepherd; and I know My own, and My own know Me, even as the Father knows Me and I know the Father; and I lay down My life for the sheep (John 10:11-14).

How illustrative of a man with a true pastoral or shepherd heart! He is willing to give himself to the members of the body of Christ that inhabit His fold. He stands by them no matter what the cost. He *knows* His sheep. He calls them by name! And the sheep know Him; they know His voice.

There is no way to escape the implication of what it means to be a true elder. He must be *with* his people—not separate from them. He must know them personally—their needs, their concerns, their problems! He must be willing to leave the ninety and nine in the fold, and go out into the darkness of the night to find the straying lamb who has wandered away from the safety of the flock, and has been caught up in the thicket of disillusionment and sin (Matt. 18:12-13).

His door must be open to the flock. No good shepherd excludes a single sheep from the fold. He must be available—not in word only, but truly available! His personality must say in no uncertain way, "I love you, I care about you, and I'm here beside you; you can talk with me *anytime, anywhere* and about *anything* you wish. I won't condemn you! I won't hurt you! I will help you become the person you really want to become—a mature member of the body of Christ."

This concept of shepherding is true for both staff and nonstaff elders. For the elder "worthy of double honor"—the elder "who works hard at his preaching and teaching" and who receives wages (1 Tim. 5:17-18)—must in no way circumvent people. The sacred desk must *not* become a barrier between shepherd and flock. It must never become a place to hide, a place to defend personal weakness, a vantage point from which to unload a barrage of biblical ammunition and then a trench in which to drop out of sight so that there's no danger of getting hit by return fire.

Nonstaff elders should also be shepherds. To function biblically, they must not merely be members of a board that meets to make administrative decisions. True, this is part of managing God's people. But it is only one aspect of being a good pastor. In fact, elders who are "decision makers" and "administrators" only will not make adequate decisions because they are out of touch with people's needs. They don't really "know the sheep."

Managing and pastoring also involves *teaching* (3:2; Titus 1:9). This means that an elder must *know* the Word of God and be loyal to it. He must be able to share its dynamic truth with members of the body of Christ. This is a charge to both staff and nonstaff elders.

Obviously, the staff pastor will have a ministry that is more public than the nonstaff elder. He is the one who is working hard at preaching and teaching (1 Tim. 5:17). But the Scripture teaches that *all* elders must be involved in the teaching process. Unfortunately, we have superimposed our own ideas of what teaching and preaching involve. To understand the biblical process, we must go back and look at the biblical examples. Jesus Christ, of course, becomes the supreme example in carrying out this process.

As we travel through the Gospels, following the Man of Galilee, we see a Teacher reflecting many varied characteristics. He taught individuals, small groups, large groups—and even several different groups at the same time (Luke 15:1—7:11). He was not limited to a classroom, but rather taught anywhere He saw people in need— on a hillside, in an upper room, in the synagogue, by a well, on a rooftop, on a boat in the middle of a lake, on a mountaintop, and even as He hung between two thieves on a cross. Sometimes they came to Him; other times He went to them. At times He delivered a discourse and at other times He asked questions. Sometimes He told stories. Frequently, He visualized His words by referring to the fowls of the air, the water in the well, the sower on the hillside, or even to people themselves. He was never stereotyped; never rigid; never without the right words. He was always meeting the needs of listeners, getting them intellectually and emotionally involved, and always penetrating to the deepest recesses of their personality. He was indeed the *Master Teacher!*

How different from our stereotyped approach to teaching in the church today, particularly among those of us who are staff pastors. We often mount our platforms and deliver our packages which we hope are homiletically perfect. We seldom go to the people; they come to us and to the usual place, where they settle into their comfortable pews and wait to be stimulated. There is seldom opportunity for response, very little variation in the process and visualization is seldom used. Furthermore, with this limited definition of teaching, we eliminate those opportunities for teaching that are personal, one on one—and which can be carried out effectively by nonstaff elders.

Don't misunderstand. I am not suggesting that we cannot be effective unless we go back to the exact pattern of Jesus' example of teaching. We are living in a different culture, a different world. But may I suggest that in many instances we are not even coming close to applying New Testament principles. We assume our present forms and structures are adequate to create a dynamic learning experience. We almost worship at the shrine of the transmissive approach to communication—"preaching" particularly.[2] We glorify the scholar who knows the content of the Bible, while we ignore the body of Christ and its many members who also have something to contribute to the ministry and the building up of the body.

Do we want a dynamic church? A dynamic ministry? Then I suggest that we must develop a philosophy of leadership that grows out of the Scriptures. We need spiritual leaders who are shepherds—men who teach God's people in an intimate and personal way. Furthermore, we need structures that permit these men to be and do what God intended them to be and do.

PRIORITIES AND DELEGATION

4. *Spiritual leaders should maintain their priorities and delegate cultural responsibilities to other qualified men and women.*

The apostles of old, when confronted with the problems in Jerusalem, said to the people, "It is not desirable for us to neglect the Word of God in order to serve tables." They solved the problem by establishing priorities, by having seven men appointed to handle this matter, and they continued to give themselves "to prayer and to the ministry of the Word" (Acts 6:2, 4). Not that these matters were unimportant, nor were they matters that did not call for leaders with spiritual qualifications (6:5), but they were matters that could have taken the apostles away from their primary work.

Local church elders too are given priorities. They are to effectively manage the flock of God, which means shepherding, teaching, and praying for people. Their primary responsibility is to meet the *spiritual needs* of people.

Therefore God has established a plan for delegation. Thus, we see the role of the deacon and deaconess as important. Their responsibilities and functions are basically cultural, as pointed out in an earlier chapter. Though their qualifications are pointed out in Scripture, their functions are open-ended.

Failing to maintain priorities and delegate responsibilities is one explanation as to why elders often become typical administrators and decision makers. Their time is totally used up attending board and committee meetings, making administrative decisions, and handling other routine details. When this happens, elders are not functioning as God intended them to function.

The staff elders and pastors, of course, oftentimes become victims of this syndrome. Many men get bogged down with administrative details and neglect to serve people as shepherds and teachers. Personal contacts with the members of the body of Christ are limited to large group meetings where, separated from people by a pulpit, they expound the Word.

As a church grows large, this is why multiple leadership is so important. No one staff pastor, or even several pastors, can meet the needs of all the people in the body. There are unique and creative ways for staff leaders to utilize nonstaff elders to help them minister to people's spiritual needs.

In many of the churches which I've helped establish—as well as in the church which I presently pastor—all of our elders and their wives are required to minister to people in small groups, which we call minichurches. In addition, we have a large corps of men who serve as pastors, though they are not identified as elders. But they too with their wives are ministering under the guidance and leadership of the elders and other staff pastors. In this way, the staff pastors are able to concentrate on ministering to the elders, other spiritual leaders in the church, and to concentrate on effective teaching and preaching to the body at large.

It is important to realize that in our culture that is permeated by large centers of population, churches are going to grow in numbers. This obviously calls for strong spiritual leaders to serve as staff pastors. God needs multitalented men who can lead these large dynamic churches. But we must remember that God also designed a multitalented body—a body made up of people who all contribute in a special way to the building up of the church.

At this juncture I must add a word of warning. One of the most tragic things happening in our culture today is that highly gifted men are attempting to train ordinary men to be like themselves. Unfortunately, these ordinary men (who make up the majority of us) have neither the capacity nor the ability to become this kind of leader. The result is frustration. Or even more tragic, these men attempt to imitate the life of a multitalented man and end up a total failure—often splitting the church, hurting the body of Christ, and eventually leaving the ministry.

Does this mean a highly gifted pastor shouldn't train other men to be pastors? Not at all! But in training them, he must recognize they may not all be able to do what he is capable of doing. It is possible to get a person "in over his head," thinking he can function in all respects as his mentor. When he cannot, he is doomed to failure.

Strong leaders must be careful, then, not to think unrealistically. At the same time they must inspire others to rise to the highest level of achievement possible, but not to set their goals based on another man's capabilities.

APPOINT AND REMUNERATE
5. *Churches should appoint certain spiritual leaders to serve in staff positions and adequately remunerate them for their efforts.*

This principle is clear in Scripture. A "laborer is worthy of his wages" (1 Tim. 5:18). Unfortunately, many pastors and other

Christian workers are not remunerated adequately. There are some Christians who believe that full-time Christian workers should live more sacrificially than themselves. Unfortunately, this often leads to discouragement. Also, it creates hardship for the children of Christian workers, leading to negative feelings and even rebellion against spiritual things.

It is true that a few pastors take advantage of their flocks. They are not accountable financially to a group of godly elders. But these men are in the minority. It is far better to be on the "high side" in caring for spiritual leaders financially than on the "low side." God will honor this generosity. Furthermore, God will also deal with those few who "serve" for "sordid gain" (1 Peter 5:2).

A good rule of thumb is that a pastor and other Christian leaders should be cared for financially based on the average income of families in the congregation. Furthermore, the person's age, tenure, experience, education, and capabilities should all be considered, just as is true in any well-managed business organization. Furthermore, special attention should be given to benefits (insurance, retirement plan, etc.), just as is also true among the average people in the congregation.

Yet we must realize that there are times that spiritual leaders must give up rights because they are in the ministry. The Apostle Paul illustrated this often. But on the other hand, Christians should not take advantage of their spiritual leaders. If they do, God's ultimate blessing will not be upon that ministry.

PRIMARY LEADER
6. *When feasible, churches should be led by more than one spiritual leader, but it is important to designate one spiritual leader as the primary leader.*

The Bible definitely teaches multiple leadership. In fact, the more godly leaders we have in a given local church who measure up to the qualities of 1 Timothy 3 and Titus 1, the greater impact on the members at large. A group of godly elders and pastors serve as a multiple model of Christlikeness.

However, there are those who teach that a church should be led by "a committee." No one is to be designated to be the primary leader. Generally, this has resulted in recent years from an overreaction to men who have emerged as authoritarian personalities in the church. Some pastors are in absolute control. Their elders and deacons are merely figureheads doing their bidding.

It is true that we do not have structural models in Scripture for our present patterns involving the appointment of senior pastors, associate pastors, assistant pastors, etc. But neither do we have structural models of multiple leadership as we often try to practice it in our twentieth-century churches today. We must remember, as pointed out in a previous chapter, that it was impossible in the early days of the church to meet in central locations. Though there were the elders at Ephesus, they no doubt were in charge of numerous house churches. The same was true of the church in Jerusalem. Thus, we do not know who was in charge of this church. Though we read about the elders in Jerusalem, it seems evident that James eventually emerged as the primary leader.

There is a lot of biblical evidence pointing to the fact that lines of authority need to be established for effective church life to take place. For example, Paul was definitely recognized as having authority over Timothy and Titus and other men who helped establish churches. In turn, Timothy and Titus were definitely recognized as having authority in given cities to appoint elders. It is only logical that certain elders were given authority to give direction to the ministry in a certain location.

Remember, too, that the New Testament church was probably influenced significantly by the synagogue. Though there was a counsel of elders over a given synagogue, the Bible also speaks of those who were the primary leaders in the synagogues (Acts 18:8, 17).

Not only is there biblical evidence pointing to the fact that someone must be appointed as a primary leader in a given situation, there is plenty of evidence from practical experience. This is particularly true as a church begins to grow and staff pastors are added to the leadership team. Without designated lines of authority, insecurity frequently surfaces among the members of a church staff. Furthermore, the door is open for a power struggle to take place which always results in disunity.

True, when a church is small and there is only one staff pastor, it is possible for that staff pastor to function with a group of nonstaff elders as if *they* are the leaders of the church. And, indeed they are. But even then, the staff pastor will emerge as an elder to the elders, a pastor to the pastors. And when an additional staff pastor is added, it is very important that that person be responsible to the senior spiritual leader. He cannot be equal in authority, for if he is, it usually leads to inefficiency and eventual conflict.

Take for example one practical consideration. Who determines salary structures in a church where there are no lines of authority among the paid staff? It is impossible for men who are on staff to meet together to determine their own salary structures. Someone has to be the primary leader who recommends salary increases because of an obvious awareness of those who are on staff. Nonstaff elders do not have enough exposure to the day-to-day operations of a church to be able to make wise judgments regarding who is and who is not responding well to his tasks.

But it is important to underscore that the more authority and the more position a spiritual leader is given, the more he is to be a servant. He is not to lord it over those who are to respond to his leadership. It is possible to be a senior pastor and yet to be a servant to the total paid staff, to the nonstaff leadership, as well as to the body of Christ at large. Jesus demonstrated this principle in His own life when He taught that he who was greatest is to be servant of all.

FREEDOM TO DEVELOP

7. *Churches should be free to develop creative forms and structures to apply the functions and principles just outlined.*

There are many "form" questions that are not answered specifically in Scripture when it comes to leadership. Some of those questions are as follows:

1. How old should spiritual leaders be?
2. How should these leaders be selected?
3. How many leaders should there be in a specific church?
4. How long should these leaders serve?
5. What is the best way for these leaders to carry out their functions?
6. When there is more than one spiritual leader, who takes primary leadership?

7. What titles should we give to these spiritual leaders?

Though there are not specific answers to these questions, the Scriptures do give specific principles and the lenses of history and culture yield additional guidelines. They are as follows:

1. Spiritual leaders should be chosen from among those who've learned from years of experience, making them wise and discerning.

2. A system of selection should be developed that discovers and appoints qualified leaders who are highly respected by the people of the church. In our own church, elders are selected from men who have successfully ministered to a small group of Christians for a substantial period of time. Furthermore, they must be approved by the small group as being qualified to serve as an elder. After all, it is the people who have been ministered to who know this person best.

3. The board of elders should be small enough to make decisions quickly, yet wisely. In my own experience, I have seen the result of a board getting too large. When it does, attendence patterns vary at board meetings. Communication begins to break down. Eventually, it is difficult to maintain unity in decisions and when you do, the process becomes long, laborious, repetitious, and inefficient.

4. If the church board size is limited for effective decision making, then a system should be developed to allow leaders to rotate off the board in order to make room for other qualified leaders to serve. Otherwise, the board becomes "ingrown."

5. A plan should be developed to allow spiritual leaders to carry out their functions effectively as pastors. If we do not, they will become administrators only, which leads to decisions that are out of touch with people's needs.

6. Finally, it is logical and practical for the local church elders to designate the primary leadership role in the church to the "senior" staff pastor or elder. It is doubly important to establish lines of authority when more than one elder is added to the paid staff, so these people are responsible to the primary staff pastor.

AN EXAMPLE

Following is a presentation we have prepared for use at Fellowship Bible Church North. This document was developed after ten years of church planting experience, attempting to apply the principles outlined in this chapter.

LEADERSHIP
. . .a philosophy of form and function

You may wonder why we at Fellowship Bible Church North have a completely separate publication on *leadership* and the *forms* and *functions* of leadership within the church. Reason: We distinguish between *form* and *function* in the New Testament. The Bible is very specific on the functions of New Testament leadership but leaves us free to develop forms. In describing our forms, we do not believe we have the *only* way or even the *best* way. We have developed forms based upon our needs and our experiences.

The following is an outline of the leadership forms at FBCN. Obviously, since these represent *nonabsolutes,* they are always subject to change.

Age. How old a man must be in order to qualify as an elder is not specified in Scripture. However, the word *elder* in itself means "older man." But, again the Bible does not specify what "older" means chronologically.

Age is relative. Some men, because of experience, develop qualities of maturity and wisdom earlier than others. However, the Scriptures imply and most people agree that there are certain capabilities that we do not develop apart from experience. And experience takes time.

At FBCN, we have decided that an elder should be approximately forty years of age or older. We realize this is arbitrary and nonabsolute. However, it serves as a guideline for selecting elders. Since this is a nonabsolute, exceptions can be made at any time by the elders themselves.

Procedure for Selecting. The Scriptures do not specify *how* elders should be selected or appointed. We know that Paul and Barnabas appointed elders (Acts 14:23), and we know that Timothy and Titus must have appointed elders (1 Tim. 3:1 and Titus 1:5).

The problem for us today, however, is that we are not "apostles" in the primary sense, nor do we have men appointed by apostles, such as Timothy and Titus who stayed in certain locations and helped develop churches that were founded on the missionary journeys.

Nevertheless, there is a principle that emerges to guide us. In a new church, elders may be appointed by someone who is already recognized as a qualified spiritual leader.

There are other situations in the New Testament that illustrate another principle. In a church where there is already a sizable body of believers, it seems wise to gain the approval of those involved in the selection and appointment of elders. It does not seem appropriate to "vote" in the sense that the selection is made between or among possible candidates. Rather, it seems that the people should "approve" or "disapprove" of an individual who has been recommended to the position based on his qualifications. In other words, if a man is recommended by other qualified leaders in the church, it seems wise to gain the approval of the body at large.

In view of these principles, we have set up the following procedure:

1. Initially, elders should be recommended by the senior pastor and approved by the majority of the body.

2. From that point forward, elders should be recommended by the other elders and approved by the majority of the body.

Number of Elders. Again, the Scriptures do not specify how many elders should serve a local church. Since the New Testament church often involved a number of household churches in a given city (they could not own church buildings as we do in our culture), we are not sure how this worked out. Did they have one elder per house church? Perhaps, but we do not know for sure. They may have had more than one elder in larger house churches, since there is evidence that some of the homes in the New Testament could accommodate up to 500 people.

One thing we do know—they usually had *more* than one elder in a single church. However, the New Testament church was scattered into a number of units but was still called a single church (e.g., the *church* in Jerusalem and the *church* in Ephesus).

The principle of multiple leadership in the New Testament is very clear. The specific number for a particular church is not clear. This involves form. At FBCN, we have decided to have a minimum of seven elders and a maximum of twelve serving on the board at any given time. Through experience, we have learned that a large group is ineffective in the decision-making process. Furthermore, it is difficult to operate by consensus, though again, the Bible does not specify *how* to make decisions. It is much easier, however, to come to a unified decision through discussion when the group is small than when it is large.

Term of Service. Once again, we come to the conclusion through studying the Word of God, specifics are not given regarding how long an elder should serve in the church. It does seem that the Bible implies that once a man becomes an elder, it is an open-ended opportunity, and he can serve in this position as long as he has time to do so and is qualified. Certainly this particular "form" is allowed. However, this creates some serious problems in our present culture when our churches grow to be large. One problem is that in order to keep the opportunity for eldership open, the elder board becomes subject to growing so large that it cannot function effectively in the decision-making process. And it must be stated that when a "closed" elder system is adopted, serious problems result also. First, there is the danger of becoming "ingrown." Second, this system does not present the opportunity for other men in the body to serve as elders.

There are various forms that can be developed to resolve this problem. One is that the elder board is open-ended but that a smaller group of elders are selected to serve as a decision-making group. One of the problems with this system, however, is that those elders who are not selected to serve on the smaller group may feel left out. Since they *are* elders, they tend to feel that they should be involved in all decisions.

At FBCN, we have chosen another form. Elders appointed to the board at Fellowship Bible Church North will serve for three years, with the exception of the initial elder board. One-third of the men will rotate off the board each year which means that a third of the initial board will serve only one year and another third for two years.

After one year's absence, a man can serve as an elder for another three years. It should also be stated that a man may resign from the board any time he feels he must or should the other elders feel he has disqualified himself in some way.

Eligibility. Any man who (1) is approximately forty years of age or older; (2) is qualified according to the Pauline specifications found in 1 Timothy 3 and Titus 1; and (3) has served effectively as a minichurch pastor for a substantial period of time is eligible to serve on the board of elders. Furthermore, an elder must continue to be an active pastor serving in a minichurch while concurrently serving on the elder board. We believe this is important, since a man who is not an active pastor tends to make decisions that are out of touch with the real needs of people. We do not believe that there is allowance in Scripture for a purely "administrative" elder.

SUMMARY

1. In discerning and practicing God's plan for leadership in the church today, we must carefully distinguish between the two leadership phases in the New Testament, but yet understand the applicability of both an "apostolic" ministry and a local church ministry in carrying out the Great Commission in the twentieth-century world.
2. The first step in assisting local churches in their spiritual growth is to appoint spiritually qualified people to lead these churches. These leaders must be first of all selected on the basis of spiritual qualifications—not gifts, talents, and abilities.
3. Spiritual leaders must function as managers and pastors and not merely as administrators and decision makers.
4. Spiritual leaders should maintain their priorities and delegate cultural responsibilities to other qualified men and women.
5. Churches should appoint certain spiritual leaders to serve in staff positions and adequately remunerate them for their efforts.
6. When feasible, churches should be led by more than one spiritual leader, but it is important to designate one spiritual leader as the primary leader.
7. Churches should be free to develop creative forms and structures to apply the functions and principles just outlined.

Footnotes

[1]It is true that some people today claim to have the same power as the apostles and other first-century leaders. Some claim to have experienced and/or observed this power. Personally, I have not read about or observed anything that has convinced me that what is claimed today *measures up* to the manifestations revealed in the New Testament. This does not mean God could not do so or has not done so. But I have seen many claims that lack immediate or lasting authenticity which makes one cautious about these claims.

[2]Unfortunately, we have even superimposed stereotypes on this biblical word. New Testament preaching was never only a transmissive approach. Peter's sermons in the Book of Acts demonstrate the presence of group dynamics, interaction, and response.

THIRTEEN

BIBLICAL EXAMPLES OF ADMINISTRATION AND ORGANIZATION

The Bible is relatively silent regarding organizational and administrative patterns. But this is not without design, for nothing becomes obsolete so quickly as structural forms. They are but a means to divine ends. Furthermore, life is made up of so many variables and unpredictable events that creativity in this area must be constant.

But the Bible *does* speak in this area, and when it does, its examples yield some dynamic and powerful principles.

Both Old and New Testament illustrations of organization and administration surface the same basic principles. This again helps to show that the patterns are not absolute, but the principles are.

The purpose of this chapter is to present four structural examples—two from the Old Testament and two from the New Testament. First we'll look at an Old Testament example and a New Testament example in close alignment, to show how clearly they compare in the nature of the problems, the solutions, and the results. The second two examples are uniquely different but again demonstrate similar principles.

A COMPARATIVE STUDY

Two of the most obvious problems calling for organization and administration are found in Exodus 18 and Acts 6. The former involved a mass of people, no doubt 2 million plus, camped in the wilderness. The latter involved a rapidly multiplying group of Christians in Jerusalem, by then numbering in the thousands.[1]

The following chart will help to isolate the *problems,* the *solutions,* and *results* recorded in these passages.

Moses in the Wilderness (Ex. 18:13-27; Deut. 1:9-18)	The Neglected Widows (Acts 6:1-7)
Problem	Problem
Exodus 18 v. 13—The people stood about Moses from morning until the evening. v. 14—Moses sat alone trying to do the job all by himself. vv. 15-16—Moses was attempting to resolve the problem of the people; he served as the judge in matters of interpersonal relationships and taught the people the laws of God. v. 18—This laborious process caused undue stress for Moses and for the people as well.	Acts 6 v. 1—The disciples were increasing rapidly. With such growth: —the communal system was put under stress. —certain individuals among the Hellenistic Jews were being overlooked in the daily serving of food. —consequently, the Hellenists began to complain. v. 2—The twelve Apostles got involved in the details of this discussion and the results of this discontentment caused them to begin to neglect their primary responsibility . . . to teach the Word of God.
Solution	Solution
Exodus 18 v. 19—Moses' father-in-law, Jethro, served as his consultant. Jethro advised Moses to establish priorities —to serve as a mediator between the people and God.	Acts 6 v. 2—The Twelve called a meeting of the disciples. vv. 3-4—In this meeting they informed the people regarding their major task as the twelve apostles — prayer and the ministry of the Word.

—to teach them as a group the statues and laws of God.

vv. 20-21—To delegate the responsibility for handling the interpersonal problems of everyday life to a select group of qualified men—"able men, who fear God, men of truth, who hate dishonest gain."

v. 22—These men were to handle the minor matters, and only the major problems would be filtered through to Moses.

Deuteronomy 1

vv. 9-12—Moses communicated his problem to the people.

v. 13—Moses instructed each tribe to "choose wise and discerning and experienced men"; Moses in turn appointed them as heads.

vv. 16-18—Moses carefully instructed the leaders in everything they were to do.

v. 3—They instructed the Christians to select seven qualified men to care for the need that existed ... "men of good reputation, full of the Spirit and of wisdom."

v. 5—The congregation chose seven men—obviously Helenists.

v. 6—The apostles confirmed the choice of the people through prayer and the laying on of hands.

RESULTS	RESULTS
Exodus 18 v. 22—Moses was assisted in his responsibilities. v. 23—Moses was able to endure the demands of his leadership role. —The people's needs were met and they were satisfied.	Acts 6 v. 7—the needs of the people were met; unity was restored; the apostles were able to fulfill their primary work —the Word of God kept on spreading —the number of believers kept on increasing greatly.

Though these two events took place at different times, in different settings, and under a different set of circumstances, and though there were many other differences surrounding the details of these two situations, the nature of the problems, the way in which the problems were solved, and the results are strikingly similar.

THE NATURE OF THE PROBLEM

Both Moses and the apostles had more than they could do personally, and both were becoming involved in details that kept them from fulfilling their primary responsibilities. Moses particularly was unable to endure the physical and psychological stress.

Furthermore, in both situations the people themselves were under stress and became discontented because their personal needs were being neglected. The Children of Israel came to Moses to be instructed, to have him work out problems among them, to state their grievances, and to make their petitions. Evidently, some people stood in line all day long and pehaps even then did not get a chance to have a hearing with their leader (Ex. 18:13).

In view of the previous problems Moses had with these people—their desire to return to Egypt, their complaints against him for getting them into this wilderness experience, their carnality and sin—it does not take too much imagination to reconstruct the tense mood and emotional outbursts that must have taken place among these people.

The disciples in Jerusalem must have faced similar problems. Though hopefully more "spiritually mature" than their forefathers, these new Christians also became very unhappy when their physical needs were not met. Furthermore, it may be that we see, in Acts 6, favoritism being shown toward a certain class or group.

It was the Hellenistic Jews against the Hebrews. The Hebrews were Palestinian Jews, whereas the Hellenists were residents of other countries, such as Syria, Egypt, and Asia Minor. The Palestinian Jews spoke their own language, whereas the Hellenists spoke Greek. Furthermore, the Hebrews probably composed the majority of Christians, and the Grecians were in the minority. Added to this, the Palestinian Jews no doubt reflected the more rigorous aspects of pure Judaism, whereas the Hellenists reflected the influence of Greek customs.

Consequently, we have a combination of factors that may be strongly parallel to some of the problems of prejudice that exist in the church in the twentieth century. But perhap of more importance was the fact that the growth of the church was so rapid that the natural tendency to neglect certain people may have become the primary factor in causing this problem.

THE WAY THE PROBLEM WAS SOLVED
Though the specific steps taken to solve the problems that existed differed in certain particulars, there were four important similarities. First, both Moses and the apostles *established priorities.* In Moses' case it was his father-in-law, Jethro, who helped him to see and analyze the problems. He advised Moses to give primary attention to serving as a mediator between the people and God (Ex. 18:19), and to be the one who taught the people the Word of God (Ex. 18:20).

When the apostles became aware of the problems in Jerusalem, they immediately communicated to the multitude of Christians that they could not be burdened with the details of waiting on tables, but must continue to give primary attention to teaching the Word of God and to prayer (Acts 6:2-4). They were not negating the importance of these details, but knew they would be unable to carry out their primary spiritual objectives and be personally involved in meeting the physical needs of the people as well.

The second similarity is the *delegation of responsibility to qualified men.* Moses chose able men—men who were *God-fearing, honest,* and also men who *hated dishonest gain* (Ex. 18:21).[2] The apostles instructed the people to select seven men who had a *good reputation,* who were *filled with the Holy Spirit,* and who were *wise* (Acts 6:3). Here it is important to note the high spiritual standards set for selecting men to fulfill the responsibility of meeting the physical needs of people.

Actually, these high standards in both situations were a secret to the effectiveness in solving the problem. Moses and the apostles needed men they could trust. Men who were dishonest, unspiritual, selfish, and tactless would have only accentuated the problem. Qualified men, on the other hand, would resolve the problems.

The third similarity is that they *organized to meet the need that existed at that moment and in those peculiar circumstances.* In the Old Testament situation, "Moses chose able men out of all Israel, and made them heads over the people, leaders of thousands, of hundreds, of fifties, and of tens" (Ex. 18:25). This was the best strategy for the occasion. This organizational plan was a fitting structure for a nation on the move, and "this arrangement was linked on to the natural division of the people and the tribes and families, etc."[3]

Robert Jamieson comments:

> The arrangement was an admirable one, and it was founded on a division of the people which was adopted not only in civil but in military affairs; so that the same persons who were officers in war were magistrates in peace (see Num. 31:14). . . . Care was thus taken by the minute subdivision to which the judicial system was carried, that, in suits and proceedings at law, every man should have what was just and equal, without going far to seek it, without waiting long to obtain it, and without paying an exhorbitant price for it.[4]

The apostles, on the other hand, instructed the people (no doubt the Hellenistic Christians only) to select from among themselves seven men. This was a wise move, for the people themselves knew those who would meet the qualifications that the apostles had prescribed. Moreover, if the people selected these men, there would be no accusation of a prejudicial choice on the part of the Twelve (note that all seven men chosen had Greek names).

Again the structure set up on this occasion was appropriate to the situation. The number seven is significant only in that it was recommended because the apostles estimated that this was the number it would take to do the job.[5]

A fourth similarity is that in both of these circumstances, the *structure set up was temporary.* When the Children of Israel settled in the land, the organizational plans changed. Also in a relatively short period of time, persecution drove the Christians out of Jerusalem, and some of the men who were serving tables became evangelists (Acts 7–8). The whole situation changed, creating new needs, and called for new forms and structures, particularly as permanently located churches were established in various communities.

THE SIGNIFICANCE OF THE RESULTS

The results of the organizational steps taken to resolve the problems in Exodus 18 and Acts 6 are clearly delineated in the Word of God. Simply stated, the problems were resolved—at least for the time being (organizational problems are never permanently solved). Moses and the apostles were able to carry out their primary tasks. The people's needs were met and they were satisfied. Moses' physical and psychological needs were also met, and as a result of the appointment of the seven men in Acts, the "Word of God kept on spreading; and the number of the disciples continued to increase greatly in Jerusalem, and a great many of the priests were becoming obedient to the faith" (Acts 6:7).

REBUILDING THE WALLS The Book of Nehemiah	
The Problem	
1:2-3	Nehemiah, cupbearer to the king of Persia, received a report that the remnant in Judah who had returned were in great distress and reproached because the walls of Jerusalem were broken down and burned with fire.
1:4	Nehemiah's response was one of depression and sadness.
The Solution	
1:4-11	Nehemiah fasted and prayed.
2:1-2	He did not hesitate to reveal his sadness to the king.
2:3	He told the king why he was depressed.
2:4	The king asked Nehemiah: "What would you request?"
2:4	Nehemiah asked God for guidance in responding to this question.

2:5	He asked the king to send him to Judah to rebuild the walls.
2:6	The king responded positively.
2:7-8	Nehemiah asked the king for official letters so he could travel freely and also obtain timber from the king's forest.
2:12-16	When Nehemiah arrived he spent three nights secretly surveying the situation. At this time he developed a strategy for rebuilding the walls.
2:17-20 3:1-32	Nehemiah then revealed his plan and asked the people to help him rebuild the walls.
4:1-13	When the enemies of Israel tried to stop their work, the people did two things: they prayed and set up a guard day and night.
4:14	When the people grew fearful, Nehemiah told them (1) not to be afraid, (2) to remember the greatness of God, and (3) to fight for the sake of their families.
4:15	As soon as the word got out to their enemies that they were ready to defend themselves, they returned to the wall to continue building.
4:16-23	Nehemiah devised a new plan for working and guarding so that they could continue building, but also be ready for war.
6:15	They completed the walls in fifty-two days.

The Immediate Results

12:27-29, 31-42	The people sang and praised God.
12:30	The people purified themselves and the city.
12:43	They offered sacrifices to God.
6:16	When the enemies of Israel witnessed this impossible feat and heard the rejoicing of Israel, "they lost their confidence." They recognized that this could have been achieved only "with the help of God."

THE NATURE OF THE PROBLEM

The problems in Jerusalem focused on the broken walls. This condition resulted in ridicule, reproach, and humiliation for the people of Judah. They were mistreated and abused. Many of the Jews were afraid to even live within the city. They remained a scattered, fearful people, even though they were living in the land of Judah. They had little security from their enemies round about, and lived in constant fear and anxiety.

Consequently many were living out of fellowship with God. They did not worship God nor were they being exposed to the laws of God. Some of the Jews were even taking advantage of their own people (Neh. 5). Neither did they pay tithes, nor did they keep themselves pure and separated from the paganism and idolatry that surrounded them.

THE WAY THE PROBLEM WAS SOLVED

Nehemiah's approach to solving this problem was a tremendous example of organizational and administrative skill that included both the human and divine dimensions. They are so carefully blended throughout the narrative that it is difficult to separate the two, but they are both there.

First, Nehemiah sought wisdom and help from God (1:4-11).

Struck with the terrible plight of his people, Nehemiah's initial step was to pray and fast. He acknowledged God's greatness, confessed their sins (including his own), reminded God of His promises to regather the Children of Israel if they repented, and then asked the Lord to grant him mercy before the king whom he served.

Second, Nehemiah built bridges to the king (2:1-10).

He had already laid the groundwork for this bridge. He had been a good servant. His sadness was very obvious to the king against a backdrop of his constantly happy countenance. And furthermore, Nehemiah was not afraid to reveal his true feelings to the king, evidence of a certain degree of rapport—and faith.

Nehemiah's prayer was answered. The king asked why he was so downcast. But even at this moment Nehemiah relied on God. Moving from a purely human factor (revealing his sadness), he breathed a prayer to God for wisdom to answer the king's question. Here was the opportunity he had been hoping for. His response and the *way* he answered and *what* he said were critical!

God answered Nehemiah's prayer as quickly as he had prayed. Nehemiah's answer was clear-cut but tactful. He asked that the *king* might send him to rebuild the walls.

When given a favorable reply, Nehemiah took another step—a bold one! He asked for official letters from the king to be able to pass through various countries unhindered. He even went so far as to ask for the privilege of cutting down trees from the king's forest.

Request granted! And with these credentials Nehemiah had not only built bridges to the king, but he had built bridges all the way to Jerusalem and to his own people. To the surprise of the enemies of Judah, he even arrived with army officers and horsemen assigned to him by the king.

Third, Nehemiah secretly surveyed the situation in Jerusalem and developed his strategy (2:11-16; 3:1-32).

On three successive nights he quietly but carefully inspected and evaluated the damage to the walls. Here, read between the lines, is administrative wisdom personified. Nehemiah knew that he needed to have his facts in hand before he challenged the people to rebuild the wall. Furthermore, to even let them know the purpose of his coming before developing his strategy would be lethal. Humanly speaking, he might have lost the people before he even got the plan off the ground. And furthermore, to release the information early would have unveiled the plan to the enemies of Israel, who would have scoffed even more.

The people, of course, didn't need any more demoralization. They were already at a low ebb. Nehemiah's great challenge was to build their moral and convince them the job could be done. So he proceeded to develop a strategy that was unique. The priests were to work on the Sheep Gate, inferring that this was an assignment that appealed to them personally. Some scholars feel that this gate was near the temple and it would be through this gate that they would bring small cattle for sacrifice. The men of Jericho were assigned to work on the part of the wall that was nearest to their city. In like manner, if archeological speculation is correct, the goldsmiths and perfumers were assigned a section of the wall nearest their shops.

Whatever the specifics, it is clear that Nehemiah had mapped out his plan carefully and with wisdom. Over twenty-five times the phrase "next to him" (or "them") or "after him" (or "them") is used to designate the organizational structure. Every person or group who could work, including some women, was assigned to a task.

Fourth, Nehemiah revealed the plan to the people, motivating them with both human and divine factors (2:17-20).

He appealed first to their wretched condition—the *reproach* they were bearing because of the broken walls, and the *desolate condition* of Jerusalem. Next, he told them how *God* had helped him to win the favor of the king and his support in this venture.

The results were positive. "Let us arise and build!" was the response; and so they did. When their enemies heard about it and saw the people taking their places around the wall, they responded with mockery and hatred! But the people were prepared. Their goals were set—their strategy outlined! They did not succumb to their enemies' demoralizing attacks.

Note how Nehemiah said "we" will arise and build (2:20). he *was* their leader, but he was also "one" with them. He was a part of the team, and he too was on the front line engaging in the same difficult work (5:16). This is dynamic leadership. This is a basic reason why these people saw this project through to completion against almost impossible odds. Nehemiah's example went far beyond what is ordinary expected. His life was such a contrast to those of "the officials" and "leaders" around him that he generated unusual loyalty and motivation.

Fifth, Nehemiah supervised the work closely, facing and solving unforseen problems as they arose during the process (4:1-12; 6:15).

Laying the groundwork for any venture is only part of the organizational-administrative picture. Even though the people "had a mind to work," they were to face constant ridicule and hostility. The work went on; and when it became obvious the enemies were planning to attack in order to stop the work, Nehemiah prepared for the battle by placing people all around the wall. He stationed them by families (4:13). This was shrewd—but necessary. It guaranteed performance if attacked. If their families had been in another place in the city or outside the walls, the temptation would be to run to them. Now they would have to fight to protect them—on location!

This is exactly what Nehemia knew would motivate them. So when he saw their fear, he gave them three charges: (1) "Do not be afraid of them"; (2) "Remember the Lord who is great and awesome"; and (3) "Fight for your brothers, your sons, your daughters, your wives, and your houses" (4:14).

Fortunately the battle never materialized. The enemy, evidently overawed by this determination and the bold stand of the Jews, backed away from their threat (4:15). And everyone once again took up his task at the wall.

Nehemiah devised a new strategy. From then on some worked and some guarded; some worked with one hand and carried their weapon in the other; those who had to work with both hands kept their swords at their sides. And a trumpet would be used to gather the people together quickly in case of attack. No one was to go out of Jerusalem at night; rather they were to stand guard. And in the final days of building, Nehemiah and many of his workers and guards never removed their clothes nor laid down their weapons, even when they stopped for a drink of water (4:23). Against almost impossible odds, *they completed the wall in fifty-two days!*

THE SIGNIFICANCE OF THE RESULTS

The results of Nehemiah's organizational and administrative skill are obvious all the way through the building program. This was a long-range project, and at every step along the way he achieved certain significant goals. He won the favor of the king, motivated the people to begin the work, kept the people at the task in spite of threats from their enemies, and finally they rebuilt the wall. And while doing all this, Nehemiah helped straighten out social and financial problems (5:1-19), and warded off a subtle attack on his own life by Sanballat and Gesham (6:1-14).

The final results of this project were intensely rewarding. Nehemiah must have been overwhelmed with thanksgiving and praise to God; for, all the way through this intense experience, he praised the God of heaven for every accomplishment.

Imagine the thrill when he heard the people singing and praising God at the dedication of the wall (12:27-29, 31:42). The two great choirs on top of the walls must have been an incredible sight to the enemies of Judah. The sounds of their voices and rejoicing were so loud that they could be "heard from afar" (12:43), and their enemies were so overwhelmed with this fantastic accomplishment that "they lost their confidence" (6:16). In the words of Nehemiah himself, "They recognized this work had been accomplished with the help of our God."

Other results followed. The people were able to develop a system of defense which provided security against their enemy (4:17). There were more social reforms, as they were able to reorganize and develop order in the community (11:1-2). And most important, there were religious reforms. The people were once again able to come together to hear the Law of God (8:1-18). And the most rewarding result for Nehemiah was to see the people—as a reunited people—confessing their sins, worshiping the God of heaven, and making a covenant with Him.

THE JERUSALEM COUNCIL
Acts 15:1-35

	Problem
15:1	Certain men were teaching false doctrines in Antioch—"you must be circumcised to be saved."
15:2	Paul and Barnabas debated the issue publicly but could not solve the problem.

	Solution
15:2-3	The church at Antioch decided to seek guidance from the apostles and elders at Jerusalem.
15:4	The Antioch delegation reported how Gentiles were being converted through faith alone.
15:6	The apostles and elders met in a closed session to discuss the matter.
15:7-11	Peter reminded the people of what God did for Cornelius and his household.

15:12	Paul and Barnabas gave specific testimony regarding the "signs and wonders God had done through them among the Gentiles."
15:13-18	James made reference to the work of the Old Testament prophets and how they had predicted Gentile conversion.
15:19-21	James proposed a solution to the problem.
15:22	The apostles, elders, and the whole church agreed to this proposal.
15:22-30	A letter was written spelling out the solution.
15:22	Judas and Silas were chosen by the church to deliver the letter.
15:30, 32	Judas and Silas delivered the letter and also a "lengthy message."

Results	
15:31	The congregation rejoiced when they heard the contents of the letter.
15:33	Judas and Silas were sent back to Jerusalem in peace.
15:35	The work of God continued unhindered.
16:4-5	The instructions in the letter were delivered by Paul, Silas, and Timothy to many of the new churches.

THE NATURE OF THE PROBLEM

Here was a problem that was destined to affect all of the newly formed churches. Antioch was a prominent center of Christian activity, and it would not be long until the news of the disagreement and debate would spread to the new believers scattered throughout the New Testament world. The result would be confusion, disillusionment, and disunity.

This was no minor eruption! Here were Paul and Barnabas in open debate against men from Jerusalem, the birthplace of the whole Christian movement. The issue was just as crucial—either man was "saved by grace through faith," or it also involved works. It could not be both. The results of this controversy would either unite the churches or split them.

THE WAY THE PROBLEM WAS SOLVED

It did not take long for the leaders in the Antiochian church to recognize the explosive nature of this problem. They *acted quickly* and *with wisdom.* They faced the problem *head on.* They met together and decided this problem was beyond their ability to handle. They needed assistance. Acting with perception, they decided to take the problem back to its original source. They chose a delegation—to accompany Paul and Barnabas—and set off for Jerusalem.

Note their approach when they arrived. *No attack on personalities!* No accusation against the Jerusalem church! They simply reported what God was doing in the Gentile world. And it was this noncritical and objective tactic that set the tone for this whole conference.

The immediate result was disagreement from certain people— whom Luke identified as coming from the "sect of the Pharisees" (15:5). But rather than allowing the issue to become a matter for public debate which would have quickly degenerated into emotional name calling, the apostles and elders went *into a closed session* to discuss the matter.

Exact sequences and what was involved are somewhat unclear in the biblical account. But there is a sufficient information to draw some accurate conclusions. There was more discussion and debate, probably within the smaller group (15:6-7).

Eventually, Peter stood up publicly before the whole congregation (15:7-12), and substantiated the initial report by reminding the people of something they already knew (15:7): his own personal experience with Cornelius. God had saved this Gentile and his household "by faith" and gave them the Holy Spirit, just as He had done at Pentecost (15:9). There were the same "signs" as at the beginning (Acts 10:44-46).

At this juncture Paul and Barnabas added more support to the case by building on Peter's testimony. They too related what signs and wonders God had done through them among the Gentiles (15:12).

The next move was crucial! James (undoubtedly the brother of Christ, and obviously the most respected leader in the church in Jerusalem) spoke on the issue. He began by adding support to Peter's testimony, and then in a marvelous demonstration of wisdom and insight, summarized the teachings of several Old Testament prophets that related directly to the problem. He then made a proposal—in actuality suggesting a compromise—one that would not violate "justification by faith," but one that would also pacify the Jewish Christians who still found it difficult to understand "freedom from the law" (15:19-21).

Whether this proposal was first made to the apostles and the elders or to the whole church is not clear. Obviously the letter had to be composed by a select group. The scriptural record *does* make it clear that the "whole church" felt good about the decision and was involved in the selection of Judas and Silas to deliver the letter.

So step by step under the leadership of men who were seeking God's will, the immediate problem was solved. No one could really predict what was going to happen in the actual process. An objective approach to the problem, being willing to face the issue squarely and openly, and using much wisdom and administrative skill—all made the meeting in Jerusalem successful. They accomplished there what they were unable to accomplish in Antioch—achieving results that were more far reaching and significant than had they merely stilled the local storm.

THE SIGNIFICANCE OF THE RESULTS

The usual results of a problem well solved are immediately obvious. People were happy and content. There was peace among the brethren, and the work of God continued without interruption and without being sidetracked onto peripheral issues. It is perhaps most significant that the Apostle Paul was happy with the decision. He, personally, with his missionary team, delivered the letter from Jerusalem to all the churches which he had established. Previous encounters with Paul had evidently convinced Peter and James that he would tolerate no inconsistency in crucial theological matters. Legitimate compromise was one thing, but to vacillate and be inconsistent was another (Gal. 2:1-21).[6]

SUMMARY

Here, then, are four biblical examples of organizational and administrative structure and skill. Though all vary, they all have several things in common: a problem arose, a solution was sought, and results were achieved. More than that, each problem was attacked with a variety of approaches which yielded basic principles. And it is to these principles we turn in the chapter to follow.

Footnotes

[1]It is interesting to note the references to numbers in the first part of the Book of Acts. The church was launched with approximately 120 (Acts 1:15); in 2:41 about 3,000 were added to the original 100: in 4:4 we are told that "the number of men came to be about 5,000." Some believe that the mention of "men" refers to 5,000 households. If so, the number of disciples would have been five to ten times this number, or maybe more, at the time the events in Acts 6 took place.

[2]In Deuteronomy 1:13, these men are described as "wise and discerning and experienced men."

[3]C. F. Keil and F. Delitzsch, *The Penteteuch,* 2:87.

[4]Robert Jamieson, *Genesis-Deuteronomy,* Eerdmans, pp. 348-49.

[5]It is true that a committee or board of approximately seven is a very workable number for efficient operation, particularly when group decision making is involved.

[6]Some believe the account given by Paul in Galatians 2 is also a description of the Jerusalem meeting recorded in Acts 15. Because of certain "seeming" discrepancies in this account as compared with Luke's account, there are some serious problems with this view. Consequently, some believe the Galatian account took place earlier, when Paul and Barnabas delivered the contribution to the Jerusalem brethren (Acts 11:27-30). Still others believe it took place after the event in Acts 15.

FOURTEEN

PRINCIPLES OF BIBLICAL ADMINISTRATION AND ORGANIZATION

As Christian leaders functioning in the twentieth century, we face a multitude of problems. The rapidly changing world has not helped to reduce the number of problems nor their complexity. But God's people have always faced problems, and in many instances those that face us today are—in their roots—the same old problems. But all problems—old or new—call for certain administrative actions and organizational structures to solve them. This was true both in the Old and New Testaments.

There are relatively few examples of administrative action and organizational structure in the Bible; and those that do appear vary greatly. Because of the lack of conformity, these patterns and structures cannot be classified as normative. But what do appear, however, are several well-selected examples which provide us with profound and normative principles of organization and administration. It is these biblical principles which can provide us with guidelines in developing patterns and structures, and in turn can help us carry out biblical directives.

PRINCIPLES OF ADMINISTRATION

FACE REALITY
First, face the reality of problems. Do not ignore them. If we do, they will not go away! They get worse! We may "sweep them under the rug," but eventually they reappear—in double measure.

We can "hide our heads in the sand," but when we develop enough courage to "look up," they will be bigger and more foreboding than ever. And if we manage to "imagine they are not there," eventually the people to whom we minister will painfully remind us that reality exists.

It does not take much creative imagination ro project what could have happened in Israel if Moses had ignored Jethro's advice, or if the apostles had closed their eyes to the murmuring of the Hellenists. What if the Antiochian Christians had "looked the other way" and not faced the heresy that was being taught by the Judaizers? It could have had negative repercussions all over the New Testament world.

Nehemiah's problems were different! He could have conveniently ignored the plight of his people. But he could never have gotten away from his conscience and the pain he felt in his heart. Though the task was tough and filled with unpredictable events— some that even threatened his very life—he fulfilled the will of God. And the people benefited from his selfless efforts.

There are occasions—but very few—when we, as Christian leaders, can ignore problems in the church—sometimes without too many outward repercussions. But, in our hearts we must live with the decision to withdraw from desperate situations in order to have an easier path to walk. When people's needs go unmet because of our selfishness and our unwillingness to face problems, we must live with our decisions. And as often happens, God bypasses us to achieve His purposes through another vessel, who is far more sensitive to human needs as well as to His Spirit.

Today, as in the New Testament, churches are facing problems. Some are purely organizational; some are theological; some are cultural. Many, of course, involve all three. Though some of these problems are as old as man himself, and though some are new and contemporary, they *are* problems and they must be solved for God's richest blessing to rest on the local church.

Never ignore problems. For if you do they may overwhelm you, defeat you and cause you to leave the work of God, feeling hostile and bitter or depressed and discouraged. and worst of all, you may rationalize your failure, putting the blame on others for your own unwillingness to face problems head on.

DEVELOP A PROPER PERSPECTIVE
Second, develop a proper perspective on the problem before reaching a concrete solution. Sometimes this can be done quickly, and at other times it takes a period of careful evaluation.

In Acts 6 it did not take the apostles long to pinpoint the nature of the problem and to arrive at a solution. The cause was obvious, as well as "what was" and "what was not" the best approach to solving it. It did not take a long period of prayer, evaluation, and seeking God's will to arrive at a solution.

For Nehemiah it was a different story. He was far removed from the actual environment in which the problem existed. His only source of information was an oral report (Neh. 1:1-2), and what he actually learned from this report was very limited (1:3). Consequently, he spent a lengthy period of time seeking God's guidance, and his first step when arriving in Jerusalem was to spend three nights carefully inspecting and evaluating the walls of Jerusalem. Because of the complexity of the problem and the explosive nature of the situation, he in wisdom decided to get "personal perspective" before publicly announcing his strategy.

For the leaders in the Antiochian and Jerusalem church, the problem in Acts 15 was yet different. It was a theological problem—one that had grown out of Judaism and the Law of Moses. It emerged in the transition from Old Testament days to the New, as the apostles themselves attempted to clarify even in their own minds "how a man is saved." God's choosing these men to "be with Jesus," and "to launch the church," and "to speak the truth of God," did not automatically guarantee them "complete perspective" on the whole redemptive plan. We often fail to realize this factor, which is so obvious in biblical revelation.

In Jerusalem it took time to solve the problems of Judaism versus Christianity. It involved a process of reports, debate, and discussion, both in private and in public. It involved historical and biblical research as well as an analysis of what God was doing on the contemporary scene. And it was the result of this process that led to perspective and an "organizational and administrative" answer—a letter and its deliverance to the churches.

Moses, as he led the people through the wilderness, appears to have been totally unaware that he even had a problem, or that it could be solved with a good organizational and administrative plan. It took his father-in-law, Jethro, to solve the problem.

One of the problems of being a leader is that sometimes we get so close to a situation that "we can't see the forest for the trees." This was Moses' difficulty. He knew he had a lot of work to do and that he was working with a group of "unspiritual" and "unpredictable" people, but he did not have the "big picture" that would have helped him facilitate his responsibilities. Here is where others can help us solve a problem. It took a "Jethro" to help Moses to even *see* his problem. It took the Jerusalem church to help the Antiochian church solve the problem they were *already* aware of. Pinpointing it more specifically, it took the assistance of Peter and James to help Paul and Barnabas to bring the problem of law and grace into clear focus.

A great danger that faces every Christian leader is to become threatened by advice. Somehow we feel it is a reflection on our competency, and so we proceed to try to solve the problem alone. Unfortunately, if the problem is beyond us, we will probably end up a failure, far more humiliated than if admitting we needed help. To seek advice is a sign of strength and not weakness. This does not mean that we execute every bit of advice we get from others. Rather it means listening, sorting ideas carefully, and selecting a course of action in dependence upon the Spirit of God.

ESTABLISH PRIORITIES

Third, establish priorities. This may actually be one of the main reasons we cannot solve our organizational and administrative problems. We try to solve them all by ourselves.

This was Moses' problem until he took his father-in-law's advice. He was in the process of physical and psychological deterioration caused by undue stress. He could not do everything; fortunately he recognized this fact and did something about it.

The apostles too in Acts 6, were aware of this principle. They quickly established their priorities and made them known to the people. This did not mean that "serving tables" was unimportant—far from it—but it did mean that they had certain spiritual responsibilities that they had to fulfill. They could not do both.

Today pastors and other spiritual leaders are bombarded with many demands on their time. Contemporary culture and its pressures have complicated the lives of people, creating greater needs. A "big society" and "big business" have created a "big mentality." We automatically demand more of our leaders and ourselves. Therefore, it is absolutely essential, especially for spiritual leaders in the church, to establish priorities. If we don't, we will neglect our primary calling to "shepherd" and to "teach."

DELEGATE RESPONSIBILITY

Fourth, delegate responsibility to qualified people. This principle follows naturally the "establishment of priorities." We have seen it demonstrated by Moses, by the apostles, and by Nehemiah.

This principle, we can conclude, has been the secret to *every* leader's success. Peter Drucker, who has made a careful study of executives, concludes that a significant mark of every successful leader—whether he be the President of the United States or the president of General Motors—is that he knows how to "use all the available strengths—the strength of associates, the strength of supervisors, and one's own strength."[1]

But notice that the Bible clearly emphasizes that delegation of responsibility must be to *spiritually qualified* people. This is what Moses and the apostles did in Exodus 18 and Acts 6. They looked for men who were honest and full of faith, men who were wise and discerning and experienced. They knew that to appoint men of weakness rather than men of strength would be devastating to the whole operation. They also knew that men of quality could handle organizational problems.

Nehemiah, of course, had a similar problem. However, he needed every available person to rebuild the walls, and he used them. But when it came to administering the affairs of Jerusalem after the walls were rebuilt, he appointed Hananiah, who had been commander of the forces, to be "in charge of Jerusalem." Nehemiah chose this man because "he was a faithful man and feared God more than many" (Neh. 7:2). He had already proved himself as a qualified leader.

The selection of spiritually and psychologically qualified people for leadership positions in the church is one of the most important administrative principles in the New Testament. This is why most all of the qualifications of elders and deacons in 1 Timothy 3 and Titus 1 relate to the man's reputation, ethics, morality, temperament, habits, and spiritual and psychological maturity.

Many churches today are guilty of filling positions with *people* —but not *qualified* people. We often make judgments based on "skills," but if these skills are practiced in a context of carnality it can be devastating. Unfortunately, "ability" and "carnality" mix well, for ignoble ends. It is much better to have a person with undeveloped skill but who is strong spiritually.

MAINTAIN A PROPER BALANCE
Fifth, maintain a proper balance between divine and human factors.

The temptation for all leaders is to go to extremes. On the one hand, we may rationalize indecision and inaction on the basis of God's sovereign will and grace. This can easily become a "cop out" for irresponsibility and—God forbid—even laziness. On the other hand, we may take matters into our own hands and ignore the will of God, His power, wisdom, and guidance.

Both extremes are inappropriate. Nehemiah, of all the biblical examples, demonstrates most forcefully the balance. He prayed and then "acted." And sometimes he "acted" and then "prayed." And at times he prayed *while* he acted. As he consistently sought guidance from God, he at the same time proceeded to use the mind and energy that God had given him to do what he *knew* needed to be done.

Perhaps the clearest example of this principle in the life of Nehemiah was when he arrived in Jerusalem. He "arose in the night" and went out and surveyed the walls. But, said Nehemiah, "I did not tell any one what my God was putting in my mind to do for Jerusalem" (Neh. 2:12). Here it is clear that he was formulating his plans as he inspected the walls, but he was also fully convinced that God was guiding his thoughts.

Christian leaders functioning in the twentieth-century church must maintain the same balance. How easy it is to go to extremes, to attempt to solve problems in our own strengths and with our own abilities; and to neglect prayer, God's help, and direction and blessing. On the other hand, how easy it is to withdraw, spend time in prayer or in Bible reading; and to neglect human responsibility. May God help us to put a proper emphasis on both the divine and human—and in that order.

CONSIDER ATTITUDES AND FEELINGS
Sixth, take an approach to problem solving and decision making that takes into consideration the attitudes and feelings of those who are directly involved.

Basic to effectively applying this principle is *communication.* Before taking specific steps to solve his problem, Moses *explained* to the people he was not able to bear up alone under the heavy responsibility (Deut. 1:9). At the appropriate time, Nehemiah called the people together and *explained* his strategy to rebuild the walls (Neh. 2:17). The apostles in Jerusalem "summoned the congregation" and *explained* the situation (Acts 6:2), and in Acts 15 the whole church was ultimately involved in solving the problem of "law and grace." Organizational and administrative problems cannot be satisfactorily solved without proper communication. Circumstances vary (as they did in the scriptural examples), affecting what is said, how much, when, and to whom. But there was always communication with as many people as necessary.

Another factor which appears in all four biblical case studies is group involvement in the decision-making process. Again we see variance in the particulars, but there was always group participation and ultimate agreement. Moses instructed each tribe to select leaders to represent and rule them (Deut. 1:13). The apostles charged the "congregation" to choose seven men to serve tables (Acts 6:1-3). And though the apostles and elders evidently met in closed session to hammer out some of the aspects of the problem of law and grace that could not be handled in a large group, the whole church helped make the final decision (Acts 15:22).

Nehemiah's problem was a different one indeed. The primary responsibility of rebuilding the walls lay on his shoulders. He was *the* leader. It was *his* idea and strategy. But Nehemiah knew he could *never* achieve his goal without the cooperation of the people. Consequently, he carefully communicated his ideas and then issued a call to "come" and as a team to rebuild the walls of Jerusalem. The results of his success as a leader are reflected in their response: "Let *us* arise and build" (Neh. 2:18).

Many problems are created in the twentieth-century church by ignoring this important biblical principle. We are only asking for trouble if we attempt to railroad things through and operate as a dictator. Even the apostles—direct representatives of the Lord Jesus Christ—did not use their apostolic authority to bypass this principle. Naturally there are many problems which need not be brought to the whole congregation for debate and discussion, but again our biblical examples give us significant guidelines in applying the principle of "congregational involvement."

In Exodus 18 and Acts 6 minor details were solved by *people selected by the group*. This was the crucial point at which there was group involvement. Note, however, that in Acts 6 it is conceivable that *only* the Grecian Christians were involved in solving the problem. There was no need to call the *whole* Jerusalem church together to solve a problem that affected only a certain segment of the church.[2] In Acts 15 the whole church seemed to be involved in being made *aware* of the problem, but the basic proposal was formulated as a result of debate and discussion by the apostles and elders. But it was the *whole* church that affirmed the proposal and was involved in the selection of men to implement the plan.

Here in Scripture we see four significant guidelines in determining when the whole group should be involved:

1. In general, it is best to involve only people who are directly related to and affected by a particular problem.

2. Clearly communicate the nature of the problem.

3. Involve this group in selecting qualified people to represent them in helping to solve the problem.

4. Secure the group's approval of the final solution.

BE CREATIVE

Seventh, solve every problem creatively under the leadership of the Holy Spirit. Never allow yourself to get locked into administrative routines that may have worked before.

We must remember that in the Bible there was no one way of either attacking or solving a problem. Every situation was different. Circumstances varied, the nature of the problem varied, and solutions varied.

Christian leaders today frequently allow themselves to get locked into administrative patterns. They attempt to "borrow" patterns and approaches from other churches, or they continue to use patterns that have worked before. When we do, we are closing our minds and hearts to God, who has always used creative means throughout history to administer His work. In order to find the will of God in every matter, we must be guided by biblical principles, current circumstances, and the Holy Spirit.

One thing is clear from a study of administration in the Word of God—*principles are normative! Patterns are not!*

PRINCIPLES OF ORGANIZATION

SET PRINCIPLES AS GOALS

First, organize to apply New Testament principles and to reach New Testament purposes.

Throughout these chapters principles are stated which are believed to be biblical principles. If the principles are applied, they will give the twentieth-century church New Testament guidelines.

Organizational structures in the Bible are always presented as a means to an end. They were never ends in themselves. Therefore, the first and most important biblical principle of organization is always to develop structures for the church which will help us to reach New Testament objectives.

This, in fact, becomes one of the criteria whereby we are able to evaluate our organizational structures. Are we truly functioning according to New Testament principles? Are we reaching New Testament purposes?

MEET NEEDS

Second, organize to meet needs. This was a distinctive mark of the New Testament church. The church did not just organize to organize. Rather it organized when the need arose, whether it was to "feed the people in need" or to "solve a theological problem."

The first and most all-inclusive and continuous need faced by the New Testament church was to carry out the Great Commission. They were under obligation to "make disciples" and to "teach those disciples." They organized to do so. But as pointed out already, very few illustrations are given as to "how" this was done. Unfortunately some today interpret the lack of organizational detail in the New Testament as an indication that the church is to function without structure. This is, of course, an impossibility. To quote Dr. George Peters, professor of missions at Dallas Theological Seminary, "Wherever there are people, there is function; and wherever there is function, there is form." This is a reality.

True there *is* limited reference to organizational structure in the Scriptures, but again this is not without design. There *are* sufficient illustrations to show it *is* necessary and there is sufficient *variance* to show that particular structures *are not absolute*. And the illustrations we *do* have yield dynamic principles that are applicable to any culture, and at any time in history. All of this points to freedom to design and create organizational structures that will be the most effective to reach New Testament objectives in today's world.

Donald Guthrie has spoken to this issue in his commentary on the Pastoral Epistles:

> There is, therefore, considerable evidence to show that Paul was not unmindful of church organization. The absence of uniformity of government in Pauline churches is capable of other explanations than that Paul was completely disinterested. He appears to have been sufficiently flexible in his approach to allow any system which suited local conditions and was dictated by the Holy Spirit.[3]

It has already been demonstrated that Paul was more concerned about qualified men than specific patterns of organization. Nevertheless, he was also interested in organization for he charged the Corinthians to "let all things be done properly and in an orderly manner" (1 Cor. 14:40). He also instructed Titus to remain in Crete so he could "set in order what remains" (Titus 1:5).

But he also knew that every culture (even the various subcultures in the New Testament world) called for different approaches to specific organizational problems. He therefore bore down on the absolutes—qualifications for leadership positions—knowing that men of God who are wise and prudent could develop the structures necessary to meet the specialized demands of any culture at any time in history. As Dr. Francis Schaeffer has said,

"Anything the New Testament does not command, and regard as church forms, is a freedom to be exercised under the leadership of the Holy Spirit for that particular time and place."[4]

KEEP IT SIMPLE

Third, keep organization simple. This principle is closely aligned with the former; that is, organizing to meet needs. If organization is to be functional, it must be as simple as possible. Complicated organizational patterns frequently become "ends" in themselves.

This does not mean that organizational patterns are never complex. For example, the pattern in Exodus 18 was very intricate, but it was also designed for over 2 million people who were traveling through the wilderness. But though complex, it *was* functional, and carefully designed to meet the needs of the Children of God at that particular time in their lives.

A good test of whether or not simplicity is being lost, even in a complex pattern, is whether or not the structure is serving biblical objectives. If it is not, it needs to be carefully evaulated in the light of scriptural criteria.

It is important for every Christian leader to realize that a "smooth running church" does not mean it is successful as measured by the Word of God. The world, and many Christian groups as well as pseudo-Christian groups, have produced dynamic organizational structures. Some because of their efficiency are reaching more people and raising more money than evangelicals.

Reaching objectives? Yes, but the wrong ones! You see, good organization can be used to reach any purpose or end—noble or ignoble, biblical or nonbiblical. And unfortunately, some non-Christians use biblical principles to reach nonbiblical objectives.

KEEP IT FLEXIBLE

Fourth, keep organization flexible. The structures set up in the wilderness for a people "on the move," were changed when they "settled in the land." When the walls were complete, a new approach was devised to govern Jerusalem. When persecution hit Jerusalem, the structure of Acts 6 was terminated, and when the specific "law and grace" problems recorded in Acts 15 were solved, they went on to *new* ways of solving *new* problems. Biblical leaders were never locked into organizational structures.

Organizational patterns that develop rigidity and "hardening of the categories" are in danger of being treated as authoritative, and absolute. This is wrong. We are not free to make unchangeable what God intended to be changeble. "In a rapidly changing age like ours," said Dr. Schaeffer, "an age of total upheaval like ours, to make nonabsolutes absolute guarantees both isolation and the death of the institutional, organized church."[5]

There are many areas today where the evangelical church needs to rethink its organizational structures—areas that we have allowed to become absolute and inflexible. The following questions are designed to probe our thinking and to "break us loose" from rigidity and inflexibility.

HOW MANY MEETINGS AND WHEN?

Who is to say *how many* meetings should be conducted in a given week in the church? The Bible certainly does not dictate any patterns in this area.

Furthermore, who is to say *when* these meetings are to be held? Other than a few references to meetings on the "first day of the week" (Acts 20:7; 1 Cor. 16:2), there is little said in Scripture about when the New Testament church met. Some would even question that meeting on Sunday is an absolute guideline for the church, but rather an example of when the church met. Remember that the Jerusalem church met daily in its initial days.

The Corinthians, no doubt, met on Sunday evening to partake of the Lord's Supper and to exercise their spiritual gifts (1 Cor. 11), but is this an absolute pattern? I think not! If so, the majority of churches have been out of step with Scripture for many years. But even in view of this scriptural evidence (or lack of it) regarding *when* believers are to meet, there are many Christians who feel you are tampering with scriptural authority if it is suggested, for example, that the Sunday night service be cancelled in favor of a more qualitative meeting at some other time.

Midweek prayer meeting has probably become one of the most rigid patterns of all, for to suggest a change (in the minds of some) is synonymous with "being opposed to prayer." The fact is, there is no biblical injunction for the church to "meet for a midweek prayer meeting." It may be an excellent idea, but there is nothing sacred about a "midweek prayer meeting" per se. What makes it sacred is what happens there, for there is no question but that believers are to *pray*. But *when* they meet to pray is but a means to an end.

It is interesting, too, that many Christian leaders evaluate the spiritual climate of the church by how many attend midweek prayer meeting. There may be some truth to this, but a more basic question is whether or not the body of believers represent a *praying* church. *When* they meet or *how many* meet at one time is not nearly so significant. A quantitative answer to "how many attend midweek prayer meeting" may be an indicator of spiritual maturity—or the lack of it. But it may also be true that a midweek prayer meeting, as it has come to be traditionally practiced, may no longer be the best means or pattern for the twentieth-century church. Because of work schedules, school activities, and other cultural changes, perhaps the hour and evening chosen in a previous era is no longer the best time. This is probably a major reason why believers are not actively attending the service as they once did.

WHAT KINDS OF MEETINGS?
In recent years the various *kinds* of meetings conducted by the church have multiplied. The twentieth-century church has meetings for children, meetings for youth and meetings for adults. We have Bible classes, fellowship meetings, training sessions, worship periods, preaching services and prayer meetings. We have Sunday School sessions, vacation Bible schools, training hour, children's church, youth church, adult church, women's missionary meetings, home Bible studies, child evangelism classes and youth rallies. We have board meetings, committee meetings, teachers' meetings and choir practice. Other types of meetings, of course, could be added to this list depending on the church and situation.

Actually it is impossible to find any pattern in the New Testament that illustrates the present approach to meetings and agencies in our average church today. We know the first-century Christians had meetings, but what kind and what the specific characteristics of these meetings were is very difficult to determine.

This, of course, does not mean it is wrong to have the different kinds of meetings and agencies we have today. The very freedom allowed in the New Testament is the basic reason there *is* so much variety. The important New Testament principle is *why* these meetings are held; in other words, do they exist to achieve New Testament objectives.

But the point I am making here is that the very freedom that has allowed us to develop the forms and structures we have today has been stifled by allowing what we are doing at the present time to become *the way*. For example, is the typical Sunday school the best form of Christian education in our contemporary society? Is the usual training hour on Sunday evening the best way to equip various members of the body of Christ for Christian service? Is our morning church service the best kind of meeting to help believers learn the Scriptures and worship God?

It is time for the church to evaluate the kinds of meetings it has, and to justify their existence on the basis of New Testament principles and purposes.

WHAT ABOUT THE PATTERNS AND FORMAT?

In some churches if you dare change the order of the morning worship service, you get the distinct feeling you are tampering with the Scriptures themselves. Who is to say how a service is to be ordered? There is very little in Scripture to suggest specific answers to this question.

We *do* have mention of what *experiences* Christians should have when the body of Christ meets, but *how* all of this is put together is not illustrated in detail. We do have some reference to what the Corinthians did in their Sunday evening meetings, but the specific format is difficult to reconstruct.

It is my opinion that what we see in Corinthians is illustrative of the way *they* met and, with the exception of certain aspects of *what* they did, provides no absolute guidelines for the church. This is logical when we realize that the whole tone of Scripture emphasizes freedom in "organizational structure." And this point becomes even more forceful when we realize that the Corinthians, who were using this freedom, were doing so as a carnal group of believers. All the more reason not to get locked into *their* patterns.

The body of Christ, therefore, needs to determine its meeting patterns and format, first of all, by setting forth clear-cut biblical objectives for these meetings. The patterns which are chosen should then be the best possible means to achieve these biblical ends within the context of the contemporary culture, taking into consideration the many variables which affect a group of people who live in a particular time in history, and in a particular part of the world, and in particular communities. This is also true in determining the *number* of meetings, *when* the meetings are held, and the various *kinds* of meetings. To allow our present patterns to lock us into a particular approach is to make nonabsolutes absolute, and this is a definite step in the direction of institutionalism.

WHAT ABOUT THE PLACE FOR MEETINGS?
An interesting trend in churches today is to conduct meetings off the church property. But more interesting than this phenomenon is the attitude of certain Christians toward this trend. Some people are highly threatened, for they feel the church hierarchy may lose control of what is happening. To some, anything that decentralizes the body of Christ rather than centralizing it (that is, bringing everyone together in one place) is a danger signal.

It is "enlightening" to get feedback from some Christians that the "church building" is *the* scriptural place to meet. This is of special interest since the New Testament Christians had no church buildings to meet in. At first they met in the temple in Jerusalem and in homes. When the Jewish leaders eventually rejected Christianity, some Christians had to meet in their homes. This is one reason why we have many references to "house churches" in the New Testament.

Does this mean that "house churches" is the New Testament way—an absolute pattern which we must go back to if God's richest blessing is to rest upon the church? Again, I think not! However, I would add that there is something unique about the "house church" that assists in creating a "family atmosphere" for the body of Christ. It is unfortunate that the strong emphasis on church buildings has led us away from also using homes as meeting places for believers to experience dynamic Christianity.

On the other hand, there are many problems created by our culture in exclusively holding a regular church meeting in a "house church." Extensive traveling for business purposes by the head of the home, vacation periods, trends in weekend living habits, the various needs of all age levels, a limited time for families to even get together as a single family in their homes—all of these factors make a "house church" difficult to maintain in many communities.

But to say that the "church building" is *the* biblical place to meet is to be totally unscriptural. To say that *any* particular place is *the* biblical place is to make a nonabsolute an absolute. Because of the various cultural changes and the needs of people today, the body of Christ needs to be flexible as to where it meets. A Sunday school class for college youth meeting on the university campus may be far more effective than meeting in the church. Using a number of homes for midweek Bible study and prayer sessions, led by a number of mature lay Christians, may be far more significant than trying to get everyone to meet at the church under the leadership of the pastor.

Then too renting facilities other than church buildings may be a greater use of the Lord's money than building a huge church plant. Some churches use YMCA buildings, public schools, college campuses, and other available buildings. On the other hand, in some locations it is difficult to function this way, particularly if the church is growing. Also, people in our culture are often hesitant to become serious about becoming involved *permanently* in a church that meets in a *temporary* place. More about this cultural implication later!

But the important point is that the body of Christ be *flexible* in determining *where* its meetings are to take place. There are no biblical absolutes dictating the answers to these questions.

SUMMARY

What forms and patterns are developed to carry out these administrative and organizational principles is a matter of creative leadership under the direction of the Holy Spirit. It is impossible to derive specific patterns and structures from the New Testament (which is also abundantly demonstrated by the many different types of church government in existence today among evangelical believers).

It seems, however, that the Holy Spirit definitely planned this "ambiguity." Because of the variety of environments, cultures, and mentalities in the world today, God knew that to issue absolutes in the area of structure and form in organization and administration would be to provide specific guidelines that would be difficult to implement in various areas of the world. In fact, if God had dictated form, He would have "locked the church into the Middle-Eastern culture in a first-century world. It would have greatly restricted the spread of Christianity to other cultures.

But God has not locked us into culture. The principles He has given us are supracultural and can and should be applied to the twentieth-century church, wherever it may be.

These principles are:

ADMINISTRATION

1. Face the reality of problems.
2. Develop a proper perspective on the problems before seeking concrete solutions.
3. Estabish priorities.
4. Delegate responsibility to qualified people.
5. Maintain a proper balance between divine and human factors.
6. Take an approach to problem solving and decision making that takes into consideration the attitudes and feelings of those who are involved.
7. Solve every problem creatively under the leadership of the Holy Spirit.

ORGANIZATION

1. Organize to apply New Testament principles and to reach New Testament purposes.
2. Organize to meet needs.
3. Keep organization simple.
4. Keep organization flexible.

Footnotes

[1]Peter F. Drucker, *The Effective Executive,* Harper & Row, p. 71.
[2]The argument for this is based on the fact that only men who had Greek names were selected. It is further supported by the fact that it was the Grecian Jews who were being neglected. It seems the apostles called *these* people together and helped them solve their particular problem.
[3]Donald Guthrie, *The Pastoral Epistles,* p. 28.
[4]Francis Schaeffer, *The Church at the End of the Twentieth Century,* p. 67.
[5]Ibid.

FIFTEEN

COMMUNICATION IN THE NEW TESTAMENT

The *way* in which New Testament Christians communicated is another broad and significant area for study. Actually, many facets of communication have already appeared in our investigation of first-century believers, and the way in which they proceeded to carry out the Great Commission.

Among the unsaved they taught, declared, spoke, proclaimed, preached, testified, witnessed, exhorted, praised, reasoned, refuted, explained, demonstrated, persuaded, and gave evidence for what they believed.

As a church "gathered" for edification they taught and exhorted one another. They engaged in fellowship, broke bread, prayed, and praised God. They encouraged and strengthened one another, and reported and described God's work and blessings in other parts of the world. And when they had theological and ethical difficulties, they wrote, implored, admonished one another, and at times engaged in heated debate.

All of these words are used in the New Testament to describe the process of communication, both as the believers evangelized (made disciples) and as they gathered to build up one another. A careful study of these words in context makes it very clear that they were used to describe a process that was characterized by variety and many different approaches. Whether it involved Peter's sermons recorded by Luke, or Paul's communication with various individuals and groups, there is no consistent pattern in the *way* their content was presented. And the New Testament letters *all* reveal a variety in literary style and form. Even among and within the Pauline epistles, there is no consistent approach in form and structure.

All of this points to "freedom" in communication. But the many examples in the New Testament, like so many other areas of first-century church life, yield some profound principles which can assist the twentieth-century church to be a "communicating" church—as a church "in the world" and as a "gathered community."

Because Paul said, "Be imitators of me, just as I also am of Christ" (1 Cor. 11:1), two basic communication models follow. The first presents Jesus Christ Himself, the supreme model! The second presents the ministry of Paul, as well as two of his co-workers. Both models yield New Testament principles of communication.

A COMMUNICATION MODEL FROM JESUS CHRIST
The communication methods of Christ have been studied and researched for many years, and the process has yielded some outstanding observations and principles. But there is an "overall" perspective that has not, to my knowledge, been explored, or at least presented in written form.

A careful listing of the specific communication situations, beginning with Christ's public ministry and up to the time He was taken into custody, yields approximately 194 examples. Assuming that all such cases recorded in the Gospels are generally representative of Christ's three-and-one-half-year ministry on earth, some very interesting observations can be made from the chart "Communication Situations in Christ's Ministry."[1]

These communication situations can be broken down into the various cases listed in table 1. When these cases are divided into two categories by identifying those who were either neutral or negative and those who were definitely positive, we have the statistics given in table 2. If these cases are divided into those involving individuals and those involving groups, table 3 is the result. By dividing the "Group" situations into those who were positive toward Christ and those who were either neutral or negative toward Him, the comparison in table 4 is made.

COMMUNICATION SITUATIONS IN CHRIST'S MINISTRY

TABLE 1

A Distribution of the Percentage of Times Christ Spent Ministering to Various Individuals and Groups (as listed in the four Gospels)

COMMUNICATION SITUATION	NUMBER	PERCENTAGE
The disciples (larger group of followers)	29	15.8
The scribes and Pharisees (as a group)	28	15.5
Two or more apostles	24	13.0
Sick people (includes only individual healings)	22	11.9
A general group (other than disciples)*	20	10.8
Individuals generally**	19	10.3
Individual apostles (the Twelve)	19	10.3
The multitudes	18	9.7
Sick people (involving group healings)	5	2.7
Totals	184	100

TABLE 2

The Percentage of Times Christ Spent Ministering to Various Individuals and Groups Positive Toward Him Compared with the Percentage of Times Spent with Those Negative

DEFINITELY POSITIVE		EITHER NEUTRAL OR NEGATIVE	
Disciples	15.8%	Scribes and Pharisees	15.5%
Sick people (individual		General group	10.8%
and group)	14.6%	Individuals generally	10.3%
Two or more apostles	13.0%	Multitudes	9.7%
Individual apostles	10.3%		
Total	53.7%	Total	46.3%

*Indicates such groups as the "Jews," the "servants," etc.
**Such as Nicodemus, the woman at the well, a scribe, etc. This does not include individuals who are definitely classified as disciples. They are included under the first item in the table. Out of twenty-nine references to the disciples, only eight are "individual" disciples.

TABLE 3

The Percentage of Times Christ Spent with Individuals Compared
with the Percentage of Times He Spent with Groups

INDIVIDUALS		GROUPS	
Sick individuals	11.9%	Disciples	15.8%
Individuals generally	10.3%	Scribes and Pharisees	15.5%
Individual apostles	10.3%	Two or more apostles	13.0%
		General group	10.8%
		Multitudes	9.7%
		Sick people (a group)	2.7%
Total	32.5%	Total	67.5%

TABLE 4

The Number of Times Christ Spent Ministering to Groups Positive
Toward Him Compared to Those with Groups Negative or Neutral

GROUPS POSITIVE		GROUPS NEGATIVE OR NEUTRAL	
Disciples	29	Scribes and Pharisees	28
Two or more apostles	24	General group	20
Sick people	5	Multitude	18
Total	58 (46.8%)	Total	66(53.2%)

From these categorizations, note the following specific observations:

1. Christ *balanced* His ministry by communicating with many different kinds of people. Taking into account all of the subgroups and individuals He ministered to, the percentage of times He spent with each of these various groups ranges from approximately 10 percent to 15 percent (table 1).
2. He spent approximately *half* of His times communicating to those who were *positive* toward His ministry and the other *half* communicating to those who were either neutral or negative (table 2).
3. He spent about *one third* of the times with individuals, and about *two thirds* of the times with groups (table 3).

4. Of the two-thirds of the times He spent communicating with groups, He spent about half of them with groups who were positive toward His ministry and the other half communicating with those who were either neutral or negative (table 4).

5. Of the 32.5 percent of the times that He spent with individuals, He spent about one-third communicating with individual sick people, one-third communicating with individuals generally, and about one-third communicating with individual apostles. Interestingly, all three categories involving individuals approximate 10 percent (see table 3).

All of these observations indicate that Jesus Christ neglected no one. He had His priorities, but He was as interested in those who were positive toward Him as those who were negative or neutral. He also divided His time between groups and individuals. And even among the kinds of individuals He ministered to, He evenly distributed His efforts.

TRAINING THE TWELVE

There is no more outstanding communication model! But more than the overall picture, the way He trained the Twelve is even more magnificent. They were His special group. Even though it appears that He spent as many times communicating with individuals generally as He did with individual apostles, in reality He spent nearly 100 percent of His time with the Twelve.

How could this be? Note His general approach to training these select men. First, after calling them to follow Him, along with the general group of disciples, He then called them to be with Him in a special way: to watch, to observe, to listen as He preached to the multitudes, as He debated with the scribes and Pharisees, taught the larger group of disciples, and ministered to individuals. Then He sent them out to do what He had been doing. Finally, He began a special concentrated ministry with them, preparing them for His death, His resurrection, and the Great Commission.

As Christ carried out His general ministry communicating with all classes of people, He, in a special way, spent His total time training these twelve men. Every time He spoke to the multitudes, the apostles had opportunity to hear what He said. Every time He healed a person, they could observe. Every time He dialogued and debated with the Pharisees, they looked on with amazement. In almost every instance when He talked with individuals, they also listened in—or at least got firsthand feedback (for example, as with the woman at the well).

Notice too the unique pattern that frequently emerged in Christ's overall ministry. At times He would be teaching the multitudes; then He would turn to the larger groups of disciples and speak to them more personally. And on occasions, He would turn to the Twelve and speak even more specifically and intimately about the truth He was teaching the larger group. Going a step further, He would at times turn to one individual or perhaps two or three of the Twelve to share with them some truth even more forcefully. (See fig. 19.)

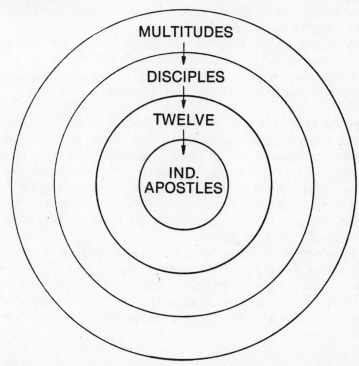

Figure 19. A Communication Pattern in Christ's Ministry

What we see in Jesus Christ is an unequaled communication model. While He reached the multitudes, He was equipping a group of twelve men for an in-depth ministry. And while He was equipping twelve men, He was especially equipping Peter and John for a more foundational ministry that would go beyond even that of the other apostles. This is obvious from the ministry of these two men as revealed in the Book of Acts, as well as by the New Testament literature they wrote. It was no secret to the Twelve that Jesus Christ had a special ministry for them, and particularly for the Apostle Peter. The way He singled out Peter for special instructions and lessons verifies this point.

Paul, Silas, and Timothy were New Testament leaders chosen for a reason. First, they represented three men who in a special way exemplified those who had the greater gifts (1 Cor. 12:31). Paul was an *apostle;* Silas was classified as a *prophet* (Acts 15:32); and Timothy was definitely a *teacher*.[2]

A second reason these men are chosen for this model is that they have left for us, through Paul's writings, one of the most comprehensive communication patterns found anywhere among those who founded and established churches.

THEIR MINISTRY IN THESSALONICA

Luke records the basic events leading to the founding of the church in Thessalonica (Acts 17:1-9). Paul himself "reasoned" in the synagogue for three Sabbaths, probably covering a three-week period (vv. 2-3). Some Jews were converted plus a large number of Greeks and leading women (v. 4). Other than these basic facts, Luke tells us very little about the actual ministry of these three men in this Macedonian city.

However, when we come to Paul's first epistle to these new Christians, a large portion of the letter is given over to describing their initial ministry with these people. These reflections by Paul give us some exciting insights into the way these men as a team communicated with these people—before and after they became Christians.

The First Thessalonian Letter

1.1 Paul and Silvanus [Silas] and Timothy to the church of the Thessalonians in God the Father and the Lord Jesus Christ: Grace to you and peace.

1:2 We give thanks to God always for all of you, making mention of you in our prayers;

1:3 constantly bearing in mind your work of faith and labor of love and steadfastness of hope in our Lord Jesus Christ in the presence of our God and Father;

1:4 knowing, brethren beloved by God, His choice of you,

1:5 for our Gospel did not come to you in word only, but also in power and in the Holy Spirit and with full conviction; just as you know what kind of men we proved to be among you for your sake.

1:6 You also became imitators of us and the Lord, having received the word in much tribulation with the joy of the Holy Spirit,

1:7-8 so that you became an example to all the believers in Macedonia and in Achaia. For the word of the Lord has sounded forth from you, not only in Macedonia and in Achaia, but also in every place your faith toward God

Communication Characteristics

Paul wrote this letter representing his two co-workers, Silas and Timothy, who served with him when the church was founded in Thessalonica.

Part of their follow up with these people was *prayer.*

The criteria for evaluating the effectiveness of their ministry was the degree of *faith, hope,* and *love* manifested by these believers.

They recognized *God's sovereign work* in the lives of people.

They did not depend upon their oratory and communication skills alone, but primarily upon the *power* of the *Holy Spirit.*

They lived in such a way as to be living *models* of the Christ-life which these people could imitate.

One of their objectives was to *multiply themselves;* they also measured the effectiveness of their work by the outreach of these believers.

has gone forth, so that we have no need to say anything.

1:9-10 For they themselves report about us what kind of a reception we had with you, and how you turned to God from idols to serve a living and true God, and to wait for His Son from heaven, whom He raised from the dead, that is Jesus, who delivers us from the wrath to come.

Paul never hesitated to give *positive feedback* in order to encourage his converts to continue to live dynamic lives for Jesus Christ.

2:1-2 For you yourselves know, brethren, that our coming to you was not in vain, but after we had already suffered and been mistreated in Philippi, as you know, we had the boldness in our God to speak to you the Gospel of God amid much opposition.

When first communicating with the non-Christians in Thessalonica, they preached the Gospel with *boldness.*

2:3 For our exhortation does not come from error or impurity or by way of deceit;

These men were *honest, open,* and *sincere.*

2:4 but just as we have been approved by God to be entrusted with the Gospel, so we speak, not as pleasing men but God, who examines our hearts.

They wanted to *please God first* of all, not men.

2:5 For we never came with flattering speech, as you know, nor with a pretext for greed —God is witness—

Their motives were *pure.*

2:6 nor did we seek glory from men, either from you or from others, even though as apostles of Christ we might have asserted our authority.

They did not demand honor because they were Christ's representatives; rather they won *respect* through their behavior.

2:7 But we proved to be gentle among you, as a nursing mother tenderly cares for her own children.

They ministered to these people in a spirit of *gentleness*—like a mother nursing her child.

2:8 Having thus a fond affection for you, we were well pleased to impart to you not only the Gospel but also our own lives, because you had become very dear to us.

They were *unselfish,* being willing to literally give their lives if necessary to win these people to Christ.

2:9 For you recall, brethren, our labor and hardship, how working night and day so as not to be a burden to any of you, we proclaimed to you the Gospel of God.

They worked night and day so as not to have their *motives* misinterpreted.

2:10 You are witnesses, and so is God, how devoutly and uprightly and blamelessly we behaved toward you believers;

They lived *exemplary lives* among those who came to Christ (see 1:5-6).

2:11-12 just as you know how we were exhorting and encouraging and imploring each one of you as a father would his own children, so that you may walk in a manner worthy of the God who calls you into His own kingdom and glory.

They maintained an *individualized ministry* among these new Christians; they literally taught and encouraged "each one," just like a father would work with each one of his children.

2:13 And for this reason we also constantly thank God that when you received from us the Word of God's message, you accepted it not as the word of men, but for what it really is, the Word of God, which also performs its work in you who believed.

They *exalted* the Word of God; not their own ideas or philosophy.

2:17-20 But we, brethren, having been bereft of you for a short while—in person, not in spirit—were all the more eager with great desire to see your face. For we wanted to come to you—I, Paul, more than once—and yet Satan thwarted us. For who is our hope, or joy or crown of exultation? Is it not even you, in the presence of our Lord Jesus at His coming? For you are our glory and joy.

They *continued their interest* in these people after they had to leave them.

3:1-2 Therefore when we could endure it no longer, we thought it best to be left behind at Athens alone; and we sent Timothy, our brother and God's fellow worker in the Gospel of Christ, to strengthen and encourage you as to your faith;

They *followed up* their ministry by having Timothy return to Thessalonica to strengthen and encourage these believers.

3:3-5 ... so that no man may be disturbed by these afflictions; for you yourselves know that we have been destined for this. For indeed when we were with you, we kept telling you in advance that we were going to suffer affliction; and so it came to pass, as you know. For this reason, when I could endure it no longer, I also sent to find out about your faith, for fear that the tempter might have tempted you, and our labor should be in vain.

They were *straightforward* and *honest* with these people about the realities of Satan, and the trials they would have to endure because of their decision to follow Christ.

3:6-9 But now that Timothy has come to us from you, and has

They *did not hesitate to share their human feelings* with these brought us good news of your faith and love, and that you always think kindly of us, longing to see us just as we also long to see you, for this reason, brethren, in all our distress and affliction we were comforted about you through your faith; for now we really live, if you stand firm in the Lord. For what thanks can we render to God for you in return for all the joy with which we rejoice before our God on your account,

people—they were desperately concerned about them, and when they received a positive report of their progress in the faith, they were encouraged in the midst of their own trials and tribulations. They did not hesitate to share these inner feelings.

3:10-13 as we night and day keep praying most earnestly that we may see your face, and may complete what is lacking in your faith? Now may our God and Father Himself and Jesus our Lord direct our way to you; and may the Lord cause you to increase and abound in love for one another, and for all men, just as we also do for you; so that He may establish your hearts unblamable in holiness before our God and Father at the coming of our Lord Jesus with all His saints.

They *wanted to return as a team* and assist these believers to go even further in their Christian development.

4:1,ff. Finally then, brethren, we request and exhort you in the Lord Jesus that, as you received from us instruction as to how you ought to walk and please God (just as you actually do walk), that you may excel still more.

Paul *used this letter as an additional means of follow up.* Certain areas needed additional instructions — about morality (4:2-8); business life (4:10-12); the second coming of Christ (4:13-17); attitudes toward their spiritual leaders, those in special need, and all men (5:12-15); as well as about their church life (5:16-21).

SUMMARY

From Christ's model, we have looked at an overall strategy in the area of communication. The Lord Jesus demonstrated in a unique way how to meet the needs of all, but at the same time to communicate in a special way with special groups for in-depth training and development.

The communication model representing Paul, Silas, and Timothy demonstrates in a more specific way how these men won people to Christ, and then how they helped them grow spiritually. In summary, their communication was marked by the following characteristics:

THE MEN AS A TEAM

1. They were living examples of the Christian way of life.
2. They were sincere and honest, and kept their motives pure.
3. They were bold and unintimidated.
4. They were gentle and loving.
5. They were unselfish and sincerely interested in people.

THEIR METHODS AT THE DIVINE LEVEL

1. They included a ministry of prayer.
2. They recognized God's sovereignty.
3. They relied upon the Holy Spirit.
4. They exalted the Word of God.

THEIR METHODS AT THE HUMAN LEVEL

1. They won respect through performance.
2. They maintained an individualized ministry as well as a ministry to groups.
3. They followed up by sending Timothy back to teach them.
4. They were honest and open about their own humanness.
5. They planned to return as a team to continue the process of edification.
6. They gave positive feedback to these new believers regarding their progress in the Christian life.
7. They maintained a written ministry by sending letters to encourage and instruct them.

THEIR EFFECTIVENESS

1. They evaluated it by the degree of faith, hope, and love present and manifested in the local body of believers.

2. They evaluated it by the way these believers were multiplying themselves in their sphere of influence.

Footnotes

[1]A.T. Robertson's *A Harmony of the Gospels,* was used for this study. The specific analysis began with "Christ's public ministry," Part VI, page 19, and was terminated at Part XIII, page 205, entitled, "The Arrest, Trial, Crucifixion, and Burial of Jesus." Before His public ministry there are no references to specific communication situations, and following His arrest the references are quite limited.

Certain judgments were made as to what was a "specific" communication situation. Furthermore, general references were excluded from this list; such as, "And Jesus was going about all the cities and the villages, teaching in their synagogues, and proclaiming the gospel of the kingdom, and healing every kind of disease and every kind of sickness" (Matt. 9:35; see also Mark 16:20).

[2]There is biblical evidence that all of these men had multiple gifts. For example, Paul classifies himself not only as an apostle but as a preacher and a teacher. Luke also classifies Paul as a prophet. There is no doubt that he was also an evangelist. Silas was not only a prophet, but seemingly a teacher and a pastor. Timothy had both the gift of teaching and that of pastor.

SIXTEEN

PRINCIPLES OF NEW TESTAMENT COMMUNICATION

A study of communication models in the New Testament, from the life of Christ and the lives of New Testament leaders, surfaces some significant principles. These principles can serve as guidelines to enable Christians to be more effective in presenting the Word of God, both to believers and others.

A HUMAN/DIVINE PROCESS

First, Christian communication is a distinctive process including both human and divine elements. As illustrated in figure 20 it can take place, and quite effectively, at the human level. God's common grace gives men ability to communicate with each other.

But Christian communication includes some unique elements that go far beyond the purely horizontal level. Even when communicating with non-Christians, the Word of God, the Holy Spirit, and God Himself are involved in the process. A leader who is sensitive and open to spiritual guidance will find God Himself waiting to communicate through His Word and by His Spirit. (See figure 21.) In turn, the believer has access to God's heart and power through prayer. At the same time all of these elements are at work in the communication process, God is working in the heart of the unbeliever through His Holy Spirit (John 16:7-8).

But Christian communication becomes a totally unique process when individuals involved are Christians. (See figure 22.) Here we have the concept of the "body." Communication can now move in all directions.

God's plan definitely calls for those who are specially qualified to communicate to the church. This is very clear in the requirements spelled out for spiritual leaders. But the Scriptures are also very explicit that God's plan calls for every member of the body to communicate with one another in order to be properly edified (Col. 3:16; Eph. 4:16, 5:19).

But, as we consider this distinctive process including both the human and divine elements, note that some Christians tend to overemphasize, on one hand, the human elements; and on the other hand, some overemphasize the divine elements. New Testament leaders demonstrated beautifully the importance of both. They maintained a unique balance.

Paul, Silas, and Timothy recognized that "no one can say, 'Jesus is Lord,' except by the Holy Spirit" (1 Cor. 12:3). This is why, in writing to the Thessalonians, they gave testimony to the fact that the Gospel did not come to these believers "in word only, but also in power and in the Holy Spirit and with full conviction" (1 Thes. 1:5). It was God who was at work in their hearts, causing them to respond to the Word of God (1:4). They knew the power of prayer (1:2) and the supernatural influence of the Word of God (2:13).

They were also aware of the importance of human effort. They were definitely cognizant of the fact that God has chosen to use human instrumentality to achieve His sovereign purposes. This is why they spent time with each one individually (2:11). After they had left Thessalonica, this is why they sent Timothy back to strengthen and encourage them (3:2). This is why Paul wanted the whole team to return to Thessalonica to continue a ministry among them (3:11-13). They did not hesitate to give positive feedback to these people. And they sat down and wrote letters to give them additional instructions and help.

All of these factors clearly point to human responsibility in Christian communication. In fact, most of the principles which follow grow out of the "human dimension" of communication in the New Testament setting. It is these factors which stand out on the pages of Scripture as you study the biblical examples. We cannot ignore them, but neither should we substitute them for the

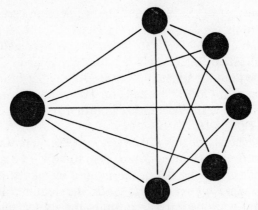

Figure 20. Communication— Effective at the Purely
Human Level

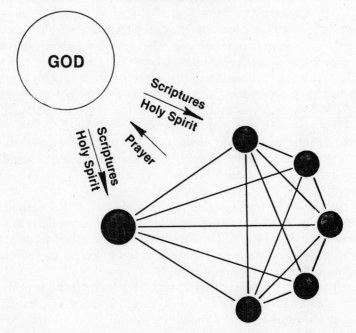

Figure 21. Christian Communication—Distinctive in the
Process of Evangelism

divine elements in the unique process of Christian communication.

COMMUNICATE TO ALL
Second, Christian communication should be to all kinds and classes of people.

Jesus demonstrated this principle forcefully. He went everywhere communicating with everyone! Whether Pharisee or disciple, apostle or another individual in need, He included them all. Whether to admirer or critic, He distributed His efforts in an amazing way.

Paul too said, "I am under obligation both to Greeks and to barbarians, both to the wise and to the foolish" (Rom. 1:14). There were no class distinctions in this man's mind. Everyone needed the Gospel. There was no one too poor or too rich, too

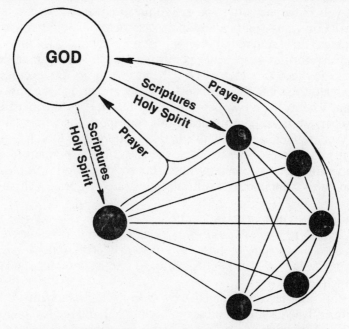

Figure 22. Christian Communication—Even More
Distinctive in the Process of Edification

religious or too pagan, or too near or too far, who did not come within the circle of Paul's concern.

Christians, like all human beings, can become prejudiced. It is easy to "pick and choose" those to whom we want to communicate.

James blasted this kind of "personal favoritism," when he said:

> For if a man comes into your assembly with a gold ring and dressed in fine clothes, and there also comes in a poor man in dirty clothes, and you pay special attention to the one who is wearing the fine clothes, and say, "You sit here in a good place," and you say to the poor man, "You stand over there, or sit down by my footstool"; have you not made distinctions among yourselves, and become judges with evil motives? (James 2:2-4)

This is wrong! These things ought not so to be, exclaimed James. "If you show partiality, you are committing sin" (2:9).

All Christians—particularly spiritual leaders in the church, should evaluate their sphere of communication. Obviously we must establish priorities—especially as spiritual leaders. Our primary calling is to "feed the flock of God." But this in no way excuses us from a ministry to the *total* flock of God, and also to the unsaved man, wherever and whoever he may be. And as shepherd and teacher, we must communicate this concept to the whole family of God. In fact, it is the whole body functioning as God intended that makes it possible to reach the spectrum of humanity. It is impossible for any one individual, but together God's people can apply this principle so beautifully illustrated by Jesus Christ.

GROUPS AND INDIVIDUALS

Third, Christian communication should be carefully balanced between a ministry to groups and a ministry to individuals. Again, Jesus Christ as well as Paul, Silas, and Timothy demonstrated this principle.

You may have wondered why these New Testament leaders frequently left a strong and thriving church. It did not just happen! If the Thessalonians are representative of their philosophy of communication, they spent a significant amount of time discipling individuals as well as speaking to groups.

The tendency today among evangelical Christians is to be satisfied to speak "to the multitudes." Pastors frequently spend most of their time behind the pulpit or in front of the group. To do so is to ignore a dynamic principle of Christian communication, demonstrated by both our Lord and the church leaders in the New Testament.

Certainly this takes time! But it is time well spent. For without this balanced approach, Christian communication becomes impersonal and wooden. It loses its dynamic and power. The individual is lost in the crowd, and we become guilty of communicating to a congregation—not individuals; to groups and not persons; to classes and not individual students.

Aren't you glad Jesus Christ died for *you*—as well as the world? Remember, in His mind you are one among many, but also the very hairs of your head are numbered!

This New Testament principle is particularly important in our present culture where technology and mass communication are in vogue. The tendency is to forget the individual.

There is no substitute for personal contact. Paul's illustration of ministering to the Thessalonians like a "mother nursing a child" and communicating with each one "as a father would [with] his own children" are powerful examples (1 Thes. 2:7, 11). People respond to personal attention. This is the way God made us. Therefore mass communication *must* never become a substitute for face-to-face interaction.

Interestingly, some evangelicals react against technology per se. It must be emphasized that technology in itself is not "evil." In fact, technology—if used appropriately and with wisdom—can greatly help us to put the personal touch back in communication. But, ironically, many of those Christians who react the most against technology are often the ones who violate the principle of personal contact. They do so by substituting a "pulpit only" type ministry. Their primary outreach is to groups, and their main approach is verbalization. Unfortunately they are striking out at the wrong thing. A deeper concern—and far more significant—is their violation of a biblical principle of communication so clearly demonstrated in the Word of God. We *must* carefully balance our ministry to groups, as well as to individuals.

In doing so, Christian leaders must establish priorities. Furthermore, it is impossible to apply this principle in a growing church without developing a team of pastors who will take this principle seriously. This is why multiple leadership is such an important concept in the New Testament. Even before elders were ever appointed in Thessalonica, Paul and Silas and Timothy beautifully demonstrated this principle in founding and establishing the church. It would have been impossible for one man to communicate with each one "as a father would his own children." But *together* they accomplished the task.

SMALL AND LARGE GROUPS
Fourth, effective Christian communication must include an in-depth ministry to a select group as well as a ministry to the larger group of Christians.

Once again we see this principle illustrated, both in the communication model of Christ and particularly in the ministry of Paul. While Jesus Christ was ministering to a variety of groups and individuals, He was at the same time preparing the Twelve for a specialized ministry. While Paul was traveling about preaching and teaching, he was building his life into Timothy, who was his traveling companion.

The results of Paul's "discipling process" in the life of Timothy were capsuled when he wrote to this young pastor-teacher while he was stationed at Ephesus: "And the things which you have heard from me in the presence of many witnesses, these entrust to faithful men, who will be able to teach others also" (2 Tim. 2:2).

In these words of Paul to Timothy we have not only a tribute to Paul's unique approach to communication, but here is also a reinforcement of the communication principle under consideration in Timothy's ministry. This process was to be continued. Timothy was to select "faithful men" that he in turn could disciple. And these men were in turn to "teach others."

We cannot communicate with all people in depth. It is a human impossibility! Even Christ, our Lord, concentrated on a select few. But we can, while "equipping all saints to do the work of the ministry," equip a few chosen individuals in a specialized way. It will be these people who will in a unique way multiply our ministry.

But here again many Christians get off balance. It is either the "multitude" or the "individual." It is either the "large group" or the "small group." It is either an "in-depth ministry" or a "general exposure." The Bible, of course, teaches it must be "both-and"—not "either-or." And again it takes a team of spiritual leaders to effectively apply this principle.

GET BEYOND THE "WORD" LEVEL
Fifth, for communication to be qualitative, it must get beyond the verbalization level. This is particularly true in training people in depth.

Christians often stop at the "word" level. We are so conditioned to thinking "verbally" that we feel awkward in a context that is characterized by total involvement.

With Christ, it was verbalization, plus visualization, plus actual involvement. (See figure 23.) He did not stop at the first level. He verbalized, yes, but visualized wherever possible, and as He trained the Twelve, He got them totally involved in the process. They learned by doing. Their failures, as well as their successes, became

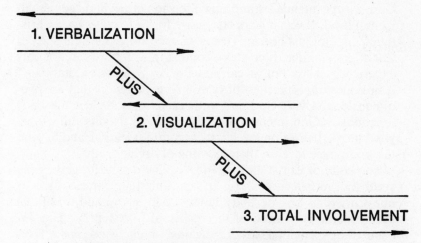

Figure 23. Biblical Communication Levels

the backdrop against which Christ spoke the deep truths of God. And even after they had *experienced* many things, He still remarked: "I have many more things to say to you, but you cannot bear them now" (John 16:12). They had not yet "experienced" the separation from Him and the trauma of His arrest, crucifixion, and His resurrection. *Then* they would understand His words even more fully.

"Words," of course, are basic to communication. They are God's unique invention, and through the *written* Word of God they have become a primary means by which He has revealed His will to mankind.

But if we are to follow the example of New Testament leaders, particularly in equipping individuals for a ministry in depth, we must get beyond the verbalization level, particularly in a culture that is more and more oriented toward sensory experience. The "Sesame Street" generation is on us, and in many respects McLuhan is correct: "The medium has become the message." No amount of criticism or reaction will change this reality. It is here! Our responsibility then is to respond to this challenge with effective Christian communication.

These "new" concepts should not be new at all to Christians. God *always* intended communication to get beyond the verbalization level. It was *always* His desire for us to *experience* Christian truth, not just hear it. This is why the concept of the body of Christ is so unique. It creates a context in which we can not only experience Christ, but we can actually "experience one another." It provides opportunities for relational experiences that are two-dimensional—with God and with each other. When the body functions as God intended it to function, Christians will get beyond the verbalization level in their communication, and beyond the knowledge level in their learning of divine truth.

The body of Christ also is God's divine means for getting beyond the verbalization level in our Christian witness. It is as non-Christians *see* the body functioning in *love* and *unity* that they become convinced of the reality of Christianity. This becomes the experiential backdrop against which "words *about* Jesus Christ" take on meaning and true significance. McLuhan's phrase then, "the medium is the message," is actually a biblical concept.

It is the *medium* (the body of Christ) that actually *becomes* the message to the unsaved world. And it is the "functioning body" that becomes the context in which believers can grow to maturity.

But this leads us to another significant New Testament principle of communication.

EXAMPLE IS BASIC

Sixth, in Christian communication, example is foundational to effective verbalization. No amount of words can overcome the power of hypocrisy. Nor will words alone do what the power of positive example can achieve.

This was the distinctive characteristic of Paul, Silas, and Timothy. This is the basic reason why these Macedonian missionaries obtained such outstanding results. "You are witnesses and so is God," they wrote, "how devoutly and uprightly and blamelessly we behaved toward you believers" (1 Thes. 2:10). No individual could point his finger at these Christian leaders and accuse them of inconsistent Christian living. They demonstrated with their lives what they were communicating with their lips.

This is why Paul laid such great emphasis on proper moral and ethical behavior as a criteria by which church leaders should be selected. This is why he chose Timothy; he was "well spoken of by the brethren" (Acts 16:2). This is why all of the New Testament writers emphasized the importance of "walking worthily" before each other, and particularly the unsaved world. It is as Christ becomes incarnate within the body of Christ that Christian communication develops its power, and "words" become meaningful. People may forget "what we say" but they never forget "what we are."

This leads to another important point when discussing the principle of exemplary living. Frequently the *way* something is said is far more important than *what* is said. "And the Lord's bond-servant must not be quarrelsome, but be kind to all ... with gentleness correcting those who are in opposition" (2 Tim. 2:24-25), wrote Paul to Timothy. Elders too must not be "self-willed" or "quick-tempered" (Titus 1:7). Many Christians have not even "been heard" because of a bad example or the tactless use of words. There is truth in the maxim: "the way we live speaks so loudly they cannot hear what we say."

Have you ever wondered why Paul could say some of the things he did and get away with it? After all, he "pulled no punches" when writing to the Corinthians, and he "minced no words" in his communication with the Galatians.

Actually the answer is quite simple. When people know "you love them," it is amazing what you can say and still be heard. But let them doubt your love, your concern, and sincerity, and your words will become "as a noisy gong or a clanging cymbal."

SACRIFICE AND HARD WORK
Seventh, effective Christian communication doesn't just happen— it takes self-sacrifice and hard work.

There is something very demanding about getting involved in the lives of people. There is a price that must be paid. You not only exert physical energy, but there is an emotional and spiritual drain that often leaves the dedicated Christian leader exhausted.

While on earth Jesus Christ was, of course, the most selfless Person who ever lived. He gave *everything*—including His life— that men might live. But at the human level, the Apostle Paul is an amazing example. While in Thessalonica, he and Timothy and Titus worked "night and day" so as not to be burdensome to these people. Paul was so intent on not communicating false motives that he at times did not take what was rightfully his (1 Cor. 9:1-15).

But Paul paid a price for his devotion to Christ's work. He himself testified that his greatest burden was "the daily pressure" upon him because of his "concern for all of the churches" (2 Cor. 11:28). He often agonized over believers who were immature and in need of spiritual growth and development (Gal. 4:19-20). He, like no other servant of Jesus Christ, bore in his body the "brandmarks of Jesus" (Gal. 6:17).

To be an effective communicator, we cannot resist hard work and involvement. To reach all classes of people—both groups and individuals—and to build our lives into certain people in depth, all of this calls for effort and hard work. God never called us to a life of ease and leisure. Our lives are not our own. We are bought with a price! Responsibility calls for accountability.

Here again we see the uniqueness of the body of Christ. God did not call each one of us to carry out the Great Commission alone. He did not call each one of us to be an "Apostle Paul" or even "a Timothy." But He does expect each member of the body to function and contribute to the work of Christ. With the grace that is given to each of us "according to the measure of Christ's gift" (Eph. 4:7), we must participate *diligently* in God's great plan.

BE FREE AND FLEXIBLE
Eighth, Christians must never get locked into certain methods of communication, but always be free and flexible.

As evangelicals we have allowed ourselves to absolutize in the use of various communication forms. We have tended to fixate on certain approaches to communication, particularly in our preaching and teaching methodology.

Where in Scripture are we told to preach three-point sermons, or to deliver thirty-minute messages without interruption?

Where are we told to prepare and deliver lectures on various books of the Bible? Or to expand on topics which we trace through the Scriptures?

Don't misunderstand! These are effective ways to communicate. But the problem is that there are some who seem to believe that their way is the *biblical* way.

The fact is that we are hard pressed to find illustrations of the way we preach and teach today. Most examples in Scripture are greatly varied and far more spontaneously developed and delivered than our particular approaches. And we certainly cannot find any consistent form or pattern in the way Scripture was written. We have a great variety of approaches to written communication from one Bible book to another, with a majority of New Testament books being personal letters. Most of these are not highly structured. Each one varies in form and literary style, depending on the need of the recipients and the background of the author.

We fail to realize that communication patterns are relative and very much related to the culture in which we live at any given moment in history. Even in our own American culture we are seeing some tremendous changes in the way communication takes place and what people respond to. As McLuhan points out, we have moved from what he calls an emphasis on "hot" to "cool" communication. Eventually we will shift in another direction, particularly in this technological age, which is creating a number of upheavals in many areas of our lives.

Many Christians have superimposed upon Scripture certain methods which they feel are biblical but which are purely cultural. For example, what do *you* think of when you hear the words of Paul to Timothy, which instructed him to "preach the word"? (2 Tim. 4:2) If you are typical, you will not think of this function per se, but you will think of the *way* you have experienced preaching taking place in your lifetime. The tendency is to equate the *way* we preach with the biblical imperative *to preach*. Actually Paul does not tell us *how* to preach, and the word here correctly means *to proclaim*. But again he doesn't tell us *how* to proclaim the Word. He did, however, demonstrate in his own way a variety of ways to carry out this injunction.

The preaching methodology, which we have come to accept as the "biblical way," has come to us through cultural and educational developments. "One-way" communication, particularly, is a product of the development of oratorical skills which have grown out of the Greek and Roman culture.

All of this is not to say that to use these methods is wrong. They have proved to be very effective in certain situations and under certain circumstances. What *is* wrong is to get locked in to a "way" of communication that is supposed to be only a means to a divine end. What makes it doubly wrong is to classify it as a biblical norm. We must be free to develop new approaches to communication and free to disband old and ineffective forms and structures. The challenge is to allow ourselves to be guided by the principles of Scripture which will keep our eyes focused on guidelines and which will help us to be contemporary though biblical.

SUMMARY

We are experiencing a communications revolution in our society. Evangelical Christians must accept the challenge of creatively communicating the message of Christ and His Word to a people who are bombarded with the latest in communication technique. In a day of satellite communication and earth-lunar dialogues, Christians need to focus clearly the New Testament principles of communication. These principles both guard us against extreme influences by science and technology and yet set us free to be creative under the leadership of the Holy Spirit.

1. Christian communication is a distinctive process, including both human and divine elements.
2. Christian communication should be to all kinds and classes of people.
3. Christian communication should be carefully balanced between a ministry to groups, as well as a ministry to individuals.
4. Effective Christian communication must include an in-depth ministry to a select group, as well as a ministry to the larger group of Christians.
5. For communication to be qualitative it must get beyond the verbalization level.
6. In Christian communication, example is foundational to verbalization.
7. Effective Christian communication doesn't just happen—it takes self-sacrifice and hard work.
8. Christians must never get locked into certain patterns and forms in communication but be free and flexible under the leadership of the Holy Spirit.

PART TWO
THE LENS OF HISTORY

The second part of this study is designed to assist you in viewing the contemporary church through the lens of history. Part I treats biblical history, particularly, New Testament history.

But Part II focuses in on a particular kind of church history—the history of forms and structures. It surveys especially the reflections of institutionalism from the pages of the past. But, perhaps most important, are the lessons we can learn from the *immediate* past, those lessons that grow out of the study of the church in the twentieth century.

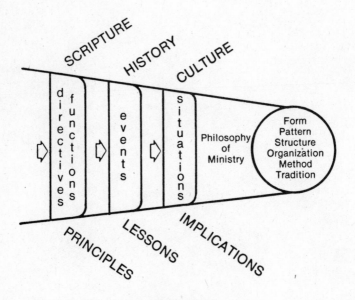

Lens of History

SEVENTEEN

INSTITUTIONALISM IN HISTORY

The process of institutionalization is a recurring phenomenon among God's people. What makes this pitfall particularly dangerous is that it is not exclusively related to the church or other Christian organizations. It happens naturally wherever you have people who band together to achieve certain objectives. People, plus structure, plus age more often than not, equal institutionalism.

And all elements are necessary, for wherever you have people, you have function; and wherever you have function, you need some kind of form and structure. And *age,* of course, is inevitable, for time marches on.

But more specifically, what is "institutionalism"? Let's look at it first as a natural phenomenon.

WHAT OF THE SECULAR WORLD?

John W. Gardner, past president of the Carnegie Corporation, has said: "Like people and plants, organizations have a life cycle. They have a green and supple youth, a time of flourishing strength, and a gnarled old age."[1]

Rather than defining "institutionalism" per se, it may be easier to look at the symptoms of institutionalism—when has it happened? Or, when is it beginning to happen?

Institutionalism is in process when:

1. The organization (the form and structure) becomes more important than the people who make up the organization.
2. Individuals begin to function in the organization more like cogs in a machine.
3. Individuality and creativity are lost in the structural mass.
4. The atmosphere in the organization becomes threatening, rather than open and free; people are often afraid to ask uncomfortable questions.
5. The structural arrangements in the organization have become rigid and inflexible.
6. People are serving the organization more than the objectives for which the organization was brought into existence. In other words, means have become ends.
7. Communication often breaks down, particularly because of a repressive atmosphere and lots of red tape.
8. People become prisoners of their procedures. The "policy manual" and the "rule book" get bigger, and fresh ideas are few and far between.
9. In order to survive in a cold structure, people develop their own special interests within the organization, creating competitive departments and divisions. The corporate objective gives way to a multitude of unrelated objectives which, inevitably, results in lack of unity in the organization as a whole.
10. Morale degenerates; people lose their initiative; they become discouraged and often critical of the organization and of others in the organization—particularly its leaders.
11. As the organization gets bigger and as time passes, the process of institutionalization often speeds up. A hierarchy of leadership develops, increasing the problems of communication from the top to the bottom and the bottom to the top. People toward the bottom, or even in the middle of the organizational structure, feel more and more as if they "really don't count" in the organization.

When you have these symptoms in an organization, institutionalism is already in its advanced stages.

But there is a note of optimism that grows out of the study of the history of organizations and institutions. Again, let me quote Gardner:

Organizations differ from people and plants in that their cycle isn't even approximately predictable. An organization may go from youth to old age in two or three decades, or it may last for centuries. More important, it may go through a period of stagnation and then revive. In short, decline is not inevitable. Organizations need not stagnate. They often do, to be sure, but that is because the arts of organizational renewal are not yet widely understood. Organizations can renew themselves continuously.[2]

The principles of organizational renewal actually work. More and more, even secularists are discovering what these rules are and are beginning to apply them in the secular community.

WHAT OF THE PEOPLE OF GOD?

Church history reveals at least three major periods of institutionalism among the people of God, with many smaller segments and periods of institutionalism in between.

Judaism. The first main period of institutionalism involves the Children of Israel after they returned from Babylonian Captivity. For a while, under the leadership of Ezra and Nehemiah, new life was evident among God's chosen people. But by the time Jesus Christ arrived on the scene, the nation of Israel as a whole, and its religious system particularly, had become so encrusted with institutionalism that it was nigh unto impossible to recognize truth from tradition.

It was at this "religious system" that Jesus directed His sharpest barbs. For example, when His disciples were criticized by the Pharisees for plucking the heads of grain on the Sabbath, Jesus retorted: "The Sabbath was made for man, and not man for the Sabbath" (Mark 2:27). In other words, He was saying, "You have taken a *means* and made it an *end* in itself. You have completely lost sight of the spirit of the Law. You have lost the individual in your religious system. All you have left is an empty form."

Again and again Jesus put His finger on the devastating results of institutionalism. He reminded the religious leaders that they had successfully preserved their religious system, their "orthodoxy," and their tradition, and had even led the majority of the people into an external conformity with the outward expressions of their religion. But they had lost the individual; they had no deep understanding of God's truth; their followers had no vital and real experience with the living God.

Roman Catholicism. In the panorama of church history, the vibrant, pulsating New Testament church that grew out of Judaism eventually gave way to a stagnant, lifeless Roman church. As always, there were pockets of vitality and pure Christianity; but as a whole, the church was doomed to hundreds of years of institutionalized religion. When the Edict of Milan gave legal status to Christianity, many became "Christians" because it was the popular thing to do.

It was against this religious system that the Reformers rose up to defend biblical truth and personalized Christianity. Religion had become a matter of form and ceremony, not of life and experience. All kinds and varieties of tradition began to overshadow biblical truth. Abuses and pagan practices became rampant.

But notice! The Roman church was preserved—in all of its "bigness" and power—even to this day. Its authoritarian approach to education and its transmissive communication preserved the church's "orthodoxy," and until very recently, very few within the system questioned its demands and dogmas.

It is important to point out at this juncture that "bigness" is not necessarily a sign of true spiritual success. "Numbers" can be very deceiving. "Followers" are relatively easy to find, if one works hard enough and shouts loud enough to make his voice heard above the many that are crying for the attention of people today. And once people are in a religious system and accepts its dogmas, most can be controlled by guilt tactics and fear of rejection.

But what are they following? What do they believe? What of their lives? Where are we leading them?

These are the crucial questions! Let us not be deceived by numbers, for if Jesus Christ's success on earth had been measured by numbers, He must be classified as a failure. There were times, of course, when multitudes followed Him, when His disciples multiplied; but there also came a time when "many of His disciples withdrew, and were not walking with Him any more" (John 6:66). The price was too great for these people to follow Jesus Christ (6:60).

This is not to say that numbers are not significant. In the early days of the church, thousands were added to the company of believers (Acts 2:41), and "the number of the disciples continued to increase greatly" (6:7). But true success was measured by the results that were being achieved in the lives of people. Just so today, we must measure our success by biblical criteria—not by how many people attend on Sunday morning, or Sunday evening, or on Wednesday night, or how many we have enrolled in our Sunday School. Some even measure success by the total number of meetings that have been conducted in a given period of time. Activity per se is not a correct measuring rod. The results of these activities (biblical results) are!

Reformation Churches. And so the reformers reacted against the institutionalism and the dead orthodoxy of the Roman church. But with what did they replace it?

For a time—life and vitality! The authority of the Bible, justification by faith, and the priesthood of every believer became cardinal doctrines once again. Conversion became a matter of personal relationship with Jesus Christ, particularly among adults who saw the light. But what of their children? What of their tolerance of others? What of their forms and structures and approaches to communication? What of their eventual outcome?

You cannot *force* Christian community. Some leaders eventually refused others the same liberty and freedom they had demanded for themselves. Education was controlled and directed by Protestant state churches, and degenerated into the same stereotyped, traditional and authoritarian system from which they came. Correct doctrine per se was not the answer!

The Free Church Movement. Out of the institutionalized religion that soon developed in the Reformation churches came a variety of groups that wished to maintain the vitality and freshness they saw reflected in the New Testament. The discovery of America provided a natural means by which many could begin anew. But in many instances, even in these early days, the same "institutionalism" was transferred from the Continent to the New World. It was a constant struggle, as it has always been, for the true believers to keep a proper focus on biblical objectives and principles, and to keep from becoming institutionalized.

An interesting phenomenon, however, hit the shores of America in the 1900s that was destined to be a blessing in disguise for the evangelical church. The stormy winds of liberal theology threatened the very life of Bible-believing Christians. Battering away at the very foundations of historic Christianity, liberal theologians and natural scientists made Bible-believing Christians study, think, pray, and act as never before.

True, the majority of seminaries went liberal and many Christian colleges followed suit, but in their place came the Bible institutes and the Bible conference movement, and eventually the evangelical seminaries. From these training institutions, came men and women who believed the Bible as the Word of God; believed in personal conversion; and generally speaking, believed in the local church as God's primary means for the edification of believers.

In the '40s and '50s liberalism began to retreat—not necessarily because of the fervor of evangelical Christians—but more because of liberal theologians themselves, who began to question the very presuppositions of their own theology. Two world wars blasted hard at the very core of their thinking—that man is basically good and that the world is destined to get better. In its place came a new theology, frequently called neo-orthodoxy, but with little in common with classic Christianity, except in its terminology. Its proponents tried desperately to be relevant, and contemporary, and to meet the needs of mankind in a world that appeared on the brink of disaster. Racial hatred, wars, pollution, overpopulation, conflicting ideologies, and the threat of nuclear disaster were common topics for discussion among the leaders of the world in both religious and secular circles.

The Church at Large. The Protestant church at large is, without doubt, institutionalized. It is criticized by young and old alike. It not only has become a victim of its form and ceremony, but it has lost its direction. It no longer has an absolute guide to determine its objectives and from which to get its principles to guide it in its function.

Many religious leaders recognize the symptoms of institutionalism in the church at large. They are trying desperately to pump new life into a dying corpse by means of "form" changes and a renewed emphasis on the individual. They really *try* to care—to interact with the issues that surround us on every hand—in some cases putting evangelical Christians to shame.

But they are no more successful than the university or the social organization in obtaining ultimate success, for even though they can meet the physical needs of people, and in some ways their psychological needs, they have no way to change the heart, the inner being. The true message of Christianity—personal conversion and a supernatural new birth through the indwelling and living Christ—has been basically eliminated from modern theology. A comfortable universalism has replaced the hard realities of eternal lostness outside of Jesus Christ and "situation ethics," which has no foundations in the absolute values of Scripture, is rampant within the religious community. Without the true message of the Gospel and God's eternal laws for Christlike living, all efforts toward helping people are ultimately doomed to failure. No amount of organizational renewal can save the church at large.

It should be noted that many of the mainline Protestant denominations as well as the Roman Catholic Church have been influenced significantly by the charismatic renewal movement. There is no question that this has impacted churches that are basically permeated either by dead orthodoxy or liberal teaching, bringing into existence pockets of spiritual vitality. Unfortunately, much of what is happening is more *experience oriented* than *Word oriented.* Theological convictions have grown more out of personal and existential factors than out of the Bible. Consequently, it is difficult to predict how long this phenomenon will continue to impact Christianity. Whenever sound and systematic Bible study and teaching is neglected, there will always be a lack of depth leading to superficial experience and various kinds of excesses.

The Evangelical Church. What of the Bible-believing church? It has grown and become more popular than ever before and *has* penetrated society. Some of its key spokesmen are household names among the leaders of the world.

Evangelicalism has come into its own as a worldwide movement. There are many signs of encouragement. In spite of the pressures of secularism and materialism, and the obvious moral decline in our culture as a whole, evangelical Christianity is continuing to make an impact. The advent of the drug culture, sensualism, and the mystical cults actually created a vacuum into which Bible-believing Christians have been able to enter with the message of Jesus Christ. Youth, particularly, who have been subtly led into a way of life that has left them in a whirlpool of despair, are responding to the authority of the Bible and its redeeming message. Campus organizations such as Campus Crusade for Christ, Inter-Varsity Christian Fellowship, and The Navigators are experiencing unparalleled opportunities to communicate the Gospel to disillusioned youth. Furthermore, these organizations are also impacting the church in its areas of weakness.

But what about the local church in the evangelical community? Here too there are some definite encouragements. Bible-believing churches are growing. Generally, there is a strong faith in the authority of Scripture and the need for personal salvation. Many Christians, though affected in their thinking by materialism and secularism, still have a deep desire to be in the will of God. There is a strong commitment on the part of many to the local church itself, including those who head parachurch organizations. Many pastors are teaching the Word of God as never before and there is general concern for evangelism and edification. Never have we had so many educational agencies within the church, and so many excellent materials and tools available to reach all age levels.

But somehow, with all of these strengths, the voice of the ancient apostle comes echoing across the centuries: "I know your deeds and your toil and perseverance. . . . I know your deeds, and your love and faith and service. . . . But I have this against you" (Rev. 2:2, 19-20). Something is wrong with the evangelical church! This, of course, is not strange language, for something is always wrong and will always be wrong with the church on earth. We can never be perfect while in bondage to mortality. But there seems to be something distinctly wrong in the local church, a lack of focus that need not be; something that can be corrected by means of making some proper adjustments.

Here we can learn a vital lesson from history. Every growing movement eventually faces the threat of creeping institutionalism. Evangelical Christianity is facing this threat today, particularly in an era of rapid church growth. It is in particular danger because it has moved from the crisis of fighting for its life into a period of unparalleled popularity—a trend that usually produces institutionalization.

At this juncture we need to remind ourselves of what happened to previous movements among the people of God. We need to look carefully at the results of institutionalized religion.

REFLECTIONS OF INSTITUTIONALISM

Judaism, Roman Catholicism and the Reformation churches preserved their religious system, but they lost sight of the individual. In fact, the system in each instance—its dogmas and traditions and its forms and structures—eventually became more important than the people themselves.

These movements also preserved their "orthodoxy," but their adherents failed to appropriate a deeper and personal comprehension of God's truth. People gave mental assent to doctrine, but there was little relationship to their daily living. Being a part of the movement was little different from belonging to a club, society, or group in the secular world. In many cases traditions overshadowed the Word of God.

These movements all gained external conformity on the part of their followers, but apart from inner experience. People religiously performed routines and rituals, but without true spiritual meaning. Their religion became a matter of form and ceremony, not life and experience. A personal relationship with God was replaced with an impersonal relationship with an organization.

All of these movements perpetuated themselves by means of an education that was authoritarian, stereotyped, and transmissive. They utilized indoctrination with little room for creative thinking and freedom. The learning atmosphere became nonpermissive.

All of these movements developed a hierarchy of leaders, who in turn developed a careful and logical system of theology. It was the leaders who did the "thinking" and the "communicating," while the ordinary people became the recipients and followers of the wisdom of the sages.

As these movements grew and enlarged, structure and form became rigid and inflexible. In fact, their means and ways of doing things eventually became ends in themselves and as sacred in the minds of people as their beliefs.[3]

SUMMARY
It is the thesis of this chapter that history can tell us something very important. As evangelicals we often confuse functions and forms and what is absolute and what is non-absolute. When we do, our churches move rapidly in the direction of becoming institutionalized.

But what are some of the specific symptoms? It is to this question we turn in the next chapter.

Footnotes

[1]John W. Gardner, "How to Prevent Organizational Dry Rot," *Harper,* October 1965, p. 20.
[2]Ibid.
[3]For a helpful treatment of the problems of institutionalism in the church, see Findley B. Edge *A Quest for Vitality in Religion* (Nashville: Broadman, 1963). Though this book was written over two decades ago, its primary message on this phenomenon is even more relevant today.

EIGHTEEN

REFLECTIONS OF INSTITUTIONALISM IN THE EVANGELICAL CHURCH

The phenomenon of creeping institutionalism in the evangelical church in the latter part of the twentieth century is unique. In some respects it is a different kind of institutionalism than at any other time in history.

True, the institutionalism we see today has many similarities to that of the past. There are certain common elements wherever and whenever institutionalization takes place.

But there are also some unique elements, the most important being our *biblical* orthodoxy. Is it possible to believe the Bible is the Word of God and to communicate it to others with expertise, and yet be a victim of institutionalism?

PROBLEMS CREATED

1. *Our greatest strength has helped create some of our greatest problems.* The strongest feature of the evangelical church has been its adherence to the Bible as its final authority in faith and practice. Though there is a variety of interpretations in some areas of theology, most evangelicals, in spite of the errancy movement, are in agreement regarding the Bible as being the inspired and inerrant Word of God.

This emphasis has helped greatly to preserve historic Christianity. Wherever groups have departed from this basic starting point, history reveals there is an eventual movement away from the clear teachings of the Scriptures regarding Jesus Christ and salvation, as well as other important fundamental doctrines.

Our valiant fight for survival in the early 1900s against the inroads of liberalism successfully preserved the fundamentals of the faith. This was really the roots of what eventually became a strong, evangelical scholarship, which has given evangelical Christianity a decided respectability and sophistication.

But something has happened, particularly in our strong Bible-teaching churches. By emphasizing the Bible as the Word of God—and rightly so—as well as its doctrinal teachings, we have put a strong emphasis on studying the Bible and transmitting it to others. This, in turn, has become a primary objective of many evangelical churches, a worthy objective, to say the least.

Several things have transpired. First, to carry out this objective, we began to train qualified people to teach the Bible. Evangelical schools—first Bible institutes and colleges and later seminaries—designed curriculums to teach young men and women a knowledge of the content of the Scriptures so that they might transmit it to others.

Second, the people trained in these schools went into churches and taught as they were taught. Many became ardent expositors (in some instances, "little professors") and the people were their "students." In Sunday morning services, on Sunday evenings, during the midweek service, and in Sunday School classes, some people have listened to three or four or even five expositions a week. In the '20s and '30s, when people were starved for the Word of God, which had been ripped from the pulpits of the land, this was a refreshing breeze from heaven.

However, a problem has emerged. Many laymen have become ardent "listeners." There is little opportunity for personal interaction with other members of the body of Christ, or little opportunity for expressing the Word in their own lives. In many churches the functioning body has been replaced with a trained and talented individual.

Fortunately, young pastors can take what they have learned in schools and transmit it to others as they turn their churches into miniature Bible schools and seminaries. But, for the most part, those who are on the listening end in the churches absorb the Word but have no similar outlet.

Third, church structures and patterns are often designed to carry out this Bible-teaching objective. Church sanctuaries, functionally speaking, often become "lecture halls," and educational buildings become academic centers. Preaching well-organized sermons (or put another way, delivering high-powered Bible lectures) has become the primary means of teaching the Word of God.

Thus our concentration on biblical authority and the importance of learning and transmitting its message has led some evangelicals to neglect some other extremely important emphases in the Scriptures. As we've already observed in our study, learning the Word of God is foundational to Christian growth. But what of other experiences Christians need to become mature believers? What about the New Testament emphasis on the importance of the body of Christ functioning in all of its parts in order to build itself up? How can all members of the body participate in this process when they are consistently "forced" to sit and listen to one man teach or preach? In many instances there are no opportunities for mutual ministry.

And what about the New Testament atmosphere that emphasizes *koinonia,* that unique fellowship with one another where Christians bear one another's burdens and "thus fulfill the Law of Christ"? To what extent do our church structures and patterns lend themselves to bringing about this kind of New Testament experience?

And what about that unique New Testament experience of worship and fellowship with God that grows naturally out of a heart full of gratitude to God, not only for His Word, but for fellow believers? To what extent do our typical "worship services" and "prayer meetings" result in true worship?

In many churches our failure to provide balanced New Testament experiences for believers has resulted in an emphasis on correct doctrine and a knowledge of the Scriptures, but has neglected other important needs that create mature Christian personalities. Consequently, we have moved toward a sterile, though biblical orthodoxy, a very dangerous move in the direction of institutionalized religion. One well-meaning layman put it well when she said, "I take notes in my Bible at every meeting of the church and I have all of this wonderful Bible information, but something is really lacking in my life. Something is wrong in my Christian experience."

THE SOUL-WINNING STATION

2. *Emphasizing the church as a soul-winning station has also contributed its share to the process of institutionalization.* This is really a different kind of problem than the one just described. In a sense, it is an opposite-type problem, one you don't really find in the strong Bible-teaching church. In the "evangelistic-oriented" church we often find a decided lack in good Bible teaching. The frequent complaint is that "all the preacher ever preaches is the simple Gospel message." And often he preaches these "Gospel messages" to a church full of Christians. Pastors of these churches put a strong emphasis on bringing unsaved people to the church to "hear the Gospel." The church becomes the center of all activity in reaching the unsaved world. Laymen are taught by word and example that their evangelistic task is to "bring them in" to hear the Gospel.

This approach brought rather successful results in the early 1900s, primarily because then many unsaved people were religiously oriented. Many had already been exposed to the fundamentals of the faith and were at one time "church people." But times have changed! Many neighbors and work associates are pure pagans. They could care less about ever going to church—especially evangelistic meetings. And as times have changed, so have the number of non-Christians who consent to come to a church building. But in many instances the "preacher" is still preaching the Gospel as if they were there. Consequently, Christians are starving for good Bible teaching.

Incidentally, this is why many Christians leave these churches and seek out good Bible-teaching churches. Their initial response in their new environment is one of great satisfaction. But over a period of time they become saturated with Bible truth, and then their experience parallels that just described in the previous section.

But what about the church as an evangelistic center? First of all, one of the basic objectives of the church *is* to reach the unsaved world. But the purpose of the "church gathered" as described in the New Testament is not to provide a setting for the pastor to preach evangelistic sermons to unsaved people who are brought to church by church members.

Again, don't misunderstand—this does not mean that unsaved people should not be welcomed in the church or even invited. Otherwise, they may not see the body of Christ functioning in love and unity, a vital means of reaching non-Christians. However, there is not a single reference in the New Testament to structuring a church service for unsaved people. Only in 1 Corinthians do we see Paul instructing the Christians to be orderly in their service, lest some unsaved person come in and think these Christians are out of their minds (1 Cor. 14:23). But here again Paul was emphasizing the importance of a service properly ordered for Christians (14:24). The non-Christian, observing the body of Christ functioning properly to build up itself, would then be in a position to become convicted by the Holy Spirit and respond to the message of the Gospel (14:24-25).

Many churches that function as evangelistic centers often have greater problems with institutionalism than the Bible-teaching churches. Without a good diet in the Word of God, activity and meetings become even more superficial and void of real scriptural meaning. Even fellowship opportunities degenerate into social contacts that are little different from social gatherings in the world. Fellowship, or *koinonia,* in the biblical sense is *more* than "coffee and doughnuts" and human beings relating to each other on the human level. Within the context of *biblical koinonia,* even partaking of food will become a more meaningful experience (Acts 2:42).

In addition to superficial experiences (a distinct reflection of religious institutionalism), many Christians in these churches have their eyes focused on the church as a meeting place. They hear and experience so frequently that the church is the place for spiritual activity that they become "building oriented."

An emphasis on the "church gathered" is commendable and biblical. But a church in the biblical sense is not a building or simply an organization, or even a place of meeting—but an organism, a body of believers meeting together. And "why" Christians meet is of utmost importance! From a biblical point of view, it is *not* to listen to a pastor preach an evangelistic sermon. Nor is it to just listen to the pastor-teacher expound the Word. Rather, the total structure of the church is to provide an opportunity for believers to be edified through total body function. There will need to be a time when the Word of God is taught. But there must also be times when believers can experience true "family of God" relationships. As a result of these vital experiences, they are in turn to minister to their own families, minister to other believers, and be effective witnesses for Jesus Christ in the unsaved world.

EXISTENCE VS. CAUSE

3. *We are beginning to support the "institution" rather than its reason for existing.* Put another way, we are more concerned *with* existence than our *cause* for existence.

This problem is reflected in the way we evaluate success. As long as we have lots of activity, lots of people coming, lots of "decisions," an enlarging income, a growing pastoral staff, and an ongoing building program, we feel comfortably successful and evangelical. "The Lord is blessing," is our repeated evaluation. "The Holy Spirit is at work," echo the church-growth people.

Frequently, we show little concern for the content of our activities, as long as they are "going on." Whether or not "decisions" result in mature discipleship is often overlooked in the midst of everything else that is "happening."

And the people who come? Well, so long as *new* people are coming, it really doesn't matter *who* they are and *where* they come from and how long they stay. When they come, we report we are reaching people. The facts seem to be that many churches grow *only* because Christian people are on the move—from the center of the city to the suburbs, and from city to city, and from church to church. Few seem to be new Christians, reached for Christ by the local body of believers as they share their faith with neighbors, friends, and work associates.

Yet we feel successful because we are *growing*—and really without reaching a New Testament objective of penetrating the pagan community in which we live.

The problem of being concerned with "existence" more than our *reason* for existence is also reflected in the way we evaluate "spirituality," particularly as a pastoral staff. Our people "measure up" as long as they come and listen to our sermons, bring their children to all the activities we've planned for them, support the church with their offerings, willingly serve on boards and committees, and help keep the agencies of the church functioning by filling leadership slots. In short, as long as people *support the program,* we evaluate them as spiritually mature.

But what about their home life? Is the father the spiritual head of the home, spending time with his children individually and collectively? What about the relationship between mother and father? What about the spiritual climate as measured by biblical criteria?

Is each home a dynamic force in the community, reflecting Jesus Christ? How is the family relating to unsaved neighbors? Is the family given to hospitality, both among non-Christians as well as Christians?

What about the father's ethics in the business world? Is he a dynamic Christian witness in the way he lives as well as in the way he talks?

What about other aspects of our church life? Are believers really ministering to other members of the body of Christ, or do they use all of their time and effort just to keep the machinery of the church running smoothly? Are they really growing and developing in their Christian life? Or are they frantically running on a religious treadmill, getting wearier and more numb as each week passes by, and at the same time keeping their guilt level down because of their "Christian service"?

What about the overall climate in the church? Is it warm and inviting and personal, or do people come Sunday after Sunday, sit side by side in long pews, take notes in their Bibles, say "Amen," drop their money in the offering plate, and walk out without really coming to know other members of the Christian family, and without making any contribution to other members of the body of Christ?

All of these questions can go unanswered in many evangelical churches—can even be answered negatively—and yet we can evaluate our church as successful. The truth is, it may be existing beautifully as an organization but woefully lacking as a function-

ing New Testament organism. It is not achieving certain fundamental, biblical objectives.

BELIEF VS. CONDUCT

4. *We are emphasizing correct doctrine and frequently neglecting
the quality of one's life.* An important criterion for evaluating
spiritual maturity is often "what a man believes" and not "the
way he lives."

To be sure, what a person believes is basic and fundamental,
but the Bible is explicit and clear that it is "both/and," not "ei-
ther/or." The first eleven chapters in Paul's letter to the Romans
emphasize doctrine and the last five, Christian living. Likewise,
the Ephesian Epistle presents doctrine in the first three chapters,
and the last three chapters present the Christian's walk. The Bible
is clear that we are to be "doers of the Word, and not merely
hearers" (James 1:22).

It is possible to go into some evangelical churches and discover
there is little difference in the lifestyle of its members and that of
non-Christians. They may know the Bible, but their lives reflect
little of the fruit of the Spirit. On the other hand, many evangelical
churches have developed false criteria for evaluating spirituality—an unfortunate legalism that reflects the same spiritual sickness of the Pharisees. Spiritual depth is measured primarily by
externalities—certain "thou shalt nots" that have become standard in some Christian circles. If Christians *don't do* certain things,
they are automatically classified as spiritual. It is possible to re-
frain from many activities and be extremely carnal and yet to feel
"comfortably spiritual." And when it comes to basic Christian
attitudes toward both fellow Christians and unsaved people, particularly an attitude of love, there is a decided lack.

This is not to advocate total freedom—a concept that is very
nonbiblical. But both extremes—license or legalism—are a reflection of institutionalized Christianity. Again, we must evaluate
spiritual maturity by means of proper biblical criteria. And Jesus
stated the most important criterion. "By this all men will know
that you are My disciples, if you have love for one another" (John
13:35).

WHEN NONABSOLUTES BECOME ABSOLUTES

5. *We have allowed nonabsolutes to become absolutes.* This way of thinking is the most subtle of all in leading the church into institutionalism. That which is meant to be a *means* to an end, becomes an *end* in itself. We allow ourselves to get locked into patterns and structures that are no longer relevant and adequate to help us minister to the people who live in our contemporary culture.

It is vitally important for every believer to be able to differentiate between those areas of the Word of God that are absolute and never changing, and those areas that are relative and simply illustrative of the *way* the people of God in years past attempted to reach biblical objectives.

It is obvious from a careful study of the Scriptures that New Testament Christians considered certain doctrines absolute: that God exists; that He is a Spirit; that Jesus Christ was God in the flesh and that He came to die for the sins of the world; that man is in need of a Saviour; that salvation is by grace through faith; that there is a diabolical spiritual world which includes Satan and his evil forces; that Jesus Christ died, arose, ascended to heaven, and will come again. These and many other truths should never be changed if a church is to be "Christian" in the biblical sense.

Another area of obvious absolutes has to do with directives and objectives. The New Testament church consistently took the Great Commission seriously, both in the task of evangelism and edification. And there were certain qualifications for Christian leaders! There was to be no "give and take" in these matters.

But there is also much scriptural evidence to show that New Testament Christians did not consider certain forms and patterns and structures to be absolute. Rather, these were but means to carry out New Testament directives and reach New Testament objectives. When patterns do appear, they vary from situation to situation in the areas of communication and organization and administration.

But it is very important to note that these biblical examples are given for a purpose: to yield absolute principles for the church. A careful study of the *way* the first-century church proceeded to carry out the Great Commission reveals certain obvious guidelines that will enable the twentieth-century church to function in harmony with the New Testament church—*absolute in the essentials,* and *free and creative in devising contemporary approaches* to evangelism, edification, leadership, communication, and organization and administration. An important task facing Christian leaders of every generation is to make sure these principles and guidelines are accurately formulated and correctly focused.

SUMMARY
Evangelical churches in the twentieth century have a unique challenge to break the shackles of institutionalization that have already begun to bind and inhibit many organisms. One of the most encouraging lessons from history is that we need not be "locked in" to a continuous cycle of institutionalism. It can be broken; renewal can and must be constant. True believers, as no other group of people on earth, have the resources always to be what God wants us to be. If secular organizations can apply the principles of renewal and be successful, how much more can the family of God, particularly when it has principles that emerge from the eternal Word of God? And this is what renewal is all about.

PART THREE
THE LENS
OF CULTURE

Section III is a brief treatment of some of the most crucial problems in contemporary culture and how they affect the church. It is not designed to be exhaustive, but it is a place to begin.

This is a challenge that faces every generation of God's people. To ignore the changing world is to ignore reality and biblical responsibility.

If any lesson is clear from the New Testament, it is that the first-century church did not withdraw from society. Rather, it existed, expanded, and even thrived in a pagan culture. The twentieth-century church must do the same!

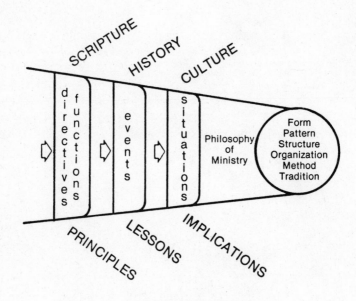

Lens of Culture

NINETEEN

CULTURAL IMPLICATIONS FOR THE TWENTIETH-CENTURY CHURCH

Prominent Christian personalities who walk across the pages of the New Testament *could not* and *did not* ignore cultures. Jesus Christ took into consideration cultural backgrounds, effectively demonstrated in His dealings with such people as the woman at the well, or in contrast, with Nicodemus. We see this demonstrated by the apostles, as they faced and solved the problem between the Hellenistic Jews and the native Hebrews in Jerusalem. We see it demonstrated by the church at Jerusalem, as they were confronted with the circumcision controversy. And we see it demonstrated in a most unusual way by Paul, both in his methodology and language, as he moved from the Jewish community out into the Greek culture.

WE MUST NOT IGNORE CULTURE

"Culture is a stern reality," acknowledged Dr. George Peters, professor of World Missions at Dallas Theological Seminary. "It is as extensive as man and as comprehensive as his ways, thoughts, sentiments, and relationships. It is the all-encompassing nonbiological atmosphere of his being as well as the institutions that make his life tolerable and mold him into the being he actually is."[1]

The twentieth-century church, then, must not ignore culture. If we do, we are neglecting a significant factor in formulating a

273

philosophy of the ministry that is truly biblical, and a contemporary strategy that is relevant, practical and workable.

What then are some cultural implications for the twentieth-century church?

MULTIPLE FACTORS AT WORK
First, and basically, the church of Jesus Christ must develop a correct perspective regarding the multiple factors at work in our American society. We must be realistic without being pessimistic. We must also be aware of reductionistic thinking, which causes us to say that our problems are caused by "this" or "that," or "something else." We are in trouble because of many factors.

Some Christians (along with many Americans who are Christian in name only) make the mistake of believing that a return to the "good old days" would solve our American problems. We must face the fact that those days are gone forever. They no longer exist. The population explosion, developing technology, and a big society have changed everything. We cannot return to a simple culture—apart from a nuclear holocaust which would simplify things fast, but not to our liking.

Some believe that if we could once again become a "Christian nation," we would be on our way back to stability. Again we must face reality. We never *were* a "Christian nation" in the true sense of the word. We were only a nation built on certain Christian principles; a nation that was soon populated by a majority who knew nothing of a "personal relationship with Jesus Christ." We can never, therefore, go back to something that never existed.

Some Christians believe that if we destroy the forces of Communism we will save America. Or if we clean up pornography and eradicate homosexuality we will turn the tide. All of these approaches—though some are noble an worthy objectives—are not based on realistic thinking regarding the overall problems. For Christians to exert their primary efforts in attempting to achieve these objectives, sidetracks them from more basic biblical injunctions. We must realize that apart from an unusual, supernatural intervention by God Himself, the church cannot save America. Our deep-rooted institutionalization, our departure from our founding principles, and our pluralistic thinking have so weakened us politically, morally, and spiritually that we stand on the brink of total decadence and disintegration.

But realism must not lead to pessimistic thinking on the part of a Christian. There is much we can do to minister to the needs of humanity and to penetrate culture, just as the New Testament Christians penetrated their culture. And though it seems impossible, humanly speaking, to turn the overall tide in America, we can make a tremendous impact for Jesus Christ.

A little careful reflection makes it difficult for those of us who have been privileged to live in the American society to understand why God has granted us this blessing. Many Christians before us and many of our contemporaries have never experienced the religious freedom and material blessings that we enjoy. But one thing is sure—with privilege goes responsibility, the responsibility to be totally Christian in all of our relationships and activities. We must, as Jesus commanded, love the Lord with all our hearts, and all our souls, and with all our minds, and our neighbors as ourselves (Matt. 22:37-39). This, of course, means both vertical and horizontal responsibilities. At the divine level we are to maintain a dynamic relationship with God, keeping ourselves untainted from this world system (1 Peter 2:11). At the human level we must love all men, both Christians and non-Christians.

DEVELOP A CORRECT VIEW OF HISTORY
Second, the church must develop a correct view of history. Life on this earth will not continue indefinitely. History is inevitably moving toward a great culmination. Eternity, for all men collectively, will eventually begin. Time as we know it will cease to exist. Most Christians, of course, "know" this "theologically," but we seem to live as if it is not true.

Many forces and factors seem to be combining and emerging in the total world environment, which point to the fulfillment of prophetic statements regarding the end of this age. The establishment of the nation of Israel is probably one of the most significant signs that could mean the soon return of Jesus Christ.

This correct view of history gives the Christian hope, no matter what happens in our society. It was a significant factor in sustaining the New Testament Christians, including the Apostle Paul. From their perspective they were looking for the return of Christ, within their lifetime, to deliver them from their cultural environment, and in many instances, the persecution that existed in the first century.

The twentieth-century church, then, must develop a correct philosophy of history, recognizing that when time runs out, our sojourn in space-time history will cease to exist. We will stand before Christ, to give account of what we have done with the time He has alloted us to carry out His purposes on earth. As American Christians, we will no doubt be evaluated in the light of the opportunities we have had to live in a culture that has provided us with more blessings and resources in life than any other people before us. We need to remind ourselves of the words of the Lord Jesus Christ Himself, who said while on earth, "And from everyone who has been given much shall much be required; and to whom they entrusted much, of him they will ask all the more" (Luke 12:48).

This concept leads us naturally to the next cultural implication.

Third, the church must understand clearly why God has left us on earth, and strive with His help to fulfill that purpose. Cultural problems can blur our purpose and sidetrack us onto peripheral issues.

The Bible is clear-cut at this point. We are not here *primarily* to make a living, or to build material security for ourselves and our families, both legitimate objectives. Furthermore, we are not on earth to save America from destruction, or to perpetuate the democratic system, again both noble goals. Our *primary task* is to fulfill the Great Commission of our Lord Jesus Christ, to both "make disciples" and to "teach those disciples." We are to be everlastingly busy at this task until Jesus Christ comes again.

This primary task does not mean we should not have earthly concerns: to provide for our families, both presently and in the future. It does not mean we should not be good citizens and do what we can to preserve our nation from moral and spiritual decay. Christians should be the *best citizens.* But all of these concerns must be kept in proper perspective, and must be subordinate to our ultimate purpose for being on earth. The sooner we realize—not just in our heads, but in our hearts—that we are but "aliens and strangers" on this earth (1 Peter 2:11; Heb. 11:13), the better we will fulfill the purpose God has left us on earth to fulfill.

SHOW CONCERN FOR LEADERS

Fourth, though "America is not our real home," the church must recognize it has a divine mandate to show a vital concern for our government leaders in the life of our nation. One of our primary responsibilities specified in Scripture is to pray for our national and international leaders. Paul made this clear to Timothy when he instructed him regarding the function of the New Testament church in relation to the political structure of his day. "I urge," he said, "that entreaties and prayers, petitions and thanksgivings, be made on behalf of all men, for kings and all who are in authority." But notice why we are to pray: ". . .in order that we may lead a tranquil and quiet life in all godliness and dignity. This is good and acceptable in the sight of God our Saviour, who desires all men to be saved and to come to the knowledge of the truth" (1 Tim. 2:1-4).[2]

The church, as it proceeds to carry out the Great Commission, must not neglect to *pray* for our national and international leaders, with a view that they may be able to lead in such a way as to maintain a cultural environment that is conducive to living for Jesus Christ, and also conducive to sharing Him with all men.

It is also clear from Scripture that "governing authorities" and the position they hold are related to God's sovereign wishes (Rom. 13:1). We must recognize this fact and fulfill our responsibility to them, even though they may be in error. This does not mean that we meekly tolerate sin and digression from the laws of God without voicing our disagreement. Assuredly, "we must obey God rather than men" (Acts 5:29), particularly when the two are in contradiction. But it also means respecting our leaders and praying for them, and recognizing their God-ordained appointments and responsibilities.

A correct view of American culture should put all Christians on their knees for the President of the United States and his associates. Their ultimate task is seemingly insurmountable and many of their problems almost insoluble. They, like the American people, seem to be shackled by the same big institutionalized machine that rumbles on and keeps them from bringing about needed changes that could, at least to a certain extent, ameliorate the American situation. And obviously they are not unaffected by the moral and ethical degeneration that is taking place in our culture. There has probably never been a time in our history when there has been more corruption and sin in high places. Abortion is at the top of the list. In my opinion, we have legalized murder, and unless we repent of this sin and turn from it, these atrocities against the unborn will bring God's ultimate judgment on us.

But, in addition to praying for our leaders, as Christians we must also function as good citizens. We must be aware of cultural issues and problems both in local and national elections and use all available channels to implement changes that will right what is wrong in our society.

Whatever our position and vocation in American life, whether in a government role or at an ordinary job, we must remember our primary task. We are God's witnesses in this world and we are part of the functioning body of Christ, with the responsibility to contribute to the health and welfare of that body. In so doing, the church can become a dynamic force against many of the environmental factors that are leading America away from truth and justice.

HELP BELIEVERS RELATE

Fifth, the church must provide an atmosphere where Christians can relate to one another in a noninstitutionalized environment. Unfortunately many local churches have become as institutionalized as the American structures. People who are fed up with an impersonal society often find an impersonal atmosphere in the church as well. People who are tired of being "cogs" in a secular machine find they become "cogs" in a religious machine.

The "church gathered" must realize that it can become a haven for lonely and frustrated people. Through providing a place that is a dynamic and loving community, it can counteract the plastic environment in which people live. Francis Schaeffer comments graphically relative to this point:

Our Christian organizations must be communities in which others see what God has revealed in the teaching of His Word. They should see that what has happened in Christ's death and reconciliation on the cross back there in space and time and history is relevant, that it is possible to have something beautiful and unusual in this world in our communication and in communities in our own generation. . . .

The Christian community and the practice of that community should cut across all lines. Our churches have largely been preaching points and activity generators. Community has had little place. In the New Testament church this practiced community was not just a banner, but cut all the way down into the hard stuff of the material needs of the members of the community. . . .

I want to see us treating each other like human beings. . . . Every Christian community everywhere ought to be a pilot plant to show that we can have horiontal relationships with men and that this can result in a community that cares not only for Man with a capital "M," but for the individual, not only for the upper case human rights, but for the whole man and all of his needs.

Unless people see in our churches not only the preaching of the truth but the practice of the truth, the practice of love and the practice of beauty; unless they see that the thing that the humanists rightly want but cannot achieve on the humanist base—human communication and human relationship—is able to be practiced in our communities, then let me say it clearly: they will not listen and they should not listen.[3]

PROVIDE STABILITY AND SECURITY

Sixth, the church must provide stability and security for people—something which culture is increasingly failing to do. In a day of unprecedented change, Christians can give people something to believe that is true and trustworthy.

America—as a nation—has abandoned its absolutes. It is like a ship at sea, caught in a storm without an anchor or a compass, with dangerous reefs nearby.

Not so with Bible-believing churches. Some may have lost their focus. Some may have become institutionalized. Others may not be fulfilling their primary purpose for existence. But we have not lost our anchor or compass. We have a foundation to which to return. We have a body of literature that can give us directives and a philosophy of life that allows us to look into the future realistically and with certainty. This, of course, cannot be said of the liberal church, the church that has—like America—abandoned its absolutes. Whether it represents the church that has returned to the use of "Bible words," or the old liberal who has abandoned even biblical terminology, both have left their authoritative base and have nothing solid to offer.

Thus the evangelical church must recognize with renewed vision that we have the *only* authoritative answers to our society's deepest needs. We must realize that the pluralisms and many uncertain voices in our society today provide us with unprecedented and unparalleled opportunities for evangelism. Men everywhere are confused, but they have the potential to differentiate truth from error. The Holy Spirit is still at work in the world, enlightening the hearts of men and honoring the Word of God.

Parents—many of whom hold to absolutes "in memory only"—are experiencing tremendous insecurity regarding their children. They see their own flesh and blood floundering in the mire of relativism. Though they do not understand it completely, they see the effects of movies, literature, friends, and professors. And many inwardly (and some outwardly) are crying out for stability—something to really believe in. When they attempt to give answers to their youth, their own children point their finger and cry "hypocrite," for they see clearly that the answers their parents are giving are not based on convictions believed as well as lived.

People need what the church can provide: stability and security, something to believe and to make a part of their total lifestyle and that squares with reality. Never has there been a more "teachable moment" than in America today. Our national problems can be a blessing in disguise—one that can bring many people into the kingdom of God.

A CHRISTIAN VALUE SYSTEM

Seventh, the church must help Christians to "live in the world" without being a "part of the world." Christians must not consciously or unconsciously adopt the aspects of the American value system that are contradictory to the Christian value system.

God has not yet called the church "out of the world" (1 Cor.

5:9-11). He never intended for Christians to withdraw from society and to live in a Christian community. For how else can we carry out Christ's commission to reach all nations with the Good News than to be "in the world." This is one reason why we are here on earth. How unfortunate when Christians confuse "separation" with "isolation." We are not to become a part of the world—living like the world lives—but neither are we to become isolated from the world. Others need to (they must) see in us what it means to be disciples of Jesus Christ.

Church leaders must also help Christians who live in the midst of our American culture to understand the conflicting value sys-tems. In days gone by, when most Americans held to a cultural value system compatible with biblical values, there was little conflict. In the business world most men were honest. In school few students cheated on exams. Moral and sexual mores were basically Christian. Generally speaking, Christians and non-Christians could trust one another and relate to one another harmoniously, at least at the social level.

But not so today. And the problem is not just one of being unable to trust one another. In some cases it is a problem of being able to survive financially or academically or socially. Today there are some Christian businessmen who are pitted against shrewd and dishonest individuals who walk off with all the profits because they tell boldfaced lies. In colleges and universities, some students receive top grades because they cheat on exams and plagiarize, thus putting the honest person at an extreme disadvantage. And some youths today are bypassed, or isolated socially, because they will not participate in nonbiblical practices and activities.

These conflicting value systems are separating the committed Christians from the uncommitted. Coexistence when value sys-tems were almost identical presented very little difficulty for Christians of yesteryear. But today it is a different story. In some in-stances, there is a "great gulf" between the person who is a "Christian" and a person who is simply an "American." Again this is a blessing in disguise. It used to be that it was difficult to explain to people why being "born in America" was not equal to "being a Christian." But today this is no problem. Most people clearly see the difference. And again this provides us with unlimit-ed opportunities in evangelism.

THE COMMUNICATIONS REVOLUTION

Eighth, the church must recognize, and understand and adapt to the cultural effects of the communications revolution.

John Culkin, a McLuhan interpreter, points out that "each culture develops its own balance of the senses in response to the demands of its environment. The most generalized formulation of the theory would maintain that the individual's modes of cognition and perception are influenced by the culture he is in, the language he speaks, and the media to which he is exposed. Each culture, as it were, provides its constituents with a custom-made set of goggles."[4]

The important issue facing the church today is *how* the present communications explosion in America is modifying cognition and perception, on the part of both the Christian and the non-Christian. It is already possible to conclude that the "Sesame Street" generation is a new breed. They are used to exciting and stimulating approaches to learning. In living color, the characters of "Sesame Street" have reached out and almost touched their viewers. As noted by Culkin, "in the process of delivering content the medium also works the sensorium of the consumer. . . . It takes hold of them, it jostles them, it bounces them around, it massages them. It opens and closes windows in their sensorium."[5]

For proof of this statement, Culkin asks that we "look out the window at the TV generation. They are rediscovering texture, movement, color, and sound as they retribalize the race." Television particularly, he says, "is a real grabber; it really massages those lazy, unused senses."[6]

Again the important issue is that the church must not—it cannot—overlook the cultural implications that grow out of our current communications revolution. Like Paul of old, who was faced with the challenge of a new mentality as he encountered the Greek culture, we, too, must adapt our communication approaches to reach people where they are. We cannot ignore their perceptive apparatus by proceeding to communicate in ways that once appealed to us, but no longer to the new generation. Whether we are ministering to children, youth, or adults, we must adapt and change in order to communicate effectively. Our message, of course, remains unchanged; our methods must be contemporary.

This, of course, raises another problem! In the church we have both the old and new generation. On the one hand, the older generation (not necessarily in age) is threatened and feels insecure and uncomfortable with new communication forms; and on the other hand, the new generation is "turned off" by the "old."

This is all the more reason for all members of the body of Christ to understand culture and how it affects us all. Understanding at least helps create tolerance and acceptance and love for one another. It helps the church itself to exist in harmony and unity—an ingredient so basic to Christian growth as well as witness.

The functioning body of Christ itself is a significant answer to the communications revolution. It has always been a "form" in itself for communicating a profound message. In a real sense, McLuhan's aphorism, "the medium is the message," applies to what God intended the body of Christ to be. It is a group of people who, as they function, create an atmosphere and environment that communicates the Christian message. To other Christians, the message is one of love and reality. To the unsaved, the unified body says that here are people who are followers of Jesus Christ, the God-Man.

The church, then, can become the means that can provide what the American culture does not—an environment that radiates acceptance, security, and stability—and at a personal level. This is the challenge that faces churches in the twentieth century.

CULTURAL EFFECTS ON LIFESTYLE

Ninth, the church must understand the cultural effects on lifestyle, particularly of our youth, and learn to differentiate between what is a violation of biblical principles, and what is a violation of the cultural norms we have come to accept as absolute.

One of the most tragic consequences of cultural change is that some Christians cannot emotionally tolerate a variance in lifestyle because they have come to equate certain externalities with being biblical. For example, men's hair lengths and beards have caused unusual disturbance among some Christians. Some have equated the two as being reflective of unspiritual or sinful behavior—forgetting that some of our great Christian leaders in the early 1900s looked quite similar.

It is easy to see how this false conclusion came into existence. Those who first demonstrated this "new" lifestyle were radical youth, who also went much further in demonstrating lifestyle characteristics that were definitely non-Christian. But many Christians—as we so often do—failed to differentiate between characteristics that violated Christian values and those that did not. We fell into the subtle trap of developing caricatures and forming generalizations based on false conclusions.

Even more tragic is a Christian who allows his prejudice toward Christians to also include non-Christians. When believers will not tolerate having on the church premises non-Christian youth whose lifestyle does not measure up to certain accepted middle-class norms, we are guilty of what James specifically called it—SIN (James 2:9). Though he was speaking in this instance in his epistle regarding prejudice towards the poor, the principle is clear. Just because a person "looks" different does not mean he is immoral, effeminate, or as some would almost imply, less than human. But even if he should be all of these, he is a person for whom Christ died. He is a human being and he needs love and compassion.

The same problem, of course, has been evident among Christians towards blacks and other minority groups. We often look for scriptural rationalizations to support our prejudicial thinking, and like most pseudo-Christian cults, we can make the Bible prove anything we want it to. All we need do is take it out of context to support our subjective biases.

God forbid that we become guilty of failing to distinguish between biblical norms and cultural norms. In the words of Francis Schaeffer when lecturing at Dallas Theological Seminary, we evangelicals have tended to "lose our way." We have developed an "ugliness" that must be terribly repulsive to our Saviour, who died for all men because He loved them. Christian "ugliness" is the saddest kind of "ugliness," for it is demonstrated by those who should demonstrate it least.

It is unfortunate, indeed, when we who are to be the "salt of the earth" and the "light of the world" are so indoctrinated with a non-Christian value system that we no longer can feel compassion towards those who are in deepest spiritual need. May God help us all to shed our carnality and prejudice and become spiritual people—people who love *all men,* not just those we can tolerate intellectually and emotionally.

STRENGTHENING THE HOME
Tenth, the church must do all it can to strengthen the home, and to counteract the devastating cultural attacks upon this basic of all institutions. Family life has been hit the hardest by the American crisis. Divorce rates are increasing, while children from these broken unions are frequently the victims of an increasing adult selfishness and insensitivity, leaving children in a state of disillusionment and insecurity.

The breakdown and abandonment of the traditional approach to home life parallels a variety of marriage experiments, such as collective marriages, trial marriages, and "living together" without any legal or moral commitments.

The Christian home too is being affected. Indeed, divorce rates are increasing at an alarming rate among Christian families. But in Christian families that remain together, our homes are still—in many ways—being split apart. Vocational demands have frequently left the family "fatherless," and financial or social pressures have "forced" mothers into a working role.

The church too is guilty. Unconsciously imitating an institutionalized society, we have developed forms and structures that literally keep families apart.

The greatest contribution the church can make to our decaying society is to help build the home. Strong families build strong churches, and together strong homes and strong churches can do more than any one thing to stabilize and revitalize our culture.

SUMMARY
There are many implications for the church that grow out of an understanding of American culture. As a starter consider these:
1. Develop a correct perspective regarding the multiple factors at work in our American society.
2. Develop a correct view of history.
3. Understand clearly why Jesus Christ has left the church on earth, and strive with His help to fulfill that purpose.
4. Show a vital concern for government leaders and the state of the nation.

5. Provide an atmosphere in the church where Christians can relate to one another in a noninstitutionalized environment.
6. Provide security and stability for people.
7. Help Christians "live in a world," without being a "part of the world."
8. Recognize, undertand, and adapt to the cultural effects of the communications revolution.
9. Understand the cultural effects on lifestyle—particularly on our youth—and learn to differentiate between what is a violation of biblical principles, and what is a violation of cultural norms we have come to accept as absolute.
10. Do everything possible to strengthen the home and counteract the devastating cultural attacks on this basic of all institutions.

Footnotes

[1]George Peters, *Saturation Evangelism,* p. 193.
[2]It is recognized that there is some problem in establishing the connection between verse 2 and vers 3. However the total context seems to point to the fact that the *salvation of all men* is directly related to *both* prayer and an environment that is conducive to dynamic Christian living and witness.
[3]Francis Schaeffer, *The Church at the End of the Twentieth Century,* pp. 39-40.
[4]John Culkin, "A Guide to McLuhan," *Religious Teacher's Journal,* October 1969, p. 26.
[5]Ibid.
[6]Ibid.

PART FOUR
DEVELOPING A CONTEMPORARY STRATEGY

Thus far in our study, we have looked through three lenses in order to develop a clear focus for the church in the twentieth century: the lens of Scripture, the lens of history, and the lens of culture.

The lens of Scripture has yielded dynamic New Testament *principles;* the lens of history has reflected some significant *lessons;* and the lens of culture has surfaced important *implications.*

Our task now is to develop forms and structures in any given cultural situation that will enable us to be in harmony with New Testament guidelines and yet relevant and contemporary in our approaches to carry out the Great Commission of our Lord Jesus Christ.

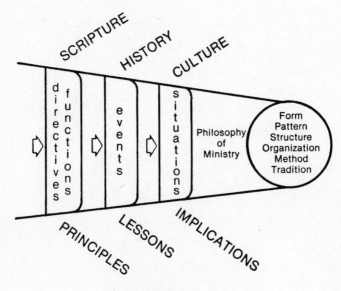

Forms and Structures

TWENTY

DEVELOPING PROPER PERSPECTIVE— STEP BY STEP

How can we renew our church? Or how can we launch a new church that is characterized by New Testament life and vitality?

These are questions that are being asked today by numerous concerned Christians: by pastors, ministerial students, and laymen representing all segments of church life.

The two chapters in this final section are designed to help answer these questions. They present a step-by-step plan for renewal—a strategy for developing proper perspective and a practical approach for implementing change.

At this juncture it is *important* to remember that church renewal within the evangelical church means dealing with the "body of Christ." Each member is part of "us"—and a part of Him. To hurt the body is to hurt ourselves and Jesus Christ, the head. Furthermore, to approach the church with brutal force and insensitivity, is to violate the very principles we believe in.

There will be those, of course, who are carnal and insensitive and inflexible. We cannot move forward for Jesus Christ without hurting someone. But this may be a necessary "hurt," and one that in the end will help transform that person into the image of Jesus Christ.

But the important concern before us is *how* can we approach the need for renewal in a way that is biblical and Christlike, and help the majority to see what must be done—and then, as a body, move forward in oneness and unity.

THE LENS OF SCRIPTURE

To start a new work or to renew an established church, it is important to begin with the perspective of the Word of God. Bible-believing Christians, particularly since they believe the Bible *is* the Word of God, are responsive to the Scriptures. It is to this Book we must turn as our authoritative base. The problem in many churches is that Christians (including both pastors and people) don't really know what the Bible teaches about New Testament church life. The principles that grow out of such a study are not clearly focused in their thinking.

You must begin, then, where we began in this study: with the *lens of Scripture.* You must start with the Great Commission and help people see *why* the church exists, both as a church "in the world" and as a "gathered community." Christians must see clearly the five important areas in the New Testament that relate to the church: evangelism, edification, church leadership, communication, and organization and administration. As they study the church's functions and the results of those activities in the Book of Acts, and as they carefully consider the directives and objectives given to the church in the Epistles, the New Testament principles we have discovered will also emerge in *their* thinking.

It should be noted, that, to this point, we have identified these concepts as *principles.* However, as will be shown later, they must be translated into New Testament purposes; that is, biblical objectives which need to be clearly focused and set up as targets for the twentieth-century church.

These New Testament principles and purposes are summarized as follows:

PRINCIPLES AND PURPOSES OF EVANGELISM

1. Every body of believers must be responsible for its own community first.
2. Corporate evangelism is basic to personal evangelism.
3. When possible, presenting the Gospel to the unsaved is to take place against the backdrop of a loving and unified body of Christians.
4. The primary target for evangelism should be adults and consequently whole households.

5. The church is responsible to identify those who have a desire to carry the Good News in a special way out into the community and beyond the immediate community, even to "the remotest part of the earth."
6. New believers, as soon as possible, should be integrated into the life of the church.
7. The twentieth-century church must develop its own contemporary forms and approaches to evangelism utilizing the principles and purposes just stated as biblical guidelines.

PRINCIPLES AND PURPOSES OF EDUCATION
1. The local church must be kept in focus as the primary means by which edification is to take place.
2. Believers must be provided with a basic knowledge of the Word of God.
3. Believers must be provided with an in-depth knowledge of the Word of God.
4. Believers must be provided with opportunities to develop capacities that go beyond knowledge.
5. Believers must be provided with the sum total of experiences, which will help them get beyond the knowledge level—vital

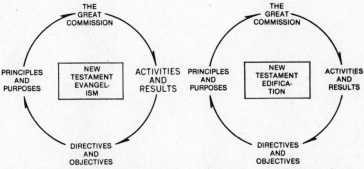

Figure 26. Principles and Purposes of New Testament Evangelism   Figure 27. Principles and Purpose of New Testament Edification

learning experiences with the Word, vital relational experiences with one another and with God, and vital witnessing experiences both individually and corporately.

6. All believers must be equipped for Christian service.
7. Believers must be helped to develop qualitative family life.
8. The twentieth-century church must develop its own contemporary forms and structures for applying the biblical principles and purposes just outlined.

PRINCIPLES AND PURPOSES OF LEADERSHIP

1. In discerning and practicing God's plan for leadership in the church today, we must carefully distinguish between the two leadership phases in the New Testament but yet understand the applicability of both an "apostolic" ministry and a local church ministry in carrying out the Great Commission in the twentieth-century world.
2. The first step in assisting local churches in their spiritual growth is to appoint spiritually qualified people to lead these churches. These leaders must be first of all selected on the basis of spiritual qualifications—not gifts, talents, and abilities.
3. Spiritual leaders must function as managers and pastors and not merely as administrators and decision makers.

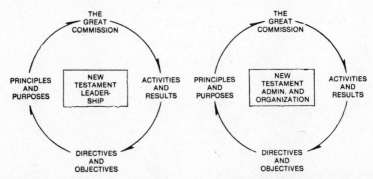

Figure 28. Principles and Purposes of New Testament Leadership

Figure 29. Principles and Purpose of New Testament Administration and Organization

4. Spiritual leaders should maintain their priorities and delegate cultural responsibilities to other qualified men and women.
5. Churches should appoint certain spiritual leaders to serve in staff positions and adequately remunerate them for their efforts.
6. When feasible, churches should be led by more than one spiritual leader, but it is important to designate one spiritual leader as the primary leader.
7. Churches should be free to develop creative forms and structures to apply the functions and principles just outlined.

PRINCIPLES AND PURPOSES OF ADMINISTRATION AND ORGANIZATION

Administration
1. Face the reality of problems.
2. Develop a proper perspective on the problem before reaching a concrete solution.
3. Establish priorities.
4. Delegate responsibility to qualified people.
5. Maintain a proper balance between divine and human factors.
6. Take an approach to problem solving and decision making that considers the attitudes and feelings of those who are directly involved.
7. Solve every problem creatively, under the leadership of the Holy Spirit.

Organization
1. Organize to apply New Testament principles and to reach New Testament purposes.
2. Organize to meet needs.
3. Keep organization simple.
4. Keep organization flexible.

PRINCIPLES AND PURPOSES OF COMMUNICATION
1. Christian communication is a distinctive process, including both human and divine elements.
2. Christian communication should be to all kinds and classes of people.

Figure 30. Principles and Purposes
of New Testament Communication

3. Christian communication should be carefully balanced between a ministry to groups, as well as a ministry to individuals.
4. Effective Christian communication must include an in-depth ministry to a select group, as well as a ministry to the larger group of Christians.
5. For communication to be qualitative it must get beyond the verbalization level.
6. In Christian communication example is foundational to verbalization.
7. Effective Christian communication doesn't just happen—it takes self-sacrifice and hard work.
8. Christians must never be restricted to certain methods of communication but always be free and flexible.

THE LENS OF HISTORY

Christians today need to "look through" the lens of history. Obviously in this study it has been impossible to treat every lesson the twentieth-century church can learn from history. We have attempted to open up the area by selecting one major area which relates particularly to church forms and structures—that of institutionalism. There are many other areas in history that will also challenge our thinking. But from the study of institutionalism in history, we can isolate at least five important lessons:

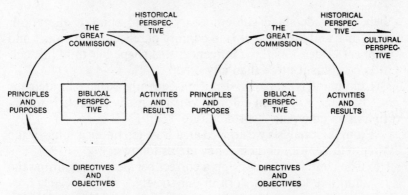

Figure 31. Lessons from History   Figure 32. Implications from Culture

1. Our greatest strength—our emphasis on teaching and learning the content of the Bible—has also helped create some of our greatest problems. In our attempt to teach the Bible we have neglected two other vital experiences: relational experiences with God and with one another and the vital experience of corporate witness.
2. We have made the church a "soul-winning" station rather than a "life-building" station, thus weakening both the functioning *body* of Christ and our witness in th world.
3. We support the institution, rather than its reason for existence. Put another way, we are more concerned *with* existence than our *cause* for existence.
4. We have emphasized correct doctrine and neglected the quality of one's life. Furthermore, the criteria for evaluating spirituality has often been based on externalities, rather than on inner spiritual qualities.
5. We have fallen into the subtle trap of allowing nonabsolutes to become absolute; of making forms and structures, methods and approaches ends in themselves, rather than means to biblical ends.

THE LENS OF CULTURE
If we are to renew the church, we must also help twentieth-century

believers understand contemporary culture—how it affects our thinking; and how easy it is to confuse purely cultural values and biblical values. Of all the influences that shape our thinking, culture can blur it more than any other.

Culture too is a large subject. Consequently we have limited our study to the American culture, which in many respects is reflective of an emerging "world culture."

From this analysis we arrived at at least ten implications for the twentieth-century church. They are as follows:

1. The church must develop a correct perspective regarding the multiple factors at work in our society.

2. The church must develop a correct view of history. We are moving on target toward the climax of history and the return of Jesus Christ.

3. The church must understand clearly why Jesus Christ has left us on earth, and strive with His help to fulfill that purpose. Culture can blur this purpose and sidetrack us onto peripheral issues.

4. The church must show a vital concern for government leaders, giving primary attention to prayer for them, as well as living an exemplary life.

5. The church must provide an atmosphere where Christians can relate to one another in a noninstitutionalized environment.

6. The church must provide security and stability for people—something which culture is increasingly failing to do.

7. The church must help Christians to "live in the world," without being a "part of the world." Christians must not, consciously or unconsciously, adopt the aspects of the American value system that are contradictory to a Christian value system.

8. The church must recognize, understand, and adapt to the cultural effects of the communications revolution.

9. The church must understand the cultural effects on lifestyle—particularly of our youth—and learn to differentiate between what is a violation of biblical principles, and what is a violation of the cultural norms we have come to accept as absolute.

10. The church must do all it can to strengthen the home, and

counteract the devastating cultural attacks on this basic of all institutions.

DEVELOPING A CONTEMPORARY STRATEGY

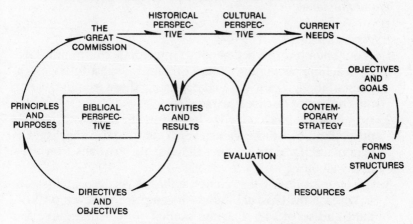

Figure 33. Contemporary Strategy in Total Perspective

Once we have clearly communicated biblical principles, significant lessons from history, and the most important cultural implications that relate to our own community, our next move in church renewal is to help Christians develop greater perspective by looking at five important steps which must be taken to develop a contemporary strategy: (1) to determine current needs in their own churches; (2) to formulate and set up both immediate and long-range objectives and goals; (3) to change, reshape, and develop functional forms and structures; (4) to discover and utilize all relevant and legitimate resources; and (5) to constantly evaluate to see if total perspective is in focus biblically, historically, culturally, and functionally. This overall, on-going process and strategy can be viewed in figure 33.

DETERMINING CURRENT NEEDS
In order to determine current needs in our local church, we need to reshape each biblical principle into significant and penetrating questions, incorporating our insights from history and culture.

These questions will form the criteria by which we can evaluate our present situation. This process will help us to spot strengths as well as weaknesses in our church.

The following section illustrates the kinds of questions which can be formulated:

EVANGELISM
1. Is our church concerned about its immediate community? Are we reaching people for Christ? Or, are we substituting a program of foreign missions and neglecting those who live within the context of our local witness?
2. Are we active "as a body" in local church evangelism? Are we providing a backdrop against which individual evangelism can take place? Or do we expect individual Christians to witness in a vacuum?
3. Are we substituting the "church gathered" as the primary place to "preach the Gospel," rather than a place to develop Christians and serve as a dynamic example of Christian love and unity to the world?
4. Are we reaching whole households with the Gospel, concentrating first on reaching parents? Or are we substituting a program of child and youth evangelism for adult evangelism?
5. Are we discovering and recognizing those in the church who feel especially called to evangelism, and are we encouraging them in their community and worldwide witness through moral and financial support?
6. Are new believers integrated into the life of the local church as soon as possible?
7. Are we utilizing contemporary strategies and approaches to carry out community and worldwide evangelism, that are distinctive and unique to our particular twentieth-century problems in reaching people for Christ?

EDIFICATION
1. Are we providing a conducive place for edification to take place? Does it provide a warm inviting atmosphere? Do we exclude people or make them feel uncomfortable because of our own cultural hang-ups and prejudices? Are we differentiat-

ing between lifestyles that are a violation of purely cultural values and those that violate true Christian values?

2. Are we providing new believers with a basic knowledge of the Word of God? Are they taught basic Bible doctrine that will stabilize them in the Christian faith?

3. Are we providing believers with an in-depth knowledge of the Word of God? Are we helping them to unerstand and appropriate the deep truths of the Scriptures?

4. Are we helping Christians to get beyond the Bible-knowledge level to develop capacities that include wisdom, enlightenment, appreciation, and awareness and sensitivity to the Holy Spirit; a sensitivity to members of the body of Christ, and a sensitivity to the needs of *all* men? Are Christians developing the sensitivity to be able to differentiate between values that are cultural and those that are Christian?

5. Are we providing believers with the sum total of experiences that will help them get beyond the knowledge level—vital learning experiences with the Word of God, vital relational experiences with one another and with God, and vital witnessing experiences, both corporately and individually?

6. Are all believers being equipped for Christian service—both in the world and within the church?

7. Are we helping husbands and wives, fathers and mothers, and children to develop qualitative Christian family life? Are we doing all we can to unite families, to encourage families, and to provide them with the spiritual equipment to combat the negative influences of the secular and materialistic culture?

8. Are we developing contemporary church forms and structures that will enable us to apply New Testament principles in the twentieth century? Do we have forms and structures that provide a sense of Christian community—an atmosphere that is in contrast to the institutionalized environment in the American culture?

LEADERSHIP

1. Are we discerning between God's two leadership phases in the New Testament, and at the same time emphasizing both an "apostolic" ministry as well as a local church ministry?

2. Are we selecting local church leadership based first and foremost on spiritual qualification rather than gifts, talents, and abilities?
3. Are the spiritual leaders in our church functioning as managers and pastors in the true sense of the word and not merely as administrators and decision makers?
4. Are our spiritual leaders maintaining their priority functions and delegating cultural responsibilities to other qualified men and women?
5. Are we appointing an adequate number of spiritual leaders to staff positions in the church and remunerating them adequately?
6. Are we practicing the principles of multiple leadership but yet designating one person as the primary leader?
7. Are we developing adequate forms and structures to enable our church leadership to adequately carry out their biblical and cultural functions?

ADMINISTRATION
1. Do we face problems realistically, doing something about them as soon as possible?
2. Do we develop a proper perspective upon problems before trying to arrive at concrete solutions?
3. Do we establish priorities, especially as spiritual leaders in the church, determining where primary attention must be given?
4. Do the spiritual leaders in the church delegate responsibility to qualified people?
5. Do leaders in the church maintain a proper balance between divine and human factors in performing their administrative roles?
6. Do we use an approach to problem solving and decision making in our church that takes into consideration the attitudes and feelings of everyone directly involved?
7. Do we solve problems creatively under the leadership of the Holy Spirit? Or are we hampered by approaches that have worked in the past or that have worked for someone else?

ORGANIZATION
1. Is organization used primarily as a means to apply New Testa-

ment principles and reach New Testament purposes? Or has organization become an end in itself?

2. Do we organize to meet needs? Or do we organize just to organize?
3. Do we keep our organizational structures simple and functional?
4. Do we keep our organizational structures flexible? Or do we get locked up by structures that are outdated, outmoded, and nonfunctional?

COMMUNICATION

1. Do we recognize both the divine and human elements in effective Christian communication? Do we recognize God's sovereign work through the Holy Spirit and the Word of God, and at the same time recognize the importance of human factors such as concern, good methods, and hard work?
2. Are we communicating with all kinds and classes of people, both Christians and non-Christians? Or are we demonstrating partiality and prejudice?
3. Are we carefully balancing our ministry to groups with that of a ministry to individuals?
4. Do we have an in-depth ministry to a select group of Christians, as well as a ministry to the total group of believers?
5. Are we communicating primarily with "words," or are we involving people totally in the process of learning? Are we getting beyond the verbalization level, to the level of visualization and total involvement?
6. Do we explore and practice the importance of Christian example as basic to verbal communication?
7. Are we "working hard" at Christian communication? Or do we expect it to "just happen"?
8. Are we being creative in developing and using twentieth-century methodology? Or are we restricting ourselves to forms that are a product of past culture, and are we unknowingly classifying them as biblical and absolute?

FORMULATING OBJECTIVES AND GOALS

Once we have evaluated the overall function of our local church, and isolated both strengths and weaknesses, we then need to formulate both immediate and long-range objectives and goals. This is a key step, and a step that will call for some very careful thinking. It will take time and effort, but it is, in some respects, the most important step in the whole process of renewal. When approached correctly, it can help to create unified thinking in the local body of Christ—an element which is basic to effective change and renewal.

On the other hand, if this step is not taken prayerfully, carefully, and thoroughly, all of the efforts put forth in focusing biblical principles, historical lessons, cultural implications, and current needs may achieve very little.

Because this is such an important step, the entire next chapter is given over to how this process can be carried out.

CHANGING FUNCTIONAL FORMS AND STRUCTURES

If formulating objectives and goals is a crucial step in the process of renewal, then changing, reshaping, and developing functional forms and structures is the most *difficult*. It is at this point that we begin to tamper with tradition and emotion. Forms and structures represent our way of doing things. And they have provided us with a great deal of security. We know what is going to happen next; that is, how things are going to be done because of our forms and structures.

But if certain forms and structures are no longer or even halfway achieving New Testament purposes because they are no longer functional, they *must* be changed. If they are not, we are failing to be New Testament. We have allowed ourselves to become chained to nonabsolutes. We are resisting the Holy Spirit. We are in bondage to ourselves. We are carnal.

If you have proceeded carefully to this point—and particularly if you have helped people clearly focus New Testament principles—most will begin to see the difference between absolutes and nonabsolutes. The Holy Spirit Himself will use the Word of God to clear away fuzzy thinking and to renew vision.

This does not mean there will not be those who will *resist* change. This is natural among all people, whether Christian or non-Christian. Management studies show that about ten percent of a group of people in an organization are *innovators*—people willing to try most any new form or structure or idea. About eighty percent are *conservative*—people who are hesitant to change, until they have all the facts and have their feet firmly planted on projections that seem to be completely feasible. Only about ten percent are *inhibitors*—people who are against any kind of change, whether they have the facts or not.

If we approach a body of believers with biblical, historical, and cultural facts, theoretically ninety percent will be ready to change when they see God's plan clearly. And hopefully, since we have the authoritative Word of God and the Holy Spirit on our side, we can reduce the number to less than ten percent who resist just to "resist." In other words, people who are Christians *should* shatter the world's statistical norms.

DISCOVERING AND UTILIZING RESOURCES

We live in a technological age that has provided the church with unusual resources. They should never, of course, be thought of as being more important than the spiritual resources available to the church; that is, the Word of God, prayer and the Holy Spirit, and the dynamic of the body of Christ itself. But to ignore the human resources available in the twentieth century is to be less than spiritually alert.

Jesus Christ used the resources available in His day. Whether it was a well, the wind, a sower, a child, or a temple, we were used to communicate His eternal message. Paul used Greek logic, various literary styles, parchments, ships, and a messenger service. Limited, yes, but he used them all to carry out the Great Commission.

Today the church needs to use every relevant and legitimate means to reach the same New Testament objectives that captured the minds and hearts of our biblical forefathers. Literature, audio casettes, videotape, films, radio, TV—whatever! We need to consider new methods, new approaches, new ideas to communicate the eternal and never-changing message. The communications revolution in our culture has set the stage for a communications revolution in the church.

This is not to say that preaching is no longer relevant or necessary. But what we need to do is "preach" in new and more creative ways. The Bible does not tell us *how* to preach; it just tells us "to preach" and gives us a variety of illustrations as to the way it was done. So it is with teaching. If we are to keep up with a media-oriented society, we cannot sit idly by and continue to perform in the same old way. Many will not listen to us. Their boredom will "win out." What's more, some will become "drop outs," especially if the problem is not counteracted by the home. At the same time we may become guilty of sitting back and complaining about the unresponsive and spiritually hardened generation.

We live in a different world. People's cognitive and perceptive abilities have changed. We think faster, know more, and ask more questions; and in many instances, ironically, we are more confused. But our hearts are the same! We still cry out for understanding, sympathy, support, and security. And what every person needs is what the church of Jesus Christ can give. Our challenge is to use every resource available to meet these human needs.

EVALUATING

The word *evaluation* is a threatening word, but it is a biblical concept. In the *King James Version,* Paul exhorted the Corinthians to "prove" themselves (2 Cor. 13:5): to put themselves to the test, examine themselves, scrutinize themselves. To the Galatians, he wrote, "Let every man examine his own work" (Gal. 6:4); and he admonished the Thessalonians to "examine everything carefully" (1 Thes. 5:21).

Paul also practiced this concept in his own ministry. He sent Timothy back to Thessalonica to evaluate the state of the church—to see how they were (1 Thes. 3:5). He was constantly anxious to get reports from various sources, as to what was happening in all the churches, regarding their problems, their needs, their concerns, and their progress.

Several things should be noted regarding the process of evaluation.

First, it should be constant. As illustrated in figure 33, it applies to every aspect of the process of developing a biblical philosophy of the ministry. We must constantly search the Word of God to see if we have clearly focused biblical principles. We must constantly reconsider history in the light of contemporary culture. We must constantly determine current needs against the backdrop of biblical principles, historical lessons, and cultural implications. We must constantly refocus our objectives and goals, particularly in the light of biblical purposes. We must constantly evaluate our forms and structures to see if they are appropriately applying biblical principles and reaching New Testament goals and objectives. We must constantly look for resources to help us apply New Testament principles in the twentieth century. And finally, we must evaluate, evaluate, evaluate!

Second, evaluation should be carried out by the whole body of Christ. It is only as *all* are involved in this process that *all* will want to change. This is why it is important to help each member of the body to know what *is* and what *is not* a New Testament principle; what *is* and *is not* a biblical norm or absolute; what *is* and what *is not* cultural. When every member of the body of Christ is involved in the process, it also provides assurance that we are arriving at a correct perspective on our problems. It is dangerous for one individual to evaluate alone. All of us are to a certain extent in bondage to subjective feelings. We need the body of Christ and its many members to help correct any incorrect perceptions.

Third, though evaluation is threatening, it is ultimately rewarding. We are afraid of evaluation, because we are afraid we will discover that we have done something wrong.

But let's face reality! Not one of us is perfect. We all make mistakes. This is why we need the "body." When all are involved, all are "to blame" when we make mistakes. "Together" we must evaluate; and "together" we must plan; and "together" we will become what God wants us to become.

SUMMARY
To renew your church step by step:
1. Help the church to focus biblical principles and purposes by looking through the lens of Scripture.
2. Help the church focus lessons of history by looking through the lens of history.
3. Help the church focus implications from culture by looking through the lens of culture.

4. Help the church determine its current needs in the light of biblical, historical, and cultural perspective.
5. Help the church formulate immediate and long-range objectives and goals.
6. Help the church develop contemporary forms and structures.
7. Help the church discover and utilize relevent resources.
8. Help the church use this step-by-step process to constantly evaluate and to "prove themselves."

TWENTY-ONE

FORMULATING OBJECTIVES, GOALS, AND STANDARDS

It was emphasized in the previous chapter that formulating objectives, goals and standards was one of the most important steps in bringing about renewal in the church. Because this is true, this final chapter is designed as a "model" for goal setting. How can this be done?

DEFINITION OF TERMS

First we must define terms.

A *purpose* is a broad statement of an aspiration. It describes the general direction we want to go. This is why the principles which have emerged in our study of the New Testament church are identified as *purposes* as well as *principles*. In each instance, they are broad, scriptural statements that apply to evangelism, edification, leadership, communication, organization and administration.[1]

An *objective* is a more specific statement of an aspiration, which, if attained, will produce progress toward fulfilling each scriptural purpose. There are usually two or more objectives for each purpose.

The *goal* is a still more specific statement of what is to be accomplished to produce progress toward an objective. There are usually two or more goals for each objective.

A *performance standard* is a measurement by which performance can be evaluated. Standards can be expressed in terms which are relative to a *purpose* or an *objective* or a *goal.* There are usually two or more standards for each goal.

THE BASIC MODEL

On the basis of these definitions, the following model is set up to illustrate how a biblical principle can be translated into a purpose, and how objectives, goals, and standards can be formulated for a local church. A principle of New Testament evangelism is used to illustrate this process.

PURPOSES

Purposes should be the same for every Bible-believing church. Since they are based on biblical principles, they are supracultural.

Example A
One of the purposes of New Testament evangelism is *to give primary attention to reaching our own community with the Gospel.*

OBJECTIVES

Objectives vary from church to church, community to community, and culture to culture. They are based upon current needs and concerns within a particular church.

Examples Under A
1. To *educate* people relative to this important New Testament principle.
2. To *motivate* people relative to this important New Testament principle.

GOALS

Goals are specific statements of steps to be taken if objectives are to be achieved. There usually are two or more goals for each objective.

Examples Under A-1
(a) To expose people to this concept of community evangelism through biblical teaching on the subject.
(b) To expose people to this concept by sharing with them what other churches are doing to reach their communities.

STANDARDS

Standards are specific statements of conditions to be met if each goal is to be reached. There are usually two or more standards for each goal.

Examples Under A-1-a
(i) The whole congregation is exposed to this concept at least once a year through a sermon.
(ii) A group of selected people will explore this concept in a small group training session once a year.

AN EXPANDED MODEL

This model includes all of the New Testament principles which have emerged in our study of the first-century church. They have been translated into purposes; and in the first section on evangelism, two purposes have been developed to illustrate what a "certain" church *might* do to formulate objectives, goals, and standards to carry out these two purposes. Hereafter, only the purposes are listed under each section, with the exception of the partial development of purpose. A in the area of edification. This process of development should be carried out for each purpose, including at least two objectives, two goals under each objective, and two standards under each goal. It should be realized, however, that some situations may call for more than two statements under each category, and some may call for less than two. Each individual church should complete this task in view of their own particular current needs. In developing each section, it will help to rethink the material covered previously in this study.

Evangelism

Purpose A. To give primary attention to reaching our own community with the Gospel

    Objective 1. To *educate* people relative to this important New Testament principle

        Goal (a). To expose people to this concept of community evangelism through biblical teaching on the subject

            Standard (1). The whole congregation is exposed to this concept at least once a year through a sermon

            Standard (2). A smaller group of people explores this concept in the Bible in a small group training session once a year.

        Goal (b). To expose people to this concept by sharing with them what other churches are doing to reach their own communities

            Standard (1). A film on the subject will be shown during a special evening session to the whole congregation to launch this emphasis.

Standard (2). Each member of the local body is encouraged to read one book on the subject by means of the church bulletin. A list of books appears once a month.

Objective 2. To *motivate* people relative to this important New Testament principle

Goal (a). To bring in guest laymen from other churches to share what they are doing to reach their community for Christ

Standard (1). One Sunday is designated every three months when laymen from other churches are invited to come in and share in a morning service.

Standard (2). One Sunday is designated every three months when laymen from other churches are invited to come and share in an evening service.

Goal (b). To provide opportunity for people to share with others what they are doing to reach their neighbors, friends, and business associates for Christ

Standard (1). Opportunity is given every Sunday evening for people to share their witnessing experiences.

Standard (2). People are regularly encouraged to share prayer needs with other members of the body, regarding unsaved neighbors, friends, and business associates.

Purpose B. To emphasize that corporate evangelism is basic to personal evangelism

Objective 1. To explain what corporate evangelism is

Goal (a). To expose people to this concept through biblical teaching.

Standard (1). The whole congregation is exposed to this concept through a sermon.

Standard (2). This concept is explored by means of a small-group Bible study in a four-part series in each adult Sunday School class, following the introductory sermon on this subject.

Goal (b). To demonstrate how this concept works

Standard (1). A dramatic presentation is made one Sunday evening to show how corporate evangelism opens up opportunities for individual witness.

Standard (2). People are encouraged each Sunday evening to share opportunities that have come to them for Christian witness because of the functioning body of Christ.

Objective 2. To explain that we must devise ways and means to expose unsaved people to the functioning body of Christ

Goal (a) To encourage people to invite unsaved people to share in a special church function that demonstrates the functioning body

Standard (1). A special church function is planned once a month that is conducive for inviting unsaved friends to see the body of Christ function in love and unity.

Standard (2). Regular body-life services are planned periodically in which any non-Christian may see the body of Christ functioning in love and unity.

Goal (b). To encourage people as families to invite their neighbors for dinner or a picnic, in order to demonstrate the functioning body of Christ at the family level

Standard (1). People are regularly encouraged to share experiences with other believers as to what they are doing to build bridges to unsaved neighbors.

Standard (2). Whenever a person comes to know Christ through seeing individual families function in love and unity, that person is invited to share his testimony with the total church family in a church service.

Purpose C. To follow the New Testament example of creating a loving and unified body of believers to serve as a backdrop against which to communicate the Gospel.

Purpose D. To reach whole households for Christ, beginning with fathers and mothers

Purpose E. To identify those in the church who desire to be involved in evangelism, and to provide both moral and financial support so they can function effectively.

Purpose F. To integrate new believers into the life of the church as soon as possible

Purpose G. To develop contemporary forms and structures to reach New Testament purposes

Edification

Purpose A. To develop a local church that can indeed serve as a primary means by which effective edification can take place for all twentieth-century believers, young and old, and Christians from all walks of life

Objective 1. To expose all believers in the church to this concept

Goal (a). To expose, first of all, the spiritual leaders in the church to this concept

Standard (1). This concept will be discussed in a series of luncheons, with key spiritual leaders in the church suggesting a series of Bible studies with the whole board.

Standard (2). This concept will then be developed in a series of Bible studies with the spiritual leaders of the church, assuming that this will be supported by these leaders.

Goal (b). To specifically expose the whole congregation to this concept after the spiritual leaders have been exposed

Standard (1).

Standard (2).

Objective 2. To expose all believers in the church to Christians who do not live in the same cultural situation as we do

Goal (a).
    Standard (1).
    Standard (2)
Goal (b).
    Standard (1).
    Standard (2).

Purpose B. To provide new believers with a knowledge of the basic doctrines of the Christian faith.

Purpose C. To provide all believers with an in-depth knowledge of the Scriptures

Purpose D. To help believers to develop capacities that go beyond the knowledge level

Purpose E. To provide all leaders with balanced New Testament experiences

Purpose F. To equip all believers for Christian service

Purpose G. To help parents develop qualitative family life

Purpose H. To develop contemporary forms and structures in the church that will serve as the best means for reaching these purposes, objectives and goals

Leadership

Purpose A. To carefully discern between God's two leadership phases in the New Testament but yet develop both an "apostolic" ministry as well as a local church ministry in carrying out the Great Commission.

Purpose B. To select and appoint church leaders based first and foremost on spiritual qualifications—not gifts, talents, and abilities.

Purpose C. To make sure our spiritual leaders are functioning in a biblical way as managers and pastors and not merely as administrators and decision makers.

Purpose D. To make sure our spiritual leaders are maintaining their priorities and delegating cultural responsibilities to other qualified men and women.

Purpose E. To appoint an adequate number of spiritual leaders to staff positions and to adequately remunerate them for their efforts.

Purpose F. To practice the principle of multiple leadership but to make sure one individual is then designated as the primary spiritual leader of the church.

Purpose G. To be free in developing creative forms and structures to enable our church leaders to function as God intended.

Organization and Administration

ADMINISTRATION

Purpose A. To face all problems immediately and realistically

Purpose B. To develop a proper perspective on all problems, before seeking a concrete solution

Purpose C. To establish priorities

Purpose D. To delegate responsibility to qualified people

Purpose E. To practice an approach to problem solving and decision making that considers the attitudes and feelings of everyone directly involved

Purpose F. To solve every problem creatively under the leadership of the Holy Spirit

ORGANIZATION

Purpose A. To devise organizational structures that will carry out New Testament principles and reach New Testament purposes.

Purpose B. To organize on the basis of needs

Purpose C. To keep organization simple

Purpose D. To keep organization flexible

Communication

Purpose A. To maintain a proper balance between divine and human factors in communication

Purpose B. To communicate with all kinds and classes of people

Purpose C. To maintain a proper balance between a ministry in-depth to a small group of Christians and a general ministry to all Christians

Purpose E. To get beyond the verbalization level in communication

Purpose F. To make sure Christian example is basic to verbal communication

Purpose G. To put forth the necessary effort to attain good Christian communication

Purpose H. To use and develop twentiety-century patterns and forms in communication

SUMMARY

Formulating objectives, goals and standards on the basis of New Testament purposes is a very important step a local church can take to bring about spiritual renewal. When this process is carried out properly—and as a body—the necessary forms and structures and the utilization of relevant resources will follow naturally.

This does not mean that every individual will cease to be threatened by change, but it does mean that "together" the body of Christ will carry out the Great Commission of our Lord Jesus Christ more effectively. On some occasions it will mean new churches must be established; for some churches have become so institutionalized and some individuals have departed so far from the Word of God, that even the Scriptures mean very little in their lives. But when Christians believe the Word of God and are committed to it, they are hardened indeed if they do not respond to the Holy Spirit as He exposes them to its teachings regarding the New Testament church.

A PRAYER

Ɔ God give us perspective! Help us to see clearly the principles in Your Word which will give us direction for our churches. Help us to see clearly the lessons from history we should learn—lessons that will keep us from repeating the errors of our forefathers; and lessons that will help us to do again, but even better, what they did right. Help us to understand our contemporary culture, and not to be in bondage to it nor totally separated from it, but to use it as a bridge to a troubled humanity. Help us not to get locked in to nonabsolutes and keep us from getting sidetracked onto peripheral issues. Above all, help us to fulfill the great purpose for which You left us here on earth—to "make disciples" of all nations and to be a functioning part of a dynamic body of New Testament believers.

"Now to Him who is able to do exceeding abundantly beyond all that we ask or think, according to the power that works within us, to Him be the glory in the church and in Christ Jesus to all generations forever and ever. Amen" (Eph. 3:20-21).

Footnotes

[1]Dr. John Alexander, president of Inter-Varsity Christian Fellowship, has in many respects set the pace in goal setting among evangelical leaders. It is from his book *Managing Our Work,* InterVarsity, that the basic definitions and model are taken (pp. 15, 22-23). The specific adaptation to the work of the church has been made on the basis of the material discussed in these chapters.

Appendix A

An Opportunity to Make Your Own Inductive Study

The commission given by Jesus Christ in Matthew 28:19-20 has been separated into two basic tasks: *evangelism* (why the church exists in the world) and *edification* (why the "church gathered" exists). Evangelism involves *going* and *making disciples,* and edification involves *baptizing* them and *teaching* them.

These two tasks have been used to develop two columns, which include Scriptures, to illustrate the way in which these tasks were carried out. The Book of Acts has been used as a basic source for this information, and the Epistles have been correlated with the basic flow of events which appear in Acts.

You will note, however, that though the basic purpose of the Epistles was edification and hence their total content could appear in column 2, they also include material that is illustrative of, and particularly pertinent to, the tasks in both columns. Therefore selected Scripture verses from the Epistles appear in both columns.

For an exciting study, work through the Scriptures which have been compiled for you in this appendix. As you study, you will note that a pattern emerges in relationship to the way in which the Great Commission was carried out. (See model chart, "Why Does the Church Exist?")

In column 1 (the evangelism column) you will see *functions* and *results* in the Book of Acts. As you move into the Epistles in the same column, you will see *directives* and *objectives.*

WHY DOES THE CHURCH EXIST?

	EVANGELISM		EDIFICATION	
	Going—Make Disciples Why the Church Exists in the World		Baptizing—Teaching Them Why the Church Exists as a Gathered Community	
	Functions and Directives	Results and Objectives	Functions and Directives	Results and Objectives
ACTS	Declaring Speaking Proclaiming Preaching Testifying Etc.	Many believed The Word of God kept spreading Some were persuaded Etc.	Baptizing Teaching Encouraging Strengthening Reporting Etc.	Were of one mind Were of one heart and soul Were being built up Etc.
EPISTLES	Love your neighbor as yourself Keep your behavior excellent among the Gentiles ---- So that . . . they may glorify God in the day of visitation		Encourage one another Build up one another We admonish and teach every man ---- That we may present every man complete in Christ	

Figure 34. A Research Model

Appendix A

In column two (the edification column) you will see the same pattern emerge: that is, functions and results in the Book of Acts and directives and objectives in the Epistles. (Again see the model which will help clarify this pattern.

Now for your specific assignment!

1. Use a color code to identify: red—functions; blue—results; black—directives; green—objectives. 2. Carefully study your findings. What do you see? Use the following questions to prod your thinking:

REGARDING EVANGELISM

   a. What kind of evangelism functions did Christians engage in in the Book of Acts?

   b. What were the results of these functions?

   c. What evangelism directives are given by the writers of the Epistles?

   d. What objectives are to be achieved as a result of carrying out these directives?

REGARDING EDIFICATION

   a. What kind of edification functions did Christians engage in in the Book of Acts?

   b. What were the results of these functions?

   c. What edification directives are given by the writers of the Epistles?

   d. What objectives are to be achieved as a result of carrying out these directives?

3. Now back off from your study and answer these two questions:

   a. As a result of your study what would be principles of evangelism for a church in the last quarter of the twentieth century?

   b. As a result of your study, what would be principles of edification for a church in the last quarter of the twentieth century?

SELECTED SCRIPTURE VERSES

Go, therefore and make disciples of all the nations, baptizing them in the name of the Father and the Son and the Holy Spirit, teaching them to observe all that I command you; and lo, I am with you always, even to the end of the age (Matt. 28:19-20).

WHY DOES THE CHURCH EXIST IN THE WORLD?	WHY DOES THE "CHURCH GATHERED" EXIST?
EVANGELISM GOING— MAKE DISCIPLES	EDIFICATION BAPTIZING THEM— TEACHING THEM
Acts 1:8. But you shall receive power when the Holy Spirit has come upon you; and you shall be My witnesses both in Jerusalem, and in all Judea and Samaria, and even to the remotest part of the earth. **Acts 2:14.** But Peter, taking his stand with the Eleven, raised his voice and declared to them: "Men of Judea, and all you who live in Jerusalem, let this be known to you, and give heed to my words."	**Acts 2:41-42.** So then, those who had received his word were baptized; and there were added that day about three thousand souls. And they were continually devoting themselves to the apostles' teaching and to fellowship, and to the breaking of bread and to prayer.

Acts 2:46-47. And day by day continuing with one mind in the temple, and breaking bread from house to house, they were taking their meals together with gladness and sincerity of heart, praising God, and having favor with all the people. And the Lord was adding to their number day by day those who were being saved.

Acts 4:1-2, 4. And as they were speaking to the people, the priests and the captain of the temple guard, and the Sadducees, came upon them, being greatly disturbed because they were teaching the people and proclaiming in Jesus the resurrection from the dead.... But many of those who had heard the message believed; and the	

number of the men came to be about five thousand.

Acts 4:31. And when they had prayed, the place where they had gathered together was shaken, and they were all filled with the Holy Spirit, and began to speak the Word of God with boldness.

Acts 5:12-14. And at the hands of the apostles many signs and wonders were taking place among the people; and they were all with one accord in Solomon's portico. But none of the rest dared to associate with them; however, the people held them in high esteem. And all the more believers in the Lord, multitudes of men and women, were constantly added to their number.

Acts 5:19-21a. But an angel of the Lord during the night opened the gates of the prison, and taking them out he said, "Go your way, stand and speak to the people in the temple the whole message of this Life." And upon hearing this, they entered into the temple about daybreak, and began to teach.

Acts 5:25. But someone came and reported to them, "Behold, the men whom you put in prison are standing in the temple and teaching the people!"

Acts 5:27-28. And when they had brought them, they stood them before the Council. And the high priest questioned them, saying, "We gave you strict orders not to continue teaching in this name, and behold, you have filled Jerusalem with your teaching, and intend to bring this man's blood upon us."

Acts 4:32. And the congregation of those who believed were of one heart and soul; and not one of them claimed that anything belonging to him was his own; but all things were common property to them.

Acts 5:42. And every day, in the temple, from house to house, they kept right on teaching and preaching Jesus as the Christ.

Acts 6:4, 7. "But we will devote ourselves to prayer, and to the ministry of the Word." ... And the Word of God kept on spreading; and the number of the disciples continued to increase greatly in Jerusalem, and a great many of the priests were becoming obedient to the faith.

Acts 8:1b, 4. And on that day a great persecution arose against the church in Jerusalem; and they were all scattered throughout the regions of Judea and Samaria, except the apostles. ... Therefore, those who had been scattered went about preaching the Word.

Acts 8:5. And Philip went down to the city of Samaria and began proclaiming Christ to them.

Acts 8:25. And so, when they [Peter and John] had solemnly testified and spoken the Word of the Lord, they started back to Jerusalem, and were preaching the Gospel to many villages of the Samaritans.

Acts 8:35. And Philip opened his mouth, and beginning from this Scripture he preached Jesus to him.

Acts 8:12. But when they believed Philip preaching the Good News about the kingdom of God and the name of Jesus Christ, they were being baptized, men and women alike.

Acts 8:36, 38. And as they went along the road they came to some water; and the eunuch said, "Look! Water! What prevents me from being baptized?" ... And he ordered the chariot to stop; and they both went down into the water, Philip as well as the eunuch; and he baptized him.

Acts 9:20. And immediately he [Paul] began to proclaim Jesus in the synagogues, saying, "He is the Son of God."

Acts 9:31. So the church throughout all Judea and Galilee and Samaria enjoyed peace, being built up; and, going on in the fear of the Lord and in the comfort of the Holy Spirit, it continued to increase.

Acts 10:42-43. "And He ordered us to preach to the people, and solemnly to testify that this is the One who has been appointed by God as Judge of the living and the dead. Of Him all the prophets bear witness that through His name everyone who believes in Him has received forgiveness of sins."

Acts 11:19-21. So then those who were scattered because of the persecution that arose in connection with Stephen made their way to Phoenicia and Cyprus and Antioch, speaking the word to no one except to Jews alone. But there were some of them, men of Cyprus and Cyrene, who came to Antioch and began speaking to the Greeks also, preaching the Lord Jesus. And the hand of the Lord was with them, and a large number who believed turned to the Lord.

Acts 11:22-26. And the news about them reached the ears of the church at Jerusalem, and they sent Barnabas off to Antioch. Then when he had come and witnessed the grace of God, he rejoiced and began to encourage them all with resolute heart to remain true to the Lord; for he was a good man, and full of the Holy Spirit and of faith. And considerable numbers were brought to the Lord. And he left for Tarsus to look for Saul; and when he had found him, he brought him to Antioch. And it came about that for an entire year they met with the church, and taught considerable numbers; and the disciples were first called Christians in Antioch.

Acts 12:24. But the Word of the Lord continued to grow and to be multiplied.

Acts 13:5a. And when they reached Salamis, they began to proclaim the Word of God in the synagogues of the Jews.

Acts 13:13-16, 42-44. Now Paul and his companions put out to sea from Paphos and came to

Perga in Pamphylia; and John left them and returned to Jerusalem. But going on from Perga, they arrived in Pisidian Antioch, and on the Sabbath Day they went into the synagogue and sat down. And after the reading of the Law and the Prophets the synagogue officials sent to them, saying, "Brethren, if you have any word of exhortation for the people, say it." And Paul stood up, and motioning with his hand, he said, "Men of Israel, and you who fear God, listen. . . ." And as Paul and Barnabas were going out, the people kept begging that these things might be spoken to them the next Sabbath. Now when the meeting of the synagogue had broken up, many of the Jews and of the God-fearing proselytes followed Paul and Barnabas, who, speaking to them, were urging them to continue in the grace of God. And the next Sabbath nearly the whole city assembled to hear the Word of God.

Acts 13:45-49. But when the Jews saw the crowds, they were filled with jealousy, and began contradicting the things spoken by Paul, and were blaspheming. And Paul and Barnabas spoke out boldly and said, "It was necessary that the Word of God should be spoken to you first; since you repudiate it, and judge yourselves unworthy of eternal life, behold, we are turning to the Gentiles. For thus the Lord has commanded us, 'I HAVE PLACED YOU AS A LIGHT FOR THE GENTILES, THAT YOU

THE EPISTLE OF JAMES
James 3:1-2. Let not many of you become teachers, my brethren, knowing that as such we shall incur a stricter judgment. For we all stumble in many ways. If any one does not stumble in what he says, he is a perfect man, able to bridle the whole body as well.

SHOULD BRING SALVATION TO THE END OF THE EARTH.' " And when the Gentiles heard this, they began rejoicing and glorifying the Word of the Lord; and as many as had been appointed to eternal life believed. And the Word of the Lord was being spread through the whole region.

Acts 14:1. And it came about that in Iconium they entered the synagogue of the Jews together, and spoke in such a manner that a great multitude believed, both of Jews and of Greeks.

Acts 14:5-7. And when an attempt was made by both the Gentiles and the Jews with their rulers, to mistreat and to stone them, they became aware of it and fled to the cities of Lycaonia, Lystra and Derbe, and the surrounding region; and there they continued to preach the Gospel.

Acts 14:19-21a. But Jews came from Antioch and Iconium, and having won over the multitudes, they stoned Paul and dragged him out of the city, supposing him to be dead. But while the disciples stood around him, he arose and entered the city. And the next day he went away with Barnabas to Derbe. And after they had preached the Gospel to that city and had made many disciples. . . .

Acts 14:25. And when they had spoken the word in Perga, they went down to Attalia.

Acts 14:21b-23. They returned to Lystra and to Iconium and to Antioch, strengthening the souls of the disciples, encouraging them to continue in the faith, and saying, "Through many tribulations we must enter the kingdom of God." And when they had appointed elders for them in every church, having prayed with fasting, they commended them to the Lord in whom they had believed.

Acts 14:26-28. And from there they sailed to Antioch, from which they had been commended to the grace of God for the work that they had accomplished. And when they had arrived and gathered the church together, they began to report all things that God had done with them and how He had opened a door of faith to the Gentiles. And they spent a long time with the disciples.

Acts 15:2-4. And when Paul and Barnabas had great dissension and debate with them, the brethren determined that Paul and Barnabas and certain others of them, should go up to Jerusalem to the apostles and elders concerning this issue. Therefore, being sent on their way by the church, they were passing through both Phoenicia and Samaria, describing in detail the conversion of the Gentiles, and were bringing great joy to all the brethren. And when they arrived at Jerusalem, they were received by the church and the apostles and the elders, and they reported all that God had done with them.

Galatians 6:10a. So then, while we have opportunity, let us do good to all men.

THE EPISTLE TO THE GALATIANS

Acts 15:22-23a, 30-32. Then it seemed good to the apostles and elders, with the whole church, to choose men from among them to send to Antioch with Paul and Barnabas—Judas called Barsabbas, and Silas, leading men among the brethren, and they sent this letter by them. . . . So, when they were sent away, they went down to Antioch; and having gathered the congregation together, they delivered the letter. And when they had read it, they rejoiced because of its encouragement. And Judas and Silas, also being prophets themselves, encouraged and strengthened the brethren with a lengthy message.

Acts 15:35. But Paul and Barnabas stayed in Antioch, teaching and preaching with many others also the Word of the Lord.

Acts 15:36, 40-41. And after some days Paul said to Barnabas, "Let us return and visit the brethren in every city in which we proclaimed the Word of the Lord, and see how they are." ... But Paul chose Silas and departed, being committed by the brethren to the grace of the Lord. And he was traveling through Syria and Cilicia, strengthening the churches.

Acts 16:4-5a. Now while they were passing through the cities, they were delivering the decrees, which had been decided upon by the apostles and elders who were in Jerusalem, for them to observe. So the churches were being strengthened in the faith.

Acts 16:5b. And were increasing in number daily.

Acts 16:10. And when he had seen the vision, immediately we sought to go into Macedonia, concluding that God had called us to preach the Gospel to them.

Acts 16:13. And on the Sabbath Day we went outside the gate to a riverside, where we were supposing that there would be a place of prayer; and we sat down and began speaking to the women who had assembled.

Acts 16:31-32. And they said, 'Believe in the Lord Jesus, and you shall be saved, you and your household." And they spoke the Word of the Lord to him together with all who were in his house.

Acts 16:33-34, 40. And he took them that very hour of the night and washed their wounds, and immediately he was baptized, he and all his household. And he brought them into his house and set food before them, and rejoiced greatly, having believed in God with his whole household.... And they went out of the prison and entered the house of Lydia, and when they saw the brethren, they encouraged them and departed.

THE THESSALONIAN EPISTLES
(Written from Corinth)

1 Thessalonians 2:7-12. But we proved to be gentle among you, as a nursing mother tenderly cares for her own children. Having thus a fond affection for you, we were well pleased to impart to you not only the Gospel but also our own lives because you had become very dear to us. For you recall, brethren, our labor and hardship, how working night and day so as not to be a burden to any of you, we proclaimed to you the Gospel of God. You are witnesses, and so is God, how devoutly and uprightly and blamelessly we behaved toward you believers; just as you know how we were exhorting and encouraging and imploring each one of you as a father would his own children, so that you may walk in a manner worthy of God who calls you into His own kingdom and glory.

1 Thessalonians 3:1-5. Therefore when we could endure it no longer, we thought it best to be left behind at Athens alone; and we sent Timothy, our brother and God's fellow worker in the Gospel of Christ, to strengthen and encourage you as to your faith; so that no man may be

Acts 17:2-4. And according to Paul's custom, he went to them, and for three Sabbaths reasoned with them from the Scriptures, explaining and giving evidence that the Christ had to suffer and rise again from the dead, and saying, "This Jesus whom I am proclaiming to you is the Christ." And some of them were persuaded and joined Paul and Silas, along with a great multitude of the God-fearing Greeks and a number of the leading women.

1 Thessalonians 1:5-10. For our Gospel did not come to you in Word only, but also in power and in the Holy Spirit and with full conviction; just as you know what kind of men we proved to be among you for your sake. You also became imitators of us and of the Lord, having received the Word in much tribulation with the joy of the Holy Spirit, so that you became an example to all the believers in Macedonia and in Achaia. For the Word of the Lord has sounded forth from you, not only in Macedonia and Achaia. but also in every place your faith toward God has gone forth, so that we have no need to say anything. For they themselves report about us what kind of a reception we had with you, and how you turned to God from idols to serve a living and true God, and to wait for His Son from heaven, whom He raised from the dead, that is Jesus, who delivers us from the wrath to come.

2 Thessalonians 3:1. Finally, brethren, pray for us that the Word of the Lord may spread rapidly and be glorified, just as it did also with you.

disturbed by these afflictions; for you yourselves know that we have been destined for this. For indeed when we were with you, we kept telling you in advance that we were going to suffer affliction; and so it came to pass, as you know. For this reason, when I could endure it no longer, I also sent to find out about your faith, for fear that the tempter might have tempted you, and our labor should be in vain.

1 Thessalonians 3:10-13. As we night and day keep praying most earnestly that we may see your face, and may complete what is lacking in your faith? Now may our God and Father Himself and Jesus our Lord direct our way to you; and may the Lord cause you to increase and abound in love for one another, and for all men, just as we also do for you; so that He may establish your hearts unblamable in holiness before our God and Father at the coming of our Lord Jesus with all His saints.

1 Thessalonians 5:11. Therefore encourage one another, and build up one another, just as you also are doing.

1 Thessalonians 5:14-15. And we urge you, brethren, admonish the unruly, encourage the faint-hearted, help the weak, be patient with all men. See that no one repays another with evil for evil, but always seek after that which is good for one another and for all men.

Acts 17:10-12. And the brethren immediately sent Paul and Silas away by night to Berea; and when they arrived, they went into the synagogue of the Jews. Now these were more noble-minded than those in Thessalonica, for they received the Word with great eagerness, examining the Scriptures daily, to see whether these things were so. Many of them therefore believed, along with a number of prominent Greek women and men.

Acts 17:16-17. Now while Paul was waiting for them at Athens, his spirit was being provoked with him as he was beholding the city full of idols. So he was reasoning in the synagogue with the Jews and the God-fearing Gentiles, and in the market place every day with those who happened to be present.

Acts 17:22-31. (Paul's sermon in Athens)

Acts 17:34. But some men joined him and believed, among whom also was Dionysius the Areopagite and a woman named Damaris and others with them.

Acts 18:4-5. And [in Corinth] he was reasoning in the synagogue every Sabbath and trying to persuade Jews and Greeks. But when Silas and Timothy came down from Macedonia, Paul began devoting himself completely to the Word, solemnly testifying to the Jews that Jesus was the Christ.

Acts 18:8-11. And Crispus, the leader of the synagogue, believed in the Lord with all his household, and many of the Corinthians when they heard were believing and being baptized. And the Lord said to Paul in the night by a vision, "Do not be afraid any longer, but go on speaking and do not be silent; for I am with you, and no man will attack you in order to harm you, for I have many people in this city." And he settled there a year and six months, teaching the Word of God among them.

THE CORINTHIAN EPISTLES
(Written from Ephesus and Macedonia)

1 Corinthians 1:17. For Christ did not send me to baptize, but to preach the Gospel, not in cleverness of speech, that the cross of Christ should not be made void.

1 Corinthians 1:21-24. For since in the wisdom of God the world through its wisdom did not come to know God, God was well pleased through the foolishness of the message preached to save those who believe. For indeed Jews ask for signs, and Greeks search for wisdom; but we preach Christ crucified, to Jews a stumbling block, and to Gentiles foolishness, but to those who are the called, both Jews and Greeks, Christ the power of God and the wisdom of God.

1 Corinthians 2:1-5. And when I came to you, brethren, I did not come with superiority of speech or of wisdom, proclaiming to you the testimony of God. For I determined to know nothing among you except Jesus Christ, and Him crucified. And I was with you in weakness and in fear and in much trembling. And my message and my preaching were not in persuasive words of wis-

1 Corinthians 1:10. Now I exhort you, brethren, by the name of our Lord Jesus Christ, that you all agree, and there be no divisions among you, but you be made complete in the same mind and in the same judgment.

1 Corinthians 4:17. For this reason I have sent to you Timothy, who is my beloved and faithful child in the Lord, and he will remind you of my ways which are in Christ, just as I teach everywhere in every church.

dom, but in demonstration of the Spirit and of power, that your faith should not rest on the wisdom of men, but on the power of God.

1 Corinthians 5:9-10. I wrote you in my letter not to associate with immoral people; I did not at all mean with the immoral people of this world, or with the covetous and swindlers, or with idolators; for then you would have to go out of the world.

1 Corinthians 9:16. For if I preach the Gospel, I have nothing to boast of, for I am under compulsion; for woe is me if I do not preach the Gospel.

1 Corinthians 11:26. For as often as you eat this bread and drink the cup, you proclaim the Lord's death until He comes.

1 Corinthians 14:23-25. If therefore the whole church should assemble together and all speak in tongues, and ungifted men or unbelievers enter, will they not say that you are mad? But if all prophesy, and an unbeliever or an ungifted man enters, he is convicted by all, he is called to account by all; the secrets of his heart are disclosed; and so he will fall on his face and worship God, declaring that God is certainly among you.

1 Corinthians 15:58. Therefore, my beloved brethren, be steadfast, immovable, always abounding in the work of the Lord, knowing that your toil is not in vain in the Lord.

2 Corinthians 1:19. For the Son of God, Christ Jesus, who was preached among you by us—by me and Silvanus and Timothy—was not yes and no, but is yes in Him.

2 Cointhians 3:2-3. You are our letter, written in our hearts, known and read by all men; being manifested that you are a letter of Christ, cared for by us, written not with ink, but with the Spirit of the living God, not on tablets of stone, but on tablets of human hearts.

2 Corinthians 4:5. For we do not preach ourselves but Christ Jesus as Lord, and ourselves as your bond-servants for Jesus' sake.

2 Corinthians 5:18-20. Now all these things are from God, who reconciled us to Himself through Christ, and gave us the ministry of reconciliation, namely, that God was in Christ reconciling the world to Himself, not counting their trespasses against them, and He has committed to us the word of reconciliation. Therefore, we are ambassadors for Christ, as though God were entreating through us; we beg you on behalf of Christ, be reconciled to God.

Acts 18:19-21. And they came to Ephesus, and he left them there. Now he himself entered the synagogue and reasoned with the Jews. And when they asked him to stay for a longer time, he did not consent, but taking leave of them and saying, "I will return to you again if God wills," he set sail from Ephesus.

Acts 18:22-23. And when he had landed at Caesarea, he went up and greeted the church, and went down to Antioch. And having spent some time there, he departed and passed successively through the Galatian region and Phrygia, strengthening all the disciples.

Acts 18:24-28. Now a certain Jew named Apollos, an Alexandrian by birth, an eloquent man, came to Ephesus; and he was mighty in the Scriptures. This man had been instructed in the way of the Lord; and being fervent in spirit, he was speaking and teaching accurately the things concerning Jesus, being acquainted only with the baptism of John; and he began to speak out boldly in the synagogue. But when Priscilla and Aquila heard him, they took him aside and explained to him the way of God more accurately. And when he wanted to go across to Achaia, the brethren encouraged him and wrote to the disciples to welcome him; and when he had arrived, he helped greatly those who had believed through grace; for he powerfully refuted the Jews in public, demonstrating by the Scriptures that Jesus was the Christ.

Acts 19:1-7. And it came about that while Apollos was at Corinth, Paul having passed through the upper country came to Ephesus, and found some disciples, and he said to them, "Did you receive the Holy Spirit when you believed?" And they said to him, "No, we have not even heard whether there is a Holy Spirit." And he said, "Into what then were you baptized?" And they said, "Into John's baptism." And Paul said, "John baptized with the baptism of repentance, telling the people to believe in Him who was coming after him, that is, in Jesus." And when they heard this, they were baptized in the name of the Lord Jesus. And when Paul had laid his hands upon them, the Holy Spirit came on them, and they began speaking with tongues and prophesying. And there were in all about twelve men.

Acts 19:8. And he entered the synagogue and continued speak-

Acts 19:9. But when some were becoming hardened and dising out boldly for three months, reasoning and persuading them about the kingdom of God.

obedient, speaking evil of the Way before the multitude, he withdrew from them and took away the disciples, reasoning daily in the school of Tyrannus.

Acts 19:10, 20. And this took place for two years, so that all who lived in Asia heard the Word of the Lord, both Jews and Greeks. . . . So the Word of the Lord was growing mightily and prevailing.

Acts 19:23; 20:1-2. And about that time there arose no small disturbance concerning the Way. . . . And after the uproar had ceased, Paul sent for the disciples and when he had exhorted them and taken his leave of them, he departed to go to Macedonia. And when he had gone through those districts and had given them much exhortation, he came to Greece.

THE EPISTLE TO THE ROMANS

Romans 1:8. First, I thank my God through Jesus Christ for you all, because your faith is being proclaimed throughout the whole world.

Romans 1:9-13. For God, whom I serve in my spirit in the preaching of the Gospel of His Son, is my witness as to how unceasingly I make mention of you, always in my prayers making request, if perhaps now at last by the will of God I may succeed in coming to you. For I long to see you in order that I may impart some spiritual gift to you, that you may be established; that is, that I may be encouraged together with you while among you, each of us by the other's faith, both yours and mine. And I do not want you to be unaware, brethren, that often I have planned to come to you (and have been prevented thus far) in order that I might obtain some fruit among you also, even as among the rest of the Gentiles.

Romans 1:14-15. I am under obligation both to Greeks and to barbarians, both to the wise and to the foolish. Thus, for my part, I am eager to preach the Gospel to you also who are in Rome.

Romans 13:8-10. Owe nothing to anyone except to love one another; for he who loves his neighbor has fulfilled the Law. For this, YOU SHALL NOT COMMIT ADULTERY, YOU SHALL NOT MURDER, YOU SHALL NOT STEAL, YOU SHALL NOT COVET," and if there is any other commandment, it is summed up in this saying, "YOU SHALL LOVE YOUR NEIGHBOR AS YOURSELF." Love does no wrong to a neighbor; love therefore is the fulfillment of the Law.

Romans 16:25-27. Now to Him who is able to establish you according to my Gospel and the preaching of Jesus Christ, according to the revelation of the mystery which has been kept secret for long ages past, but now is manifested, and by the Scriptures of the prophets according to the commandment of the eternal God, has been made known to all the nations, leading to obedience of faith; to the only wise God, through Jesus Christ, to whom be the glory forever. Amen.

Acts 20:6-7. And we sailed from Philippi after the days of Unleavened Bread, and came to them at Troas within five days; and there we stayed seven days. And on the first day of the week, when we were gathered together to break bread, Paul began talking to them, intending to depart the next day, and he prolonged his message until midnight.

Acts 20:17-21. And from Miletus he sent to Ephesus and called to him the elders of the church. And when they had come to him, he said to them, "You yourselves know, from the first day that I set foot in Asia, how I was with you the whole time, serving the Lord with all humility and with tear and with trials which came upon me through the plots of the Jews; how I did not shrink from declaring to you anything that was profitable, and teaching you publicly and from house to house, solemnly testifying to both Jews and Greeks of repentence toward God and faith in our Lord Jesus Christ.

Acts 20:22-24. And now, behold, bound in spirit, I am on my way to Jerusalem, not knowing what will happen to me there, except that the Holy Spirit solemnly testifies to me in every city, saying that bonds and afflictions await me. But I do not consider my life of any account as dear to myself, in order that I may finish my course, and the ministry which I received from the Lord Jesus, to testify solemnly of the Gospel of the grace of God.

Acts 20:25-35. And now, behold, I know that you all, among whom I went about preaching the kingdom, will see my face no more. Therefore I testify to you this day, that I an innocent of the blood of all men. For I did not shrink from declaring to you the whole purpose of God. Be on guard for yourselves and for all the flock, among which the Holy Spirit has made you overseers, to shepherd the church of God which He purchased with His own blood. I know that after my departure savage wolves will come in among you, not sparing the flock; and from among your own selves men will arise, speaking perverse things, to draw away the disciples after them. Therefore be on the alert, remembering that night and day for a period of three years I did not cease to admonish each one with tears. And now I commend you to God and to the Word of His grace, which is able to build you up and to give you the inheritance among all those who are sanctified. I have coveted no one's silver or gold or clothes.

You yourselves know that these hands ministered to my own needs and to the men who were with me. In everything I showed you that by working hard in this manner you must help the weak and remember the words of the Lord Jesus, that He Himself said, "It is more blessed to give than to receive."

Acts 22. (Paul's testimony in Jerusalem)

Acts 23. (Paul's testimony before the Council)

Acts 24. (Paul's testimony before Felix)

Acts 25. (Paul's testimony before Festus)

Acts 26. (Paul's testimony before Agrippa)

Acts 27. (Paul sails to Rome)

Acts 28:23-24. And when they had set a day for him, they came to him at his lodging in large numbers; and he was explaining to them by solemnly testifying about the kingdom of God, and trying to persuade them concerning Jesus, from both the Law of Moses and from the Prophets, from morning until evening. And some were being persuaded by the things spoken, but others would not believe.

Acts 28:30-31. And he stayed two full years in his own rented quarters, and was welcoming all who came to him, preaching the kingdom of God, and teaching concerning the Lord Jesus Christ with all openness, unhindered.

THE PRISON EPISTLES

PHILEMON
EPHESIANS

Ephesians 1:15-19a; 3:14-19. For this reason I too, having heard of the faith in the Lord Jesus which exists among you, and your love for all the saints, do not cease giving thanks for you, while making mention of you in my prayers; that the God of our Lord Jesus Christ, the Father of glory, may give to you a spirit of wisdom and of revelation in the knowledge of Him. I pray that the eyes of your heart may be enlightened, so that you may know what is the hope of His calling, what are the riches of the glory of His inheritance in the saints, and what is the surpassing greatness of His power toward us who believe. . . . For this reason, I bow my knees

Ephesians 3:8-9. To me, the very least of all saints, this grace was given, to preach to the Gentiles the unfathomable riches of Christ, and to bring to light what is the administration of the mystery which for ages has been hidden in God, who created all things.

before the Father, from whom every family in heaven and on earth derives its name, that He would grant you, according to the riches of His glory, to be strengthened with power through His Spirit in the inner man; so that Christ may dwell in your hearts through faith; and that you, being rooted and grounded in love, may be able to comprehend with all the saints what is the breadth and length and height and depth, and to know the love of Christ which surpasses knowledge, that you may be filled up to all the fulness of God.

Ephesians 2:19-22. So then you are no longer strangers and aliens, but you are fellow-citizens with the saints, and are of God's household, having been built upon the foundation of the apostles and prophets, Christ Jesus Himself being the cornerstone, in whom the whole building, being fitted together is growing into a holy temple in the Lord; in whom you also are being built together into a dwelling of God in the Spirit.

Ephesians 4:11-16. And He gave some as apostles, and some as prophets, and some as evangelists, and some as pastors and teachers, for the equipping of the saints for the work of service, to the building up of the body of Christ; until we all attain to the unity of the faith, and the knowledge of the Son of God, to a mature man, to the measure of the stature which belongs to the fulness of Christ. As a result, we are no longer to be children, tossed here and there by waves, and carried about by every wind of doctrine, by the trickery of men, by craftiness in deceitful scheming; but speaking the truth in love, we are to grow up in all aspects into Him, who is the head, even Christ, from whom the whole body, being fitted and held together by that which every joint supplies, according to the proper working of each individual part, causes the growth of the body for the building up of itself in love.

Ephesians 6:1-4. Children, obey your parents in the Lord, for this is right. Honor your father and mother (which is the first commandment with a promise), that it may be well with you, and that you may live long on the earth. And, fathers, do not provoke your children to anger; bu bring them up in the discipline and instruction of the Lord.

COLOSSIANS

Colossians 1:9-12. For this reason also, since the day we heard of it, we have not ceased to pray for you and to ask that you may be filled with the knowledge of His will in all spiritual wisdom and understanding, so that you may walk in a manner worthy of the Lord, to please Him in all respects, bearing fruit in every good work and increasing in the knowledge of God; strengthened with all power, according to His glorious might, for the attaining of all steadfastness and patience, joyously giving thanks to the Father, who has qualified us to share in the inheritance of the saints in light. And for this purpose also I labor, striving according to His power, which mightily works within me.

Colossians 1:25-29. Of this church I was made a minister according to the stewardship from God bestowed on me for your benefit, that I might fully carry out the preaching of the Word of God, that is, the mystery which has been hidden from the past ages and generations; but has now been manifested to His saints, to whom God willed to make known what is the riches of the glory of this mystery among the Gentiles, which is Christ in you, the hope of glory. And we proclaim Him, admonishing every man and teaching every man with all wisdom that we may present every man complete in Christ.

Colossians 4:5-6. Conduct yourselves with wisdom toward outsiders, making the most of the opportunity. Let your speech always be with grace, seasoned, as it were, with salt, so that you may know how you should respond to each person.

Colossians 2:2-5. That their hearts may be encouraged, having been knit together in love, and attaining to all the wealth that comes from the full assurance of understanding, resulting in a true knowledge of God's mystery, that is, Christ Himself, in whom are hidden all the treasures of wisdom and knowledge. I say this in order that no one may delude you with persuasive argument. For even though I am absent in body, nevertheless I am with you in spirit, rejoicing to see your good discipline and the stability of your faith in Christ.

Colossians 3:16. Let the Word of Christ richly dwell within you; with all wisdom teaching and admonishing one another with psalms and hymns and spiritual songs, singing with thankfulness in your hearts to God.

Colossians 3:18-23. Wives, be subject to your husbands, as is fitting in the Lord. Husbands, love your wives, and do not be embittered against them. Children, be obedient to your parents in all things, for this is well pleasing to the Lord. Fathers, do not exasperate your children, that they may not lose heart. Slaves, in all things obey those who are your masters on earth, not with external service, as those who merely please men, but with sincerity of heart, fearing the Lord. Whatever you do, do your work heartily, as for the Lord rather than for men.

PHILIPPIANS

Philippians 1:12-14. Now I want you to know, brethren, that my circumstances have turned out for the greater progress of the Gospel, so that my imprisonment in the cause of Christ has become well known throughout the whole praetorian guard and to everyone else, and that most of the brethren, trusting in the Lord because of my imprisonment, have far more courage to speak the Word of God without fear.

Philippians 1:27-28. Only conduct yourselves in a manner worthy of the Gospel of Christ; so that whether I come and see you or remain absent, I may hear of you that you are standing firm in one spirit, with one mind striving together for the faith of the Gospel; in no way alarmed by your opponents—which is a sign of destruction for them, but of salvation for you, and that too, from God.

Philippians 2:1-4. If therefore there is any encouragement in Christ, if there is any consolation of love, if there is any fellowship of the Spirit, if any affection and compassion, make my joy complete by being of the same mind, maintaining the same love, united in spirit, intent on one purpose. Do nothing from selfishness or empty conceit, but with humility of mind let each of you regard one another as more important than himself; do not merely look out for your own personal interests, but also for the interests of others.

Philippians 2:19-24. But I hope in the Lord Jesus to send Timothy to you shortly, so that I also may be encouraged when I learn of your condition. For I have no one else of kindred spirit who will genuinely be concerned for your welfare. For they all seek after their own interests, not those of Christ Jesus. But you know of his proven worth that he served me with in the furtherance of the Gospel like a child serving his father. Therefore I hope to send him immediately, as soon as I see how things go with me; and I trust in the Lord that I myself also shall be coming shortly.

Philippians 4:9. The things you have learned and received and heard and seen in me, practice these things; and the God of peace shall be with you.

THE PASTORAL EPISTLES
1 TIMOTHY

1 Timothy 1:3-7. As I urged you upon my departure from Macedonia, remain on at Ephesus, in order that you may in-

1 Timothy 2:1-7. First of all, then, I urge that entreaties and prayers, petitions and thanksgivings, be made on behalf of all

men, for kings and all who are in authority, in order that we may lead a tranquil and quiet life in all godliness and dignity. This is good and acceptable in the sight of God our Saviour, who desires all men to be saved and to come to the knowledge of the truth. For there is one God, and one Mediator also between God and men, the man Christ Jesus, who gave Himself a ransom for all, the testimony borne at the proper time. And for this I was appointed a preacher and an apostle (I am telling the truth, I am not lying) as a teacher of the Gentiles in faith and truth.

struct cerain men not to teach strange doctrines, nor to pay attention to myths and endless genealogies, which give rise to mere speculation rather than furthering God's provision which is by faith. But the goal of our instruction is love from a pure heart and a good conscience and a sincere faith. For some men, straying from these things, have turned aside to fruitless discussion, wanting to be teachers of the Law, even though they do not understand either what they are saying or the matters about which they make confident assertions.

1 Timothy 4:11-16. Prescribe and teach these things. Let no one look down on your youthfulness, but rather in speech, conduct, love, faith, and purity, show yourself an example of those who believe. Until I come, give attention to the public, reading of Scripture, to exhortation and teaching. Do not neglect the spiritual gift within you, which was bestowed upon you through prophetic utterance with the laying on of hands by the presbytery. Take pains with these things; be absorbed in them, so that your progress may be evident to all. Pay close attention to yourself and to your teaching; persevere in these things; for as you do this you will insure salvation both for yourself and for those who hear you.

1 Timothy 5:17. Let the elders who rule well be considered worthy of double honor, especially those who work hard at preaching and teaching.

1 Timothy 6:1-2. Let all who are under the yoke as slaves regard their own masters as worthy of all honor so that the name of God and our doctrine may not be spoken against.

And let those who have believers as their masters not be disrespectful to them because they are brethren, but let them serve them all the more, because those who partake of the benefit are believers and beloved. Teach and preach these principles.

2 TIMOTHY

2 Timothy 1:6-11. And for this reason I remind you to kindle afresh the gift of God which is in you through the laying on of my hands. For God has not given us a spirit of timidity, but of power and love and discipline. Therefore do not be ashamed of the testimony of our Lord, or of me His prisoner; but join with me in suffering for the Gospel according to the power of God; who has saved us, and called us with a holy calling, not according to our works, but according to His own purpose and grace which was granted us in Christ Jesus from all eternity, but now has been revealed by the appearing of our Saviour Christ Jesus, who abolished death, and brought life and immortality to light through the Gospel, for which I was appointed a preacher and an apostle and a teacher.

2 Timothy 2:2. And the things which you have heard from me in the presence of many witnesses, these entrust to faithful men, who will be able to teach others also.

2 Timothy 3:14-17. You, however, continue in the things you have learned and become convinced of, knowing from whom you have learned them; and that from childhood you have known the sacred writings which are able to give you the wisdom that leads to salvation through faith which is in Christ Jesus. All Scripture is inspired by God and profitable for teaching, for reproof, for correction, for training in righteousness; that the man of God may be adequate, equipped for every good work.

2 Timothy 4:4-5. And will turn away their ears from the truth, and will turn aside to myths. But you, be sober in all things, endure hardship, do the work of an evangelist, fulfill your ministry.

2 Timothy 4:1-2. I solemnly charge you in the presence of God and of Christ Jesus, who is to judge the living and the dead, and by His appearing and His kingdom: preach the Word; be ready in season and out of season; reprove, rebuke, exhort, with great patience and instruction.

TITUS

Titus 1:5. For this reason I left you in Crete, that you might set in order what remains, and appoint elders in every city as I directed you.

Titus 2:1-15. But as for you, speak the things which are fitting for sound doctrine. Older men are to be temperate, dignified, sensible, sound in faith, in love, in perseverance. Older women likewise are to be reverent in their behavior, not malicious gossips, nor enslaved to much wine, teaching what is good, that they may encourage the young women to love their husbands, to love their children, to be sensible, pure, workers at home, kind, being subject to their own husbands, that the Word of God may not be dishonored. Likewise urge the young men to be sensible; in all things show yourself to be an example of good deeds, with purity in doctrine, dignified, sound in speech which is beyond reproach, in order that the opponent may be put to shame, having nothing bad to say about us. Urge bondslaves to be subject to their own masters in everything, to be well pleasing, not argumentative, not pilfering, but showing all good faith that they may adorn the doctrine of God our Saviour in every respect. For the grace of God has appeared, bringing salvation to all men, instructing us to deny ungodliness and worldly desires and to live sensibly, righteously and godly in the present age, looking for the blessed hope and the appearing of the glory of our great God and Saviour, Christ Jesus; who gave Himself for us, that He might redeem us from every lawless deed and purify for Himself a people for His own possession, zealous for good deeds. These things speak and exhort and reprove with all authority. Let no one disregard you.

ADDITIONAL EPISTLES
HEBREWS, PETER, JOHN
Hebrews 3:12-14. Take care, brethren, lest there should be in any one of you an evil, unbelieving heart, in falling away from the living God. But encourage one another day after day, as long as it is still called "Today," lest any one of you be hardened by the deceitfulness of sin. For we have become partakers of Christ, if we hold fast the beginning of our

assurance firm until the end.

Hebrews 5:12-14. For though by this time you ought to be teachers, you have need again for some one to teach you the elementary principles of the oracles of God, and you have come to need milk and not solid food. For every one who partakes only of milk is not accustomed to the Word of righteousness, for he is a babe. But solid food is for the mature, who because of practice have their senses trained to discern good and evil.

Hebrews 6:1. Therefore leaving the elementary teaching about the Christ, let us press on to maturity, not laying again a foundation of repentance from dead works and of faith toward God.

Hebrews 10:24-25. And let us consider how to stimulate one another to love and good deeds, not forsaking our own assembling together, as is the habit of some, but encouraging one another; and all the more, as you see the day drawing near.

1 PETER

1 Peter 2:1-5. Therefore, putting aside all malice and all guile and hypocrisy and envy and all slander, like newborn babes, long for the pure milk of the Word, that by it you may grow in respect to salvation, if you have tasted the kindness of the Lord. And coming to Him as to a living stone, rejected by men, but choice and precious in the sight of God, you also, as living stones, are being built up as a spiritual house for a holy priesthood, to offer up spiritual

1 Peter 2:12. Keep your behavior excellent among the Gentiles, so that in the thing in which they slander you as evildoers, they may on account of your good deeds, as they observe them, glorify God in the day of visitation.

1 Peter 2:18. Servants, be submissive to your masters with all respect, not only to those who are good and gentle, but also to those who are unreasonable.

1 Peter 3:1-2. In the same way, you wives, be submissive to your own husbands so that even if anyone of them are disobedient to the Word they may be won without a word by the behavior of their wives, as they observe your chaste and respectful behavior.

1 Peter 3:15. But sanctify Christ as Lord in your hearts, always being ready to make a defense to every one who asks you to give an account for the hope that is in you, yet with genteness and reverence.

1 John 1:1-4. What was from the beginning, what we have heard, what we have seen with our eyes, what we beheld and our hands handled, concerning the Word of life—and the life was manifested, and we have seen and bear witness and proclaim to you the eternal life, which was with the Father and was manifested to us—

sacrifices acceptable to God through Jesus Christ.

1 Peter 4:10-11. As each one has received a special gift, employ it in serving one another, as good stewards of the manifold grace of God. Whoever speaks, let him speak, as it were, the utterances of God; whoever serves, let him do so as by the strength which God supplies; so that in all things God may be glorified through Jesus Christ, to whom belongs the glory and dominion forever and ever. Amen.

1 Peter 5:1-3. Therefore, I exhort the elders among you, as your fellow-elder and witness of the sufferings of Christ, and a partaker also of the glory that is to be revealed, shepherd the flock of God among you, not under compulsion, but voluntarily, according to the will of God; and not for sordid grain, but with eagerness; nor yet as lording it over those allotted to your charge, but proving to be examples to the flock.

1 JOHN

what we have seen and heard we proclaim to you also, that you also may have fellowship with us; and indeed our fellowship is with the Father, and with His Son Jesus Christ. And these things we write, so that our joy may be made complete.

Appendix B

Activities and Directives— Results and Objectives

This compilation of activities and directives with results and objectives is from the Book of Acts and the Epistles. Section 1 relates to evangelism, and Section 2 relates to edification.

EVANGELISM	
ACTIVITY AND DIRECTIVES	RESULTS AND OBJECTIVES
ACTS	
Declaring	They had favor with all the people (2:47).
Speaking	Many believed (4:4).
Teaching	The people held them in high esteem (5:13).
Proclaiming	
Preaching	The Word of God kept on spreading (6:7).
Testifying	The number of the disciples continued to increase greatly (6:7).
Witnessing	
Exhorting	Many of the priests were becoming obedient to the faith (6:7).
Praising	
Reasoning	The multitudes were giving attention to what was said (8:6).
Refuting	They spoke in tongues (10:46).
Explaining	A large number turned to the Lord (11:21).
Demonstrating	The people kept begging that these things might be spoken to them the next Sabbath (13:42).
Giving evidence	
Persuading	Nearly the whole city (Pisidian Antioch) assembled to hear the Word of God (13:44).
	They made disciples (14:21).
	Some were persuaded (17:4).
	Received the Word with great eagerness, and examined the Scriptures daily to see whether these things were so (17:11).

Epistles

For our Gospel did not come to you in word only, but also in power and in the Holy Spirit and with full conviction....	You also became imitators of us and the Lord, having received the Word in much tribulation with the joy of the Holy Spirit (1 Thes. 1:5-6).
For the Word of the Lord hath sounded forth from you ... in every place your faith toward God has gone....	For they themselves report .. how you turned to God from idols to serve a living and true God (1 Thes. 1:8-9).
Make it your ambition to lead a quiet life and attend to your own business and work with your hands ...	so that you may behave properly toward outsiders and not be in any need (1 Thes. 4:11-12).
Pray for us [Paul, Silas, Timothy]	that the word of the Lord may spread rapidly and be glorified (2 Thes. 3:1).
Whether, then, you eat or drink or whatever you do, do all to the glory of God. Give no offense either to Jews or to Greeks or to the church of God; just as I also please all men in all things, not seeking my own profit, but the profit of the many,	that they may be saved (1 Cor. 10:31-33).
Prophesy....	He is convicted by all, he is called to account by all; the secrets of his heart are disclosed ... so he will fall on his face and worship God, declaring that God is among you (1 Cor. 14:24-25).
You are our letter ... I thank my God through Jesus Christ for you all ...	known and read by all men (2 Cor. 3:2).

Love your neighbor as yourself (Rom. 13:9)

because your faith is being proclaimed throughout the whole world (Rom. 1:8).

Pray on my behalf...

that utterance may be given to me in the opening of my mouth, to make known with boldness the mystery of the Gospel (Eph. 6:19).

Conduct yourselves with wisdom toward outsiders, making the most of the opportunity (Col. 4:5).
Let your speech always be with grace, seasoned, as it were, with salt,

so that you may know how you should respond to each person (Col. 4:6).

Conduct yourselves in a manner worthy of the Gospel. . . .

so that . . . you are standing firm in one spirit, with one mind striving together for the faith of the Gospel; in no way alarmed by your opponents (Phil. 1:27-28).

[Make] entreaties and prayers, petitions and thanksgiving . . . on behalf of all men . . .

in order that we may lead a tranquil and quiet life in all godliness and dignity (1 Tim. 2:1-2).

Regard [unsaved] masters as worthy of all honor,

so that the name of God and our doctrine may not be spoken against (1 Tim. 6:1).

From childhood you have known the sacred writings

which are able to give you the wisdom that leads to salvation through faith which is in Christ Jesus (2 Tim. 3:15).

Do the work of an evangelist (2 Tim. 4:5).

Keep your behavior excellent among the Gentiles,

so that . . . they may . . . glorify God in the day of visitation (1 Peter 2:12).

Be submissive to your masters (1 Peter 2:18).

Be submissive to your [unsaved] husbands	so . . . they may be won without a word by the behavior of their wives (1 Peter 3:1-2).
[Be] ready to make a defense to every one who asks you to give an account for the hope that is in you (1 Peter 3:15).	
Keep a good conscience	so that . . . those who revile your good behavior . . . may be put to shame (1 Peter 3:16).

EDIFICATION

FUNCTION AND DIRECTIVES	RESULTS AND OBJECTIVES
ACTS	
Baptizing	Were of one mind (2:46)
Teaching	Taking their meals together with
Fellowshiping	gladness and sincerity of heart
Breaking Bread	(2:46)
Praying	Were of one heart and soul (4:32)
Praising God	Enjoyed peace (9:31)
Encouraging	Were being built up (9:31)
Strengthening	Brought great joy to all the breth-
Reporting	ren (15:3)
Describing	Rejoiced because of its (the let-
Dissenting	ter's) encouragement (15:31)
Debating	The churches were being strength-
Writing	ened in the faith (15:32)
Imploring	The Word of the Lord was growing
Exhorting	mightily and prevailing (19:20)
Establishing	
Admonishing	

Epistles	
We were exhorting and encouraging and imploring each one of you . . .	so that you may walk in a manner worthy of the God who calls you (1 Thes. 2:11-12).
We . . . keep praying . . . that we may see your face,	and may complete what is lacking in your faith (1 Thes. 3:10).
May the Lord cause you	to increase and abound in love for one another, and for all men (1 Thes. 3:12).
We request and exhort you in Jesus Christ that, as you received from us instruction as to how you ought to walk and please God . . .	that you may excel still more (1 Thes. 4:1).
You yourselves are taught by God to love one another. . . .	But we urge you, brethren, to excel still more (1 Thes. 4:9-10).
Encourage one another (1 Thes. 5:11).	
Build up one another (1 Thes. 5:11).	
Admonish the unruly (1 Thes. 5:14).	
Encourage the fainthearted (1 Thes. 5:14).	
Help the weak (1 Thes. 5:14). Seek after that which is good for one another (1 Thes. 5:15). To this end also we pray for you always that our God may count you worthy of your calling, and fulfill every desire for goodness and the work of faith with power . . .	in order that the name of our Lord Jesus may be glorified in you, and you in Him (2 Thes. 1:11-12).

All agree ... [avoid divisions] ...

be made complete in the same mind (1 Cor. 1:10),

I have sent to you Timothy ...

and he will remind you of my ways which are in Christ, just as I teach everywhere in every church (1 Cor. 4:17).

Be imitators of me, just as I ... am of Christ (1 Cor. 11:1).

Seek to abound for the edification of the church (1 Cor. 14:12).

When you assemble, each one has a psalm, has a teaching, has a revelation, has a tongue, has an interpretation.

Let all things be done for edification (1 Cor. 14:26).

Always [abound] in the work of the Lord (1 Cor. 15:58).

This we also pray for,

that you be made complete (2 Cor. 13:9).

Rejoice, be made complete, be comforted, be like-minded, live in peace;

and the God of love and peace shall be with you (2 Cor. 13:11).

I long to see you ...

that I may impart some spiritual gift to you (Rom. 1:11).

Accept one another, just as Christ also accepted us (Rom. 15:7).

I urge you ... to present your bodies a living and holy sacrifice.... And do not be conformed to this world, but be transformed by the renewing of your mind,

that you may prove what the will of God is, that which is good and acceptable and perfect (Rom. 12:1-2).

Let us pursue the things

which make for peace and the building up of one another (Rom. 14:19).

Now we who are strong ought to bear the weaknesses of those without strength (Rom. 15:1).

Now may the God who gives perseverance . . .

   grant you to be of the same mind
   with one another according to
   Christ Jesus (Rom. 15:5).

Now may the God of hope

   fill you with all joy and peace in
   believing, that you may abound
   in hope by the power of the Holy
   Spirit (Rom. 15:13).

[I] do not cease giving thanks for
you, while making mention of
you in my prayers;

   that . . . God . . . may give to you a
   spirit of wisdom and of revelation in the knowledge of Him
   (Eph. 1:16-17) that the eyes of
   your heart may be enlightened
   . . .

   that you may know what is the
   hope of His calling (Eph. 1:18).

   that you may know . . . what are
   the riches of the glory of His
   inheritance in the saints (Eph.
   1:18).

   [that you may know] what is the
   surpassing greatness of His
   power toward us who believe
   (Eph. 1:19).

   [that you may] be strengthened
   with power through His Spirit in
   the inner man (Eph. 3:16).

   that Christ may dwell in your
   hearts through faith (Eph.
   3:17).

   [that you] may be able to comprehend . . . the breadth and
   length and height and depth, and
   to know the love of Christ which
   surpasses knowledge (Eph.
   3:18-19).

   that you may be filled up to all the
   fulness of God (Eph. 3:19).

[Apostles, prophets, evangelists, pastors, and teachers are given]	for the equipping of the saints for the work of service . . .
	until we all attain to the unity of the faith, and of the knowledge of the Son of God, to a mature man,
	[that] we are no longer . . . children, tossed here and there; . . . [that] the whole body [be] held together by that which every joint supplies, . . .
	for the building up of itself in love (Eph. 4:11-16).
Children, obey your parents (Eph. 6:1).	
Honor your father and mother . . .	that it may be well with you (Eph. 6:2-3).
Fathers, do not provoke your children to anger; but bring them up in the discipline and instruction of the Lord (Eph. 6:4). Do not exasperate your children,	that they may not lose heart (Col. 3:21).
We pray for you,	that you may walk in a manner worthy of the Lord. [that . . . you may] please Him in all respects, bearing fruit in every good work (Col. 1:9-10).
We . . . [admonish] and [teach] every man . . .	that we may present every man complete in Christ (Col. 1:28).
As you therefore have received Christ Jesus the Lord,	so walk in Him, having been firmly rooted and now being built up in Him and established in your faith, just as you were instructed, and overflowing with gratitude (Col. 2:6-7).

In Him

you have been made complete (Col. 2:10).

[Hold] fast to the Head, from whom the entire body, being supplied and held together by the joints and ligaments,

grows with a growth which is from God (Col. 2:19).

And beyond all these things put on love,

which is the perfect bond of unity (Col. 3:14).

Teaching and admonishing one another with psalms and hymns and spiritual songs (Col. 3:16).
Wives, be subject to your husbands (Col. 3:18).

Husbands, love your wives (Col. 3:19).
Whatever you do, do your work heartily, as for the Lord rather than for men (Col. 3:23).

Make my joy complete

by being of the same mind, maintaining the same love, united in spirit (Phil. 2:2).

[Be] intent on one purpose.

Do nothing from selfishness or empty conceit, but with humility of mind let each of you regard one another as more important than himself (Phil. 2:2-3).

I [Paul] press on toward the goal

for the prize of the upward call of God in Christ Jesus (Phil. 3:14).

The things you have learned and received and heard and seen in me,

practice these things (Phil. 4:9).

The goal of our instruction is

love from a pure heart and a good conscience and a sincere faith (1 Tim. 1:5).

Prescribe and teach these things. ... Give attention to the public reading of Scripture, to exhortation and teaching (1 Tim. 4:11, 13).

[Appoint elders] (1 Tim. 5:17). [do] not be disrespectful to [believing masters] (1 Tim. 6:2).

And the things which you have heard from me in the presence of many witnesses, these entrust to faithful men, who will be able to teach others also (2 Tim. 2:2).

All Scripture is inspired by God and profitable for teaching, for reproof, for correction, for training in righteousness; that the man of God may be adequate, equipped for every good work (2 Tim. 3:16-17).

Preach the Word; be ready in season and out of season; reprove, rebuke, exhort (2 Tim. 4:2).

Set in order what remains (Titus 1:5).

Speak the things which are fitting for sound doctrine (Titus 2:1).

Leav[e] the elementary teaching about the Christ, press on to maturity (Heb. 6:1).

Now the God of peace . . . equip you in every good thing to do His will (Heb. 13:20-21).

Long for the pure milk of the Word, that by it you may grow in respect to salvation (1 Peter 2:2).

Submit yourselves for the Lord's sake to every human institution: whether to a king as the one in authority; or to governers as sent by him for the punishment of evildoers and the praise of those who do right. For such is the will of God that by doing right you may silence the ignorance of foolish men (1 Peter 2:13-15).

Shepherd the flock of God (1 Peter 5:2).

These things we write . . . that your joy may be made complete (1 John 1:4).

Contend earnestly for the faith (Jude 1:3).

Keep yourselves in the love of God (Jude 1:21).

AUDIO ECHOES™

LINCOLN CHRISTIAN COLLEGE AND SEMINARY

Take these best-selling books on cassette with you wherever you go:

Building Up One Another—Gene Getz
6-2654 $ 9.95

Gaining Through Losing—Evelyn Christenson
6-2653 $ 9.95

Healing for Damaged Emotions—David Seamands
6-2650   (2 cassettes) $12.95

How to Really Love Your Teenager—Ross Campbell
6-2070   (2 cassettes) $12.95

How to Say No to a Stubborn Habit—Erwin Lutzer
6-2651 $ 9.95

The Leadership Style of Jesus—Michael Youssef
6-2023 $ 9.95

Management—A Biblical Approach—Myron Rush
6-2112   (2 cassettes) $12.95

Putting Away Childish Things—David Seamands
6-2134   (2 cassettes) $12.95

Seven Deadly Sins—Anthony Campolo
6-2051   (2 cassettes) $12.95

The Success Fantasy—Anthony Campolo
6-2652   (2 cassettes) $12.95

What Happens When Women Pray—Evelyn Christenson
6-2144 $ 9.95

Windows on the Parables—Warren Wiersbe
6-2655   (2 cassettes) $12.95